THE
River
CHARM

ALSO BY BELINDA MURRELL

The Sun Sword Trilogy

Book 1: The Quest for the Sun Gem
Book 2: The Voyage of the Owl
Book 3: The Snowy Tower

The Locket of Dreams
The Ivory Rose
The Ruby Talisman
The Forgotten Pearl

THE
River
CHARM

Belinda Murrell

RANDOM HOUSE AUSTRALIA

A Random House book
Published by Random House Australia Pty Ltd
Level 3, 100 Pacific Highway, North Sydney NSW 2060
www.randomhouse.com.au

First published by Random House Australia in 2013

Addresses for companies within the Random House Group can be found at
www.randomhouse.com.au/offices.

National Library of Australia
Cataloguing-in-Publication Entry

Author: Murrell, Belinda.
Title: The river charm/Belinda Murrell
ISBN: 978 1 74275 712 4 (pbk.)
Target Audience: For primary school age.
Subjects: Barton, Charlotte, 1797–1867 – Juvenile fiction.
            Families – Australia – Juvenile fiction.
            Australia – Social conditions – 19th century – Juvenile fiction.
Dewey Number: A823.4

Cover design: book design by saso
Cover images © Yolande de Kort/Trevillion Images, © Hanis/iStockphoto.com
and © Beneda Miroslav/Shutterstock
Internal design and typesetting by Midland Typesetters, Australia
Printed in Australia by Griffin Press, an accredited ISO AS/NZS 14001:2004
Environmental Management System printer

Random House Australia uses papers that are natural, renewable and recyclable
products and made from wood grown in sustainable forests. The logging
and manufacturing processes are expected to conform to the environmental
regulations of the country of origin.

To my family, who remind me where I came from, and where I am going — especially my daughter Emily Charlotte, my sister Kate, my grandmother Nonnie and my mother Gilly. Never underestimate the power of a mother's love.

'The Light from the Mountain'
by Louisa Atkinson, 1850s

Oh! The light from the mountain is fading away
And the shadows creep over it chilly and grey,
I see the dark rocks in their sternness and pride,
But the flowers are hidden that grow by their side.

The tall trees are tossing their wild arms on high,
As the shriek of the curlew goes mournfully by,
The cold night is coming it will not delay,
for the light of the mountain is fading away.
The light from the mountain is fading away.

Oh! The light from Life's mountain is fading away
The shadows are closing o'er Earth's summer day!
The cold mists have gathered on heart and on brow,
The green leaves of friendship are lost to me now,
up the steep rugged path I must wander alone.
For the blossoms of Love and Beauty are gone:
Death's chill night is welcome why should it delay,
When the light from Life's mountain has faded away.

Prologue
The Dream Girl

Millie wasn't sure if she was asleep or awake, but there seemed to be a strangely shimmering girl standing at the end of her bed. The girl hovered there, in an old-fashioned white dress — high-necked, long-sleeved and flowing to her ankles. Her long, dark hair tumbled around her pale, pale face.

'Wh . . . who are you?' asked Millie, her mouth dry, her heart thumping. 'What are you doing here?'

The girl stared at her, quiet and mysterious, her dark eyes shining in the dim moonlight. Behind her, Millie thought she could see a shadowy forest of grey-green gum trees and silvery bark. A glimmering river flowed behind her.

'Are you a ghost or a dream?' wondered Millie out loud, hugging herself against the pillows.

The girl beckoned to Millie, as though asking her to follow her into that secret forest. Millie shrank back, shaking her head, her stomach clenched in fear. The girl smiled a little enigmatic smile and offered her a bunch of creamy-white flannel flowers. Millie reached out to take them but the vision slowly faded away.

Millie shook herself and rolled over. There was no ghost girl. No forest. No flannel flowers. It was simply a dream.

When she awoke later that morning, she remembered the girl in her strange dream. The memory was a little unsettling. The image haunted her all day.

Later in art class, when she was staring at a blank page wondering what she could possibly paint for her major project, it was the ghost girl's face that came to her, pale and shimmery against the mottled-green shadows of a dark forest.

Millie smiled and began to sketch, concentrating to remember the fleeting features of the girl's face. At the end of class, the art teacher, Mrs Boardman, stopped behind Millie's chair to check on her progress. She nodded with approval.

'Millie, that is coming along beautifully,' said Mrs Boardman. 'I'm looking forward to seeing how that looks when you begin to paint it. What are those flowers? Daisies?'

'I thought so at first, but I think they're flannel flowers,' replied Millie.

'Excellent — and have you thought of a title for it yet?' asked Mrs Boardman.

Millie gave a little shiver.

'I think it's called . . . *The Dream Girl*.'

1

Lost

'Ouch,' cried Millie as her head jolted against the door.
'Sorry,' said her mum with a wince, clinging
to the steering wheel with white knuckles. 'This road is
terrible.'

The car bounced through another pothole on the narrow
dirt road. On either side, dense scrub pressed up against
the car, blocking their view. Thirteen-year-old Millie sat
in the front, while her younger sister, Bella, was in the
back surrounded by luggage.

'Do you think this is the right road?' asked Bella,
leaning forward to peer through the windscreen. 'I hope
we haven't taken another wrong turn. We could be lost out
here for hours – days even.'

Millie glanced up at the sky – heavy with grey rain
clouds – then out at a sea of parched brown Scotch thistles,
taller than a man, stretching to their left. It felt as though
they were in the middle of nowhere.

3

'No, the sign definitely said Oldbury Road,' Mum assured them. 'We should be there any . . . minute.'

The thick scrub gave way to a hedge of prickly bare hawthorn, denuded by winter frosts. Suddenly there was a view to the right, through the lichen-spotted branches. A deep brown waterhole, fringed with reeds, then a green paddock where black Angus cattle grazed.

'There it is,' cried Mum. 'That's the old house.'

The girls craned to see. Mum stopped the car. Through a gap in the hedge they could see in the distance a large house of golden sandstone, partially hidden by a thick copse of evergreens. It looked like a house out of a fairy-tale, a house protected by thorns and hedges, like a *Sleeping Beauty* castle.

'It looks a bit scary,' said the usually irrepressible Bella. 'It looks so . . . lonely.'

'It's not scary,' scolded Mum. 'It's just old — nearly one hundred and eighty years old.'

Mum accelerated again and the view was swallowed by hedges. The car followed a wide curve, then they had to stop again. The road, flooded with muddy water, disappeared into a rivulet. Flood debris hung from a nearby barbed wire fence and from tree branches and scrubby hawthorn.

'It looks deep,' said Mum nervously, surveying the flood.

The girls took this as an invitation to scramble out of their seats and onto the road. The cold air hit Millie like a slap. It seeped into her bones.

'Brrr,' she said, digging her hands into her jacket. 'It's freezing.'

'Come on,' said eleven-year-old Bella, running towards the water.

The water rushed past, swirling in brown eddies and hiding its true depth. Millie picked up a fallen branch and poked the water. Mum followed, frowning at the wide expanse covering the road.

A massive English elm had fallen beside the road. One of its branches formed a makeshift bridge, tangled with blackberry brambles. Bella balanced like a tightrope walker across it, her arms out straight to the side.

'Bella, don't go out there,' called Mum. 'It's dangerous.'

'It's fine, Mum,' insisted Bella, balancing on one leg and wobbling a little. Millie followed tentatively, using her branch as a walking stick to give her balance.

'I can't see how deep the water is,' complained Mum. 'I don't know if there's a deep hole in the middle or if it's shallow all the way across.'

Millie probed with her branch. From the middle of the tree-bridge, the view to the bottom was clearer.

'I don't think it's very deep,' Bella assured her mother. 'I think we can make it.'

Millie held up her branch, displaying the wet stain on the bark that reached about thirty centimetres up the branch.

'What do you think?' she asked. 'It doesn't seem to get deeper than this.'

Her mother sighed, squinting down at the murky depths.

'Well, I don't feel like driving all the way home to Sydney,' she confessed. 'So I guess we'll have to try it.'

Everyone clambered back into the car, their shoes

caked with thick brown mud. Mum started the car and took a deep breath before accelerating towards the creek.

The engine revved. Millie chewed her nails, the sides of her fingers already red and raw.

Mum's hands clenched the steering wheel. The car sputtered and stuttered but eventually chugged across and up the other bank, a sheet of water surging up on either side.

'We made it!' screeched Bella.

Millie collapsed back against the seat.

On the other side of the rivulet, the scrub petered out, replaced by tall elm trees, their branches bare against the winter sky. The hedge opened up to reveal paddocks, a driveway and then a clearer view of the golden house: Oldbury. It was a grand Georgian house, built of warm sandstone with a grey slate roof, its mullioned windows reflecting a glimmer of unexpected sun.

'There it is,' announced Mum with a relieved smile. 'Oldbury. Built by your great-great-great-great-great grandparents, James and Charlotte Atkinson.'

'Five times great,' confirmed Bella, jiggling up and down on the back seat.

The sight of the old house made Millie's stomach flip. 'It's beautiful,' she sighed. 'And mysterious.'

A heavy wrought-iron gate barred the driveway, fastened with a rusty bolt and a heavy iron padlock.

'The owners are away overseas,' explained Mum. 'But Aunt Jessamine is renting one of the old farm cottages nearby and has been asked to keep an eye on the place. She said she'd take us inside for a look.'

Mum checked a piece of paper with directions on the

console. 'We keep driving up this road and the cottage is on the right — an old stone cottage called Swanton.'

Eventually they found the right place, after driving past the narrow driveway. Two golden labradors barked a loud welcome as Mum pulled in and parked the car.

The green front door was flung open, revealing a woman who seemed about eighty years old, her grey hair cropped short and her face crinkled into a welcoming smile. She wore comfortable slacks and a green jumper, with a heavy gold charm bracelet on her wrist.

'Come in. Come in,' she called. 'I thought you had forgotten.' The dogs galloped up to her and licked her hands. The charm bracelet jingled as she patted the dogs.

'Sorry we're late, Aunt Jessamine,' replied Mum, giving her a hug. 'We managed to get a little lost on the way, then the river was flooded and we missed the driveway twice — but we're here now. It was so lovely of you to invite us.'

It was school holidays and Aunt Jessamine, a long-lost relative, had written to Mum in Sydney and asked her if she wanted to bring the girls down to stay for a weekend in the Southern Highlands. Both Bella and Millie had been reluctant. Bella had been hoping to go to a friend's place for a sleepover, and Millie had been planning on spending a couple of days in her pyjamas, curled up in bed reading a book or perhaps drawing and painting. But Mum had been insistent.

'Poor Aunt Jessamine is all alone in the world now,' Mum reminded them. 'She has no children or grand-children, and she's probably very lonely. Besides, it will be lovely to get away for a couple of days — we can go for long walks and eat scones and spend time together. We hardly have any time together now that you're both so busy with school and activities.'

So Mum had taken a long weekend from work, and they had packed up the car with pillows, backpacks, a bag of books and an esky of snacks and made the two-hour drive south, through the old historic towns of Mittagong and Berrima to the farmland around Sutton Forest. Mum had been working off a map roughly hand-drawn by Aunt Jessamine and sadly lacking in detail and scale, and the satellite navigation system in the car had seemed a bit contrary today and had decided to take them a long, roundabout and thoroughly confusing route.

'Not to worry,' said Aunt Jessamine. 'I have the kettle ready to boil and I've baked some apple tarts for morning tea. And these must be your beautiful daughters? Millie and Isabella — I've heard so much about you from your grandmother.'

'Hello, Aunt Jessamine,' echoed the two sisters, one shyly, the other boldly.

Mum had explained that Jessamine was more like a second cousin than their aunt. She had never had children of her own and since her husband had died, she had endeavoured to regain contact with her more far-flung relatives.

'Well, let's not just stand here,' insisted Aunt Jessamine. 'Bring your things inside.'

Aunt Jessamine had prepared a guestroom, with a view over the gardens towards Mount Gingenbullen. Bella and Millie were to share the double bed, while Mum had a day lounge against the window. They quickly dumped their bags, unpacked a few things then returned to the kitchen to join Aunt Jessamine.

The kitchen was filled with the delicious smell of hot pastry. A table covered in a white cloth held a platter of freshly baked apple tarts, a bowl of thick clotted cream and a steaming teapot. The girls sat down beside their mother and sipped on the hot tea, which warmed their cold hands.

'I believe Millie has inherited the family talent for art?' asked Aunt Jessamine, sitting at the head of the table.

Millie blushed and quickly examined the apple tart on her plate. The pastry was warm and flaky, while the moist apples were sticky with caramelised brown sugar. Millie took a forkful of tart so that she didn't need to answer. It was delicious.

Mum beamed with pride. 'Millie came top of her year with a painting she called *The Dream Girl*. Her art teacher entered it into the local art competition, and she has been announced as a finalist,' she boasted. 'Millie has to go to the announcement of the winners in the city next weekend.'

Millie's stomach churned with fear. She was absolutely dreading it. Mrs Boardman, her art teacher, had explained that there would be a huge cocktail party with hundreds of people at the Art Gallery of New South Wales, including TV cameras and media photographers, as well as a who's who of dignitaries, politicians and local celebrities. Then the mayor would announce the winners of each category. Millie was seriously considering coming down with a bad case of stomach bug so she could stay at home in bed and read a book.

'Look, I have a photo of it here,' offered Mum, rummaging around in her handbag.

She pulled out her notebook computer and opened the photo of Millie's painting, which filled the screen. It was a figure of a dark-haired girl, her pale skin in stark contrast to the shadowy silvery-greens of the forest behind. In a corner perched the almost invisible outline of a dragonfly, while a creamy profusion of flannel flowers sat in the foreground.

'I think the girl looks kind of spooky,' said Bella, wrinkling her nose. 'She looks scared.'

'No,' Mum contradicted, smiling at Bella. 'She looks *ethereal*.'

Aunt Jessamine turned the screen towards her and examined it closely, then glanced sharply at Millie.

'It's very good,' she said. 'Exceptional for a child of your age.'

'Oh, not really,' mumbled Millie, scuffing her toe on the wooden floor under the table. 'I don't know why they entered it in the competition. I wish they hadn't.'

Aunt Jessamine lifted Millie's chin with her forefinger and gazed into her eyes. Her heavy gold charm bracelet jingled. 'Millie, did you know that the lineage of talented female artists and writers in our family goes back nearly two hundred years? It's a heritage you should be proud of.'

Millie frowned. 'I didn't know that,' she replied.

'Oldbury, the house we are going to see later today, was built by your ancestors James and Charlotte,' explained Aunt Jessamine. 'Charlotte Waring, as she was before she married James, studied art and drawing under John Glover, the famous English landscape painter.

'She then taught her own four children — Charlotte Elizabeth, Jane Emily, James John and Caroline Louisa — and they all went on to become talented painters and writers. I have a book here that has reproductions of some of their paintings and sketches. Sadly, though, most of their work was destroyed in the late nineteenth century.'

In the car on the journey down from Sydney, Mum had explained that Aunt Jessamine was fascinated with the family history.

'Actually, Millie, I think you are the one who looks most like an Atkinson,' decided Aunt Jessamine. 'With your wavy brown hair and grey eyes, you look a bit like Emily or Louisa Atkinson. Emily was said to be the prettiest of the three girls. '

Millie blushed again. She really didn't like to be the centre of attention.

'What about me?' demanded Bella. 'Do I look like an Atkinson?'

Aunt Jessamine examined her closely. 'No,' she replied, shaking her head. 'Not really. I think you must take after your father's side of the family.'

Bella looked momentarily crestfallen.

'You're pretty too, Bella,' added Mum reassuringly.

'I'll show you a picture of Emily Atkinson.' Aunt Jessamine left the room and came back with a pile of books and a manila folder filled with photocopies.

'Here is a bundle of old newspaper articles, and that's a copy of a journal that Charlotte Waring used on her journey out to Australia,' explained Aunt Jessamine. 'And here are the copies I made of some of the family sketches.'

Aunt Jessamine showed them four colour photocopies of a series of watercolour portraits, all in profile, of a mother and three children.

'That is Charlotte Waring Atkinson,' said Aunt Jessamine, pointing to a rather severe-looking woman in a white lace cap. 'She was reputedly very handsome in her youth, but this was painted later after her husband died and all the troubles that followed.'

Millie thought she looked rather fierce with her black eyes and black hair.

'She was an unusually independent woman for her time, with strong opinions on the importance of education for girls and women's rights,' continued Aunt Jessamine. 'You must remember that in the early nineteenth century, women had very few legal rights to education, money, property, professions — even custody of their own children.'

Mum shook her head. 'It's hard to fathom now, isn't it? You girls are so lucky to be growing up in a time when you can be anything you want to be.'

Millie tilted her head to the side. *Could I be anything I want to be?* she wondered. *What do I want to be? Nothing amazing. Maybe just . . . brave?*

Aunt Jessamine showed them another sketch. 'This one is Louisa, the youngest daughter, who became a famous naturalist, artist and writer,' she explained. 'In fact, Louisa was the first Australian-born female novelist and one of the earliest female journalists, although it was her botanical discoveries that made her work truly remarkable. She has several plants named after her. What a shame only a tiny fraction of her drawings and paintings were preserved.'

Aunt Jessamine fanned through a book of exquisite drawings of plants and animals before showing them another portrait.

'The only boy of the family, James John Oldbury

Atkinson, was named after his father and eventually inherited the estate nearly twenty years after his father's death. And this is the original Emily, the sweet second child and the family favourite.'

Millie noted the hazel eyes and brown hair parted in the middle, pulled back and braided into intricate loops around her delicate face.

'We think these were painted by Charlotte Elizabeth Atkinson, the eldest daughter, who was named after her mother, as she is the only one in the family not depicted. Sadly, we don't know what she looked like.'

'So Charlotte painted as well?' asked Millie, examining the faded prints closely.

'Yes — all the children were very clever. They only attended school for a very short time, but nevertheless topped the prize lists. Their mother was an amazing woman . . . Did you know that she wrote the first children's book published in Australia?'

Aunt Jessamine chattered on for a little while, then pushed back her chair and stood up.

'But it's such a lovely wintry morning,' she said. 'Why don't we go for a walk down to Oldbury before lunch? I need to check the mailbox and water the plants, and it's a pleasant walk.'

All four of them rugged up with thick winter coats, scarves, gloves, beanies and boots. Millie's breath was smoky in the cold air. They walked back the way they had driven — down the long, rutted, dirt driveway through the paddocks and onto the road. The roadway wound up and over a steep hill, past some cattle yards, then down into the sheltered valley.

'This land was all once owned by the Atkinson family and part of the Oldbury Estate,' explained Aunt Jessamine as they walked down the hill. 'James arrived in the colony in 1820 and was one of the first settlers in the area. When he applied for his land grants, the whole area was remote wilderness.'

Millie tried to imagine the neat farmland as wild bushland roamed by an ancient clan of Aborigines. It seemed too long ago to fathom.

'I don't know if it's true, but my grandmother said that James Atkinson was told he could have as much land as he could ride around on horseback in a day,' added Aunt Jessamine.

'He must have had a fast horse,' joked Bella.

'Can you imagine the work involved in carving farmland from utter wilderness?' asked Mum. 'We think we work hard, but it must have been a tough life for the early settlers.'

'Sadly, the estate was subdivided many years ago into smaller farmlets,' explained Aunt Jessamine.

Mum looked longingly at a pretty stone cottage that had once been a workers home on the original estate. 'I've always thought it would be lovely to have a farm down here,' she said. 'A perfect place to escape the hustle of the city on weekends. Unfortunately, we'd need to find a pot of gold to afford it.'

Aunt Jessamine laughed, waving her gloved hand. 'You know this whole area was once infested with bushrangers. Gentleman Jackey Jackey and the Berrima axe murderer John Lynch were particularly infamous in the 1840s, when the Atkinsons lived here. There are some deep caves a few kilometres away where bushrangers are reputed to have had a hide-out. When I was growing up there were stories of hidden caches of bushranger treasure, but as much as we searched we never found any.'

'Perhaps *we'll* find some hidden treasure,' suggested Bella, skipping along.

'Now that would come in handy,' joked Mum.

They walked down to the ornate front gate, with its large padlock. Aunt Jessamine unlocked the gate with a silver key. The gravel drive was covered in brown, dead leaves. A cold wind blew them in swirling eddies.

The grand house crouched among its gardens, quiet but watchful. It looked lonely and forlorn. To the right, across the paddock, Millie could see a waterhole, its banks fringed with reeds and rushes. An old, bare-leafed elm tree towered over it, with a mossy wooden garden seat underneath.

Aunt Jessamine emptied the mailbox of an assortment of envelopes, brochures and a local newspaper. Tucking the pile under her elbow, she led the way, crunching up the gravel driveway towards the house with its circular lawn, imposing steps and columned portico over the double front doors.

2

The House

Aunt Jessamine took off her tan leather gloves and drew an old-fashioned iron key out of her pocket to open the front door. They all took their boots off outside and entered in their socks. The house smelt musty and stale from being locked up.

The door opened into a large vestibule with heavy cedar doors opening off it on either side. Millie was glad of her warm coat — the air was as chilly inside as out. A stairway rose to the second storey, while a closed door obviously led to the rooms at the back of the house.

Aunt Jessamine placed the mail on top of a tottering pile on the hall table and dropped her gloves beside it.

'The power is turned off so it's a little dark,' explained Aunt Jessamine. 'But I'm sure the owners wouldn't mind us having a peek inside, especially as the house was built by our ancestors.'

Millie and Bella looked around. 'This is the dining room,'

said Aunt Jessamine, opening a door on the right of the vestibule to reveal a gracious room, with its rose-pink walls, long dining table, balloon-back chairs and fireplace. 'And over here is the sitting room.' Mum, Bella and Millie followed her into the front room with its large, empty, cold fireplace.

'The new owners have done a beautiful job renovating the house,' said Mum, looking around the spacious room. 'I remember my parents bringing me here when I was a child, and it was very run-down then.'

While Aunt Jessamine was showing Mum and Bella the fine example of the colonial woodwork on the cedar double doors at one end of the room, Millie walked over to the large picture window that overlooked the formal gardens with their clipped box hedges, sandstone walls and wide, green lawns. Over the gardens, Millie could see the grey circle of the gravel carriageway and down the straight, tree-lined driveway to the gate. A flash of white caught her eye. She realised it was a girl in a white dress running across the lawn towards the river, her long skirts and dark hair flying.

'Oh, look,' cried Millie. 'There's someone in the garden. A girl!'

Aunt Jessamine tutted and came over, followed by Mum and Bella. Millie turned towards them.

'No one should be here,' complained Aunt Jessamine. 'All the gates are kept locked while the owners are away. One of the local children must have followed us in.'

They all looked through the window over the bare garden. There was no sign of the girl.

'I can't see anyone,' said Bella, her breath fogging up the glass.

'Why don't we go down into the garden and see if she's

there,' suggested Aunt Jessamine. 'She's probably not doing any harm, but I should check.'

Aunt Jessamine opened the glass-paned front door, pulled on her boots and led the way down the wide steps to the front path.

'She ran down towards the river,' said Millie, pointing to the left.

'Technically, it's a rivulet,' said Aunt Jessamine. 'The Medway Rivulet.'

The group trudged through the paddock towards the creek. There was no one there but some wild ducks, who squawked noisily as they approached.

'No sign of your mysterious maiden,' joked Mum. 'Perhaps she jumped into the waterhole.'

Aunt Jessamine sank onto the wooden bench under the elm tree. 'Time for a little rest,' she said. 'It's quite a walk from my cottage to the big house.'

Mum sat down beside her, leaning against the back of the chair and closing her eyes.

'Oh, this is so lovely,' she said. 'A beautiful walk in the fresh country air, gorgeous scenery, my favourite girls . . . It's just what I needed.'

Bella picked up a stone from the bank and skimmed it across the waterhole. Millie followed suit, but her stone plopped and sank without a trace.

Bella laughed. 'Millie, you have to throw it on an angle, like this,' she suggested, sending another stone skipping across the still water.

'Skimming pebbles,' said Aunt Jessamine, watching with interest. 'Now that takes me back to my childhood . . . Actually, it reminds me of a lovely story.'

'Tell us,' invited Mum, her eyes still closed, soaking up the warmth of some stray winter sunrays.

'It's the story of this charm on my bracelet,' Aunt Jessamine began, showing the heavy gold charm bracelet. One of the trinkets was a polished red-and-brown streaked stone hanging from a gold loop.

Millie and Bella turned around to look. Mum opened her eyes.

'It's a beautiful bracelet,' said Mum. 'You can tell it's old by the gorgeous rose colour of the gold, and it's heavy.'

'The stone is the oldest part of the bracelet,' said Aunt Jessamine, holding the pebble between her forefingers. 'This little stone was Charlotte Atkinson's good luck charm.'

Millie looked at it closely.

'You see, Charlotte Waring, as she was then, was a headstrong, adventurous lass,' claimed Aunt Jessamine. 'Her mother died when she was a wee babe. Her father married again and had a son, who inherited all the family wealth.

'At the age of fifteen, Charlotte had to leave home and earn her living as a governess. By all accounts she was extraordinarily clever, able to read fluently by the age of two, and she had an unusually rigorous education for a girl of those times. She became a highly qualified and sought-after teacher. Eventually she was offered a prestigious post as a governess for one of the colony's leading families of the 1820s.'

Mum nodded. She had heard the story before.

'Most young ladies of those days would have been petrified at the very idea, but not Charlotte Waring,' continued

Aunt Jessamine. 'She took the post, but only on the condition that she would travel to Australia first-class.

'Just before she left on her journey, Charlotte went home to her father's family estate in Kent. The family had owned land in the village of Shoreham for generations, and Charlotte had spent most of her childhood raised by an aunt. She went down to the River Darent, which flowed through the village and on into the River Thames.'

Aunt Jessamine gestured towards the waterway in front of them.

'Charlotte leant down and picked up a small pebble that was lying on the riverbank, and slipped it in her pocket as a reminder of home and where she had come from,' Aunt Jessamine explained. 'In years to come, when life became difficult, Charlotte would rub the brown river pebble. It would give her hope, strength and courage. It would remind her where she had come from.'

Aunt Jessamine rubbed the pebble between her fingertips with a smile. 'In time, many years later, this humble river pebble was given to her daughter Charlotte, who gave it to her daughter Flora, and so on until it was set in gold and hung on this bracelet along with lots of other charms — but for me, the river pebble is the most potent charm of all. Now I wear it as a symbol, to give me hope and courage and remind me where I came from.'

Aunt Jessamine sat back and beamed at Millie.

'That's a beautiful story, Aunt Jessamine,' said Millie. 'I wish I had a charm to give me strength and courage when I need it.' Millie thought about the upcoming art show that she was dreading, and her face was so filled with yearning that Aunt Jessamine unclasped the bracelet.

'Come and try it on, Millie,' said Aunt Jessamine. 'Perhaps you could borrow the bracelet to give you courage when you most need it. Would you like to wear it to your big art show next week?'

Millie breathed in, looking at the bracelet with awe. 'Oh, could I?' she begged. 'Aunt Jessamine, that would be wonderful. Could I please, please wear it? I promise to look after it!'

'Try it on for size,' Aunt Jessamine suggested. 'I think it will look simply gorgeous on you.'

Aunt Jessamine slipped the bracelet off and clasped it onto Millie's thin wrist.

Millie held the bracelet up to the light and it slid down her arm, the gold gleaming in the weak sunlight. There were many charms, most of which looked like souvenirs from a lifetime of travel and adventures. There was a tiny Eiffel Tower, a Turkish prayer scroll, a pale-pink cameo, an amethyst heart and an oval locket with old photographs inside. The little red-and-brown stone — the River Darent pebble charm — shone with nearly 200 years of polishing and fingering.

'Be careful of it,' warned Aunt Jessamine. 'It is irreplaceable.'

Millie smiled. 'I promise.'

Aunt Jessamine rubbed her cold hands together.

'Oh, bother,' said Aunt Jessamine. 'I've left my gloves up in the house.'

'I'll get them for you,' offered Millie, jumping to her feet.

'Are you sure?' asked Aunt Jessamine. 'That would be lovely — I think I left them on the hall table.'

Millie ran back towards the house, the charm bracelet jingling on her wrist. Aunt Jessamine had left the front door open to let the house air. Millie went inside, picked up the gloves and turned to go outside again. She suddenly paused as she heard a creaking sound from the stairs above. Millie felt a flutter in her stomach.

She glanced up to see a strange girl in white running down the stairs. The girl looked oddly familiar. She had long, dark hair hanging down her back, clear, dark eyes and a long dress with full skirts that came to her ankles. The girl stared at her, startled, then hurried into the sitting room.

Could it be? It couldn't. *It was the girl from her dream.*

As if in another dream, Millie walked reluctantly to the sitting room door. Something was different. Something was not quite right. The sound of piano playing wafted through the half-open door. Millie clutched the gloves tightly to her chest.

She opened the door to find a different drawing room to the one Aunt Jessamine had shown them. Instead of the pale-cream walls, they were papered a rich avocado green. A fire now roared in the grate, filling the room with warmth and a cheery light.

The room was no longer empty. Instead, there was a group of four children gathered around the fireplace — three girls and a boy, all dressed in strange, old-fashioned clothes.

One girl, her face framed by light-brown ringlets, sat on a stool at the piano, her fingers rippling over the keys. A slow, melancholy melody rang out, which she hummed along to, pumping the pedals with her foot. The youngest girl lay on the rug, playing with a soft rag doll, her lower legs encased in lace-trimmed pantalettes. The boy had an army of tin soldiers guarding the fireplace, and he marched them back and forth, slaying them with glee.

'Ready, aim . . . fire!' he boomed, knocking over half a dozen soldiers with a lump of coal cannonball.

The dream girl was sitting in the armchair, her feet curled beneath her. She had a pencil in her hand and was writing on a sheet of paper propped on a hardback book. Her brow was furrowed as she tried to concentrate.

'Emily, play something more cheerful,' she suggested. 'That dirge is making us all feel gloomy.'

Emily obligingly began playing a country melody, singing a few lines in a sweet, strong voice.

'Is this better, Charlotte?' asked Emily with a smile. 'I thought Mozart would help you to concentrate on your *Account of the Esquimaux People of Northern America*.'

'Don't tell Mamma but I finished that,' Charlotte confessed, waving her paper in the air. 'Now I'm working on the chronicles of Princess Arabella.'

Charlotte adopted a dramatic tone, reading from her story. 'The Princess Arabella, dressed in rags, is imprisoned in the northern tower of the castle by her evil stepfather Lord George.'

'Lord George?' asked Emily, ceasing her playing and raising her eyebrows.

'The dastardly, evil villain Lord *George*,' confirmed Charlotte. She showed the paper with a sketch of a man's face, twisted and cruel.

The youngest girl looked up from her doll. 'He looks like Mr George Bart—'

'Louisa, shush,' demanded Charlotte, glancing towards the door.

Emily stood and swooped down near her sister on the rug. Pulling her onto her lap and smoothing back the girl's dark ringlets, she said, 'Let's listen to Charlotte's story, shall we, poppet?'

The boy stopped playing with his soldiers and sat up cross-legged.

'Princess Arabella has been treated most cruelly, receiving no food or water for several days,' Charlotte continued. 'Famished and weak, she falls on her knees to beg her dastardly stepfather to set her free. Kicking her so that she falls to the ground, he laughs like the Lord of the Underworld himself, and slams the door, locking it with an immense silver key.'

Charlotte paused and looked around at her siblings expectantly.

'What happens next?' asked James.

'I'm not quite sure,' confessed Charlotte, sighing.

'A handsome young prince is riding by in the Forbidden Forest, mounted on his proud dappled stallion,' suggested Emily. 'He is on a perilous quest to find a golden dragon egg and hears her wretched cries for help. James, what comes next?'

'He gallops across the castle drawbridge, leaps from his horse, takes his battle sword and with a single blow sunders the head of Lord George,' added James, miming the attack with his clenched fists.

'Princess Arabella calls for her beloved mamma, who races to her rescue and sets her free,' said Louisa, cuddling her doll to her thin chest.

Charlotte pondered the suggestions, chewing the end of her pencil.

'I think Princess Arabella removes the sheets and curtains from her vast four-poster bed and knots them together to make a flimsy rope,' decided Charlotte. 'She tosses that out the narrow window and climbs down. Twice she nearly falls to a certain death. She is nearly at the bottom when, overcome with exhaustion, she slips a third time — but this time she tumbles into the dark depths of the slimy, green moat.'

Charlotte enacted the scene, swooning on the rug.

Emily laughed and pushed her shoulder. 'So, shivering and soaked, the weary Princess Arabella crawls up the bank of the moat in the mud, where she collapses, dying from consumption,' she concluded for her sister, pretending to collapse.

'*Then*, the prince finds her and vows to avenge her untimely death with his mighty battle sword,' said James.

'No,' insisted Charlotte, pointing at him with her pencil. 'Princess Arabella crawls up the moat, steals her horse from the stables and rides off to find the handsome prince. Together they return to rescue the impoverished queen, who is imprisoned with her younger children in the rat-infested dungeon. Realising he is defeated, the evil Lord George flees to the battlements, but there is no escape. As Princess Arabella and the handsome prince pursue him, he slips off the battlements and plunges to his gruesome death.'

Louisa screwed up her face, looking distressed. 'But —' she began.

'Princess Arabella then marries the prince and lives happily ever after in the stately castle with her mamma, her brave brother and her two beautiful sisters,' concluded Emily, smoothing out the frown from Louisa's forehead with her fingertips.

'Never *ever* again to be bothered by the villainous Lord George,' declared Charlotte with satisfaction.

Millie was still standing in the doorway, mesmerised by the impossible scene before her, the gold charm bracelet heavy on her wrist. She stepped further into the room, curious to know more.

Charlotte looked up, staring straight through her. 'Quick! I think Mamma is coming back.'

Emily flew to the piano stool and resumed her playing. Charlotte stood up and ran to the table where she tucked the papers away inside a sketchbook.

She picked up an abandoned book of poetry from the armchair and opened it to a random page.

'Come and read with me, Louisa,' coaxed Charlotte. 'We'll read "Mariana" by Alfred Tennyson.'

Louisa squeezed next to her sister in the armchair. Charlotte recited the poem in a clear voice, rich with dramatic expression:

With blackest moss the flower-plots
Were thickly crusted, one and all;
The rusted nails fell from the knots
That held the pear to the gable wall.
The broken sheds look'd sad and strange;
Unlifted was the clinking latch:
Weeded and worn the ancient thatch
Upon the lonely moated grange.
She only said, 'My life is dreary,

He cometh not,' she said;
She said, 'I am aweary, aweary,
I would that I were dead!'

Millie slipped backwards from the room and pulled the door shut, her heart thumping. She paused in the hallway. *What did I see? Where have I been? Why didn't I talk to them?* She nibbled on her fingertip, tearing the quick until it bled.

Taking a deep breath, she opened the door into the drawing room and hurried in, determined to speak to the children this time — but they were gone. Instead, the drawing room was as it had been: empty and cold. Millie stepped back into the vestibule and tried opening the door again, but nothing changed. She stood in the sitting room, eyes closed, concentrating hard, willing the ghost children to return. Nothing happened.

Feeling confused and strangely bereft, Millie slowly wandered back out to the garden to join the others.

'Oh, there you are, Millie,' said Mum. 'I was beginning to think you'd lost your way.'

Millie smiled wanly and handed the gloves to Aunt Jessamine, who drew them over her cold hands.

'Are you all right, Millie?' asked Mum. 'You look very pale.'

'She looks like she's seen a headless ghost,' joked Bella. 'Is the old house haunted, do you think, Millie?'

Millie glared at Bella. 'I was feeling a little faint.'

Mum took Millie's wrist to feel her pulse. 'Perhaps we should take you home if you're not well?'

'No, no,' Millie insisted. 'I'm fine. Actually, Aunt Jessamine, I was wondering if you could tell me more about the Atkinson family. When did they live here? What happened to them?'

Aunt Jessamine's eyes lit up. 'Of course, Millie. I'd love to tell you about the family. Why don't you sit down here beside me?'

Millie sat on the old timber seat and looked up at the ancient tree, its vast branches spreading against the blue sky.

'Is there anything in particular you'd like to know?' Aunt Jessamine asked.

'I'd like to know about the children,' suggested Millie. 'About Charlotte and Emily, and James and Louisa.' She could see their faces clearly in her mind.

'Let me tell you their story,' invited Aunt Jessamine, wriggling her back against the timber seat. 'We have some time before lunch . . .'

3

Master Maugie

Oldbury, Winter 1839

The sun shone down out of a deep-blue sky, bathing the valley in a golden, late-afternoon haze. A flock of jewel-coloured lorikeets soared across the valley, swooping and diving.

The two girls rode their ponies at a walk, side by side, through the river paddock, a black dog trotting along beside them. They rode side-saddle, their long blue skirts and flounced white petticoats cascading down the horses' left sides.

A flock of 300-odd sheep were scattered over the field, grazing on the dry, golden winter grass. Lambs gambolled, playing chase and tag, their long tails wagging. A glossy black crow, perched on a fence post, watched the lambs with beady yellow eyes.

The sisters waved to the convict shepherd, who

was smoking his pipe in the sunshine. He waved back languidly, his face brown and wrinkled under his broad-brimmed hat. Samson the dog bounded over to say hello to the shepherd's dogs and received a welcome scratch behind the ears.

'Where shall we ride today?' Charlotte asked her younger sister. 'Would you like to ride along the creek towards Golden Valley, or shall we ride to the top of Gingenbullen and sketch up there?'

Emily glanced along the creek, which was flowing sluggishly without the usual winter rains.

There were a number of timber slab huts built beside the waterhole where the shepherds and stockmen lived. Two of the workers' wives were hanging up washing on a rope strung between two trees. Chickens and geese scratched among the vegetables.

'I don't mind,' replied Emily, patting her horse's neck with her gloved hand and surveying the scenery. 'It's just so lovely to be out riding instead of doing chores or studying. Where would you prefer?'

'Why don't we ride up to the top of the mountain?' replied Charlotte, pointing with her riding crop. 'It's so tranquil up there, and I'm sure we'll find something pretty to sketch. It's such a glorious day.'

Charlotte was a striking girl with large black eyes, pale skin and curly black hair that tumbled down her back, under her broad-brimmed straw hat. Her sister Emily had a daintier prettiness with soft brown ringlets and gentle hazel eyes.

'Good idea,' agreed Emily. 'I'd like to pick some wattle for Mamma if we can find some.'

Charlotte whistled for Samson, who came bounding back obediently. Then she clicked her tongue to encourage her mare and headed left towards Gingenbullen Mountain, which loomed above the farmland covered in thick, silvery-green eucalypt forest. A track had been carved through the bush, leading up to the summit. Bellbirds chimed in the treetops, their songs echoing out over the valley. The two horses panted and puffed as they plodded up the slope, their hooves sliding on the rocky slope.

The girls rode in silence, enjoying the rustling sounds of the bush. A couple of pale-grey wallabies started then bounded across the track and into the scrub on the other side. Samson barked madly after them, his tail wagging.

'Leave them, Samson,' ordered Charlotte, whistling him back to heel. Charlotte's black mare, Ophelia, arched her neck and pranced skittishly.

As the track flattened out near the grassy summit, Charlotte kicked her heels into her horse's side and broke into a gallop. Charlotte's heart soared as the wind whipped her face and tangled her flying hair. Ophelia's hooves thundered on the track, kicking up clods of earth and flying scree.

Emily followed at a much slower pace, her grey horse, Clarie, picking its way through the tussocks of grass.

'Come on, Emily,' Charlotte beckoned.

'I'm coming,' replied her sister with a smile, urging her horse into a slow jog up the slope. 'I just do not fancy having your mud flung all over me.'

At the top of the ridge was a pastured clearing with two gnarled gum trees framing the view.

The two girls pulled up and gazed back the way they had come. Below them lay cleared paddocks dotted with grazing sheep, each field bordered by carefully tended hawthorn hedges or conifer windbreaks. Graceful elms and yew trees grew along the creek line, which formed a series of wider waterholes linked by a narrower stream. On the slope above the creek was the honey-warm stone house, its outbuildings nestled among the gardens and trees. Further away on the other side of the river, in the bush, a thin plume of grey smoke snaked into the sky where the local Gandangara clan was camping.

'Isn't it lovely?' cried Charlotte, patting Ophelia's damp neck. 'I never tire of this outlook.'

'It must be the most beautiful view in the world,' agreed Emily. 'The huts look like miniature doll's houses.'

The two horses quietly cropped the grass, their reins loose. Samson, pink tongue lolling, flopped down in the long grass. His thick black coat glistened in the sunlight.

Charlotte slipped out of the saddle and rummaged in her saddlebag, pulling out her sketchbook and a bundle of pencils. A fallen tree provided a handy bench overlooking the view, as well as branches to tether the ponies to. She took a seat, removed her riding gloves and opened her sketchbook to reveal detailed drawings of dragonflies, beetles and butterflies.

Emily dismounted and wandered around the clearing, searching for wildflowers, which she gathered into a large bunch of yellows, purples and reds. A sudden, unexpected sound caught her attention.

'What was that?' asked Emily, frowning. 'Did you hear a strange noise?'

Charlotte dropped her sketchbook and came over, her ears straining. The sound came again — a soft, plaintive whimper.

'Is it a baby crying?' replied Charlotte, looking around.

'What would a baby be doing all the way up here?' asked Emily. 'Unless it is an Aboriginal baby.'

Charlotte shook her head.

'The Aborigines never come up here because of the grave mound,' replied Charlotte.

On the side of Gingenbullen Mountain, the local Aboriginal clan had constructed a large conical grave hill about twelve metres high where, until recently, they had buried their dead. The gravesite was guarded by trees, with each trunk intricately carved with the symbols of weapons — spears, shields and boomerangs. While the local people no longer buried their dead here, they still scrupulously avoided the resting place of their ancestors.

'Perhaps it's an injured animal then,' suggested Emily.

The girls searched the long grass. The cries seemed very close.

'Look there,' Charlotte pointed under a large blue gum. 'It's a native bear and her baby.'

A grey female koala lay still on her side. The joey clung pathetically to its mother, its breathing low and shallow, its furry ears flickering. Charlotte squatted by the two animals, her heart thumping in her chest. *Is the mother alive or dead? What has happened to them?*

Samson approached and sniffed the animals.

'No, Samson,' ordered Charlotte. 'Sit and stay.' Samson obeyed, looking up longingly.

Emily crouched and clutched Charlotte's arm.

'It might be better not to look,' warned Charlotte. 'I think the mother is dead.'

She stood up and took off her fitted, dark-blue riding jacket, which she wore over a white shirt. Making soothing noises, she carefully wrapped the jacket snugly around the joey. Charlotte cuddled the shivering body to her chest then examined the mother. A bloody wound through the head was the obvious cause of death.

'What happened?' Emily asked, her voice shaking.

'I think she's been shot,' replied Charlotte.

'Who would shoot an innocent creature and just leave it to die?' demanded Emily.

'Probably one of the convict shepherds,' guessed Charlotte. 'I don't know, but I think we should take the baby home and show Mamma.'

Emily nodded and packed away their sketchbooks and pencils into the saddlebag. Taking a sheet of fallen paperbark, she placed it over the dead koala and laid her bouquet of wildflowers on the makeshift grave.

'I wish we could bury her properly,' Emily said wistfully, before turning away to mount Clarie.

Using the fallen log as a mounting block, Charlotte clambered up into the side-saddle, still nursing the koala joey. 'I'll ask Mamma to send up one of the convicts to do it. Otherwise, the native dogs will find her. It is a miracle that they hadn't found her and the baby already.'

Charlotte clicked her tongue, holding the reins with her free hand, and the mare walked on. The girls rode slowly back down the steep, rough track so as not to frighten the koala. At the base of the mountain was a gate leading from the wild scrub into the smaller fenced home paddocks, where cattle and horses grazed. Emily's horse stood obediently while she leant down to open and then close the gate from the saddle.

Close to the rear of the house was an orchard planted in long, straight rows with a vast variety of fruit trees — quince, apple, pear, peach, plum, cherry and lemon. A huge poultry yard was bustling with the clucking and scratching of chickens, geese and ducks. A flamboyant turquoise peacock paraded his tail feathers for his drab, grey mate.

The back of the house was the working side of the estate — a collection of stone and wooden outbuildings, including the barn, stables and carriage shed. A gardener in a blue smock hoed between the mulched rows of the vegetable and herb beds, whistling as he worked.

In the yard a convict carpenter, Dandy Jack, worked to mend a broken cart, while an Aboriginal boy called Charley sat polishing a saddle with linseed oil and rags. Two pet wallabies were nibbling scraps of hay and looked up curiously before hopping over to say hello.

Charley jumped up as soon as he saw the girls and rushed to hold the horses' heads while each of the girls dismounted in front of the stable. Samson ran straight to Charley, ignoring the handsome young carpenter.

'Good ride, Miss Charlotte?' he asked, rubbing Ophelia between the eyes down her white star.

'Yes, but look, Charley,' said Charlotte, holding up her bundle for inspection. 'We found a baby bear. The mother had been shot. Do you think it might have been killed by one of the shepherds?'

Charley peered at the koala cuddled up in Charlotte's arms. 'Perhaps,' he agreed. 'Those shepherds like hunting.'

35

Dandy Jack stopped work and laughed. He was nick-named Dandy because he always took particular care with his hair and clothes. 'Or Mr Barton might have seen some-thing. He was up there on the mountain hunting kangaroos yesterday. You could ask him.'

Charlotte and Emily exchanged worried glances. Their stepfather, George Barton, could easily have been the one to shoot the koala.

'It doesn't matter,' replied Charlotte, tucking her jacket more securely around the joey. 'I won't trouble him.'

'You girls ought to be careful riding up in that scrub,' warned Dandy Jack, swinging down his hammer on the plank of wood. 'There's all sorts of danger that could harm a couple of young ladies like you — wild dogs, poisonous brown snakes, bloodthirsty natives . . .'

He glanced at Charley with a sneer.

Charlotte laughed and tossed her head. 'You're just trying to frighten us, Jack. The Aborigines won't hurt us — they've been friends with my family for years. Besides, the brown snakes slither out of the way as soon as they hear you. They are far more frightened of me than I am of them.'

'The dogs are fairly timid, too, aren't they, Charley?' added Emily. 'We often see them whenever Charley's family camp on Oldbury. They have lots of them, and they howl a lot, but are quite tame.'

Charley hung his head and scuffed his bare toes in the dust.

Dandy Jack grinned and put down his hammer. 'Well, you should watch out for Mr Barton up there with his shotgun. He might think you are a pair of native bears.'

'Yes,' replied Charlotte. 'But fortunately he rode into town this morning. He told Mamma not to expect him for dinner.'

'Gone into town on business?' asked Dandy Jack slyly. 'That might take a few days.'

'Mr Barton's business is his own concern,' said Charlotte haughtily. She turned to Charley with a warm smile, patting Ophelia on her sleek black neck. 'Charley, would you be so kind as to put the horses out in the paddock for us, please? We won't be riding again today.'

'Yes, miss,' replied Charley, leading Ophelia and Clarie forward by the reins.

As they walked towards the house, Charlotte whispered to her sister, 'We can only hope he's away for a few days!'

Emily smiled with relief. 'A holiday.'

A stone-flagged verandah ran across the back of the main house, separating it from the rectangular sandstone buildings of the dairy and kitchen to the left and right of the courtyard. Large pots were filled with flowers and herbs, while pale-pink cabbage roses and lavender grew against the protected kitchen wall.

Bridget, the Irish maidservant, was sweeping the paving with a stiff broom, her pale skin flushed and sweaty with the exertion.

'Bridget, where is Mamma?' called Charlotte as she hurried across the courtyard.

Bridget paused and pushed her damp, red hair back from her face, tucking it under her white cap.

'She is in the office doing the accounts,' Bridget offered in her lilting Irish accent. Bridget peered at the bundle in Charlotte's arms. 'Do no' tell me ye two have brought home another native creature? Do ye no' have enough already wit' your wallabies and your possums? No' to mention tha' dog tracking mud on my just-cleaned floors? When will ye learn that wild creatures belong in the forest, no' in the house?'

'Oh, Bridget, I'm sorry,' Emily said. 'But he would die if we left him up there. His mother had been shot. The wallabies were orphans too, their mothers killed by hunters. Surely you wouldn't rather that we left them to die?'

Bridget smiled, leaning on her broom, a long white apron covering her grey dress. 'Oh, be off wit' ye both,' she said. 'I made some shortbread this morning if ye're hungry. Take some to yer mother. And if ye need it, there is fresh milk in the dairy, for the orphan.'

'Thank you, Bridget, you are a treasure,' said Charlotte.

The girls detoured via the kitchen to find the promised snack, then entered the heart of the house through the back door. Mamma was in the office at the rear, sitting at the desk by the window, frowning down at her work. In one hand, she held a small brown pebble that she rolled between her fingers as she read a letter. The desk was littered with papers and ledgers, while the walls of the office were lined with bookshelves crowded with hundreds of leather-bound volumes.

As the girls came through the door, Mamma looked up and smiled. Her hair was tucked under a lace cap, a gold locket on a chain hung around her throat, and a blue merino shawl was wrapped around her narrow shoulders.

Mamma was a slight woman, not very tall, with the same striking black eyes and black curly hair as Charlotte.

'Hello, my loves,' Mamma greeted them, slipping the pebble in her pocket. 'What have you there? Another treasure from the bush?'

Charlotte opened her jacket to reveal the koala, which was now sleeping soundly, rocked by the constant motion.

'A native bear — *Phascolarctos cinereus*,' said Mamma. 'From the Greek *phaskolos*, meaning "pouch" and *arktos* meaning "bear", or *coola* in the native language.'

Charlotte nodded quickly. 'But will he be all right?'

Mamma stood up, dropping her shawl on the chair. She gently took the animal, deftly examining it to see if it was injured. The koala mewled in dismay.

'He's a fine little man,' she said approvingly. 'He seems strong and healthy. I think he will survive.'

Emily smiled, her hazel eyes shining with delight. 'So may we keep him as a pet?'

'He can sleep in the schoolroom in an old shawl,' Mamma assured her. 'Remember, he is nocturnal, so he should sleep all day and become active in the evening.'

Charlotte and Emily flashed each other a grin.

'We can all take turns looking after him,' said Charlotte. 'I'll ask John the dairyman if he'll save us some milk each day.'

Mamma carried the koala out into the hallway, followed by the two girls.

'You should feed him stale bread soaked in milk, with some tender blue gum shoots,' Mamma suggested. 'We should avoid handling him for a few days until he gets used to us. We want to avoid him going into shock.'

'I think we should call him Master Maugie,' Charlotte declared, removing her black straw hat and shaking her curly hair.

'Maugie — why Maugie?' asked Mamma.

'It just suits him,' Charlotte said as they walked out the back door.

Mamma shivered as the cold air hit her. 'Charlotte dearest, I left my shawl in the office. Would you fetch it for me, if you please?'

Charlotte ran back to the office and around the desk to pick the shawl up from the chair. As she leant over, her eye was caught by a letter lying on the desk. Her eyes skimmed across it.

I have received your letter of yesterday's date and beg to say that it is entirely on account of Mr Barton that I fear for the children's property. He is your Husband — his intemperance is known to the whole world and I know from yourself and others that he is a useless idler who neglects his concerns . . . There is reason to fear that everything will be squandered. Therefore, the step I intend to take is to put the remainder of the property beyond his control . . .

'Can you not find it, Charlotte?' Mamma's voice rose from outside. 'It is on the chair.'

Charlotte's stomach flipped with anxiety and she stepped back, clutching Mamma's shawl. It was a letter from the executors — the men responsible for managing her dead father's estate. The men whose letters made her mother frown and pace the floor, white-lipped with anger. *What did it mean? What did they plan to do?*

'Coming, Mamma,' Charlotte replied. She buried her face in the shawl and sniffed the warm, comforting smell of her mother. It made her feel safe.

She hurried out again.

4

The Missing
Silverware

It was warm in the stone-flagged kitchen, with the fire roaring in the deep fireplace. Plum puddings wrapped in muslin hung from the ceiling rafters, along with a leg of ham and a bunch of dried thyme.

Mamma stood at the kitchen table, her sleeves rolled up to the elbows, a long white apron covering her grey skirts. She was rolling dough on the scrubbed-pine table with a wooden rolling pin. To her left, Charlotte and Emily stood peeling and coring apples with two sharp knives, chattering and giggling, while Louisa and James made animal shapes with the remnant dough.

'I've made an iguanodon,' James told Louisa, holding up his pastry creature. 'And it is going to destroy your pussy cat. Ggggrrrr!'

James's dinosaur tussled with Louisa's cat, biting its tail off.

'Mamma,' shrieked Louisa, holding up her tail-less feline. 'James ruined my cat.'

'James?' reproved Mamma, but her face was soft, without the harried frown she often seemed to wear these days.

'Here, Louisa,' said James hurriedly. 'See, the tail is fine. We'll just squish it back onto the body and it's fixed.'

In a moment the cat had a fine tail, fatter than before. Louisa grinned and attacked the dinosaur in retaliation. Emily laughed to see the playful battle.

Charlotte took another apple from the bowl to chop. She felt a sense of peace that even the bickering of her siblings could not destroy.

'Make sure you slice the apples nice and finely,' Mamma suggested, scattering knobs of butter over the dough. She rolled this into the dough of flour and water over and over again. Then she glazed the dough with whisked egg white, before adding more butter and rolling again.

When all the butter had been thoroughly mixed in, Mamma rolled the dough out into a thin pastry and laid it over the buttered pie dish to form a base. Charlotte and Emily then placed the sliced apple over the bottom, sprinkled with sugar, lemon juice and water. Finally, Mamma sealed the pie with a pastry lid, scoring two vents to let out the steam.

Bridget came in from the main house, her freckled face furrowed with concern. 'Ma'am, have ye moved the silver serving dishes from the butler's pantry?' she asked. 'I just went to clean the silverware as ye asked and several things seem to be missing. I put them all away after Sunday dinner, but they are no' there now.'

Mamma paused, her hands sticky with dough. She wiped a tendril of hair away from her cheek, leaving a smear of pastry.

'No,' replied Mamma, frowning. 'Are you certain you put them away in the right place?'

Bridget wrung her hands in her apron, close to tears. Charlotte and Emily paused in their work. It was a serious matter when items went missing with no explanation. Their stepfather had been known to send convict servants to the lockup in Berrima for much lesser offences.

'I swear to ye, ma'am, I wiped them all and put them away safe in the butler's pantry, then locked it as ye told me,' Bridget insisted. 'I take great care wit' the silver.'

Mamma sighed and pushed away the pie. 'I know you do — thank you, Bridget. Would you mind looking in the drawing room sideboard for me, if you please?' asked Mamma. 'Perhaps . . . perhaps someone placed them there by mistake?'

'Yes, ma'am,' replied Bridget, hurrying away, head bowed.

Mamma washed her hands in the stone sink and went to the locked store cupboard in the corner. Using the keys hanging from her belt, she unlocked the door and reached right up the back, pulling out a small tin caddy wedged behind a sack of currants. Mamma opened it with trembling hands. The caddy was empty.

'All gone,' she whispered, leaning against the door, her forehead on her hands. 'It's all gone. He's taken it.'

Charlotte felt a familiar knot return to her stomach. 'Mamma, are you all right?' she asked. 'What ails you? What is taken?'

'My allowance — *our* allowance,' Mamma whispered. 'All our money for the quarter, there is nothing left.'

'Who could have taken it?' asked Emily. 'The shepherds? The stockmen?'

'Perhaps it was bushrangers,' suggested James, jumping to his feet. 'Do you remember, Mamma, when the bushrangers came and attacked Oldbury? There was the time that they murdered poor Tom Smith, the groom, and the time last year they tried to shoot Mr Barton through the window? There is still that hole in the drawing room wall.'

Louisa, the youngest, began to cry. Mamma went pale. 'No, James, I do not believe it was bushrangers,' Mamma assured him gravely. 'I think I know who it was, but I do not want you to concern yourselves about it. Charlotte, I would be greatly obliged if you could take your brother and sisters to the dairy to wash themselves. I need to help Bridget search for the silverware.'

Mamma bustled towards the door.

'That's why Mr Barton went to town, isn't it?' asked Charlotte, a surge of anger welling in her. All the joy in their unexpected holiday was gone.

Mamma smiled wearily. 'Perhaps you could make sure that young James washes behind his ears,' she suggested. 'I think he forgot to do that this morning.'

'Yes, Mamma,' replied Charlotte, ushering the three younger siblings towards the door. The apple pie lay forgotten on the kitchen table. James grabbed an uncooked pastry iguanodon to eat on the way out.

The dairy lay on the northern side of the courtyard, matching the freestanding kitchen on the southern side. Its thick stone walls kept the milk urns cooler, and this was where Mamma and Bridget churned the butter and made cream and cheese. Emily helped Louisa wash the sticky dough from her hands under the pump by the deep stone sink.

'There you go, my poppet,' soothed Emily, drying Louisa's hands. 'Does that feel better?'

Louisa, the youngest at five years old, nodded and grinned a cheerful, gap-toothed smile, her earlier tears quickly forgotten. Like Emily, she had light-brown ringlets but grey eyes instead of hazel.

'How does Mamma know it wasn't bushrangers?' demanded James as Charlotte pumped water over his hands. 'It might be that convict John Lynch, who used to work at Oldbury and then ran away to join the bushrangers?'

James's face was alight with excitement. 'It was John Lynch who killed poor Tom Smith the groom all those years ago,' he continued. 'And it was John Lynch who swore he wished he'd shot Mr Barton when he had the chance. I'll wager it was John Lynch who tried to shoot Mr Barton through the sitting room window, too, shearing the collar of his coat and knocking him over.'

Charlotte shivered in the cool dimness of the dairy. She pulled the pump handle up and down more vigorously, making cold water cascade into the sink and splash up onto James's shirt.

'That's enough, James,' reproved Charlotte, her mouth pursed. She looked remarkably similar to her mother when she was stern.

'Imagine, Charlotte, if he had succeeded?' James said, making a pistol shape with his wet hands and taking aim at an imaginary foe. 'Wouldn't our lives be different?'

Charlotte and Emily exchanged a meaningful glance.

'Hush, James,' said Charlotte more forcefully, handing him a cloth to dry his hands. 'You must not talk like that. What if someone heard you?'

James looked sullen and kicked his boot against the floor. 'Well, I do wish that pistol shot had found its mark,' he insisted petulantly. 'And I cannot see why you all pretend otherwise.'

Charlotte sighed and soaped her own hands, a weight in her stomach.

'That shot might just have easily killed Mamma,' Charlotte reminded him sharply. 'She was sitting in the drawing room too. The lead ball fell right at her feet.'

'Thank goodness it didn't,' said Emily fervently, clasping her hands together.

The children returned to the cluttered familiarity of their schoolroom, with its crowded shelves and large table covered in books, pencils, papers and sketches.

Their noisy chatter woke Maugie the koala, who stalked from his crate on all fours, shaking his furry head grumpily. Louisa picked him up and gave him a cuddle, burying her face in his soft grey fur. James grabbed a leather ball and began kicking it around the table, shooting goals between the chair legs. Emily peered dreamily out the window towards the mountain, her chin on the palm of her hand.

Charlotte carefully opened one of the double cedar doors, which led to the elegant drawing room at the front of the house, with its avocado-green walls and red-and-blue

Persian carpet. The room was furnished with several over-stuffed chintz armchairs set around the wide fireplace, red cedar side tables and a grand piano topped with a large silver candelabrum. Two of Mamma's landscape paintings hung on the walls in thick gilt frames.

It was in this room that the family gathered in the evenings to read, sew and talk, while Emily or Charlotte played the piano.

It was into this room one June evening, just over a year ago, that someone had fired a pistol, presumably aiming at Mr Barton. In one of the glass panes in the northern window was a small, round hole, its edges chipped and cracked. In the plaster wall on the far side of the room was another hole, where the shot had struck before bouncing back to the floor.

Someone had wanted Mr Barton dead. But who could it have been? Charlotte thought about what James had said. *Wouldn't our life be delightfully different without him?*

Charlotte closed the door behind her and went back to the schoolroom feeling strangely unsettled.

Oldbury, Spring 1839

On a lovely September afternoon, Mamma appeared in the schoolroom with a large wicker basket over her arm. Sunshine streamed though the easterly windows and a small fire glowed on the hearth. Low shelves along the easterly wall were filled with scientific curios — shells, fossils, dried plants, stuffed beasts and seed pods. Maugie the koala, who had grown substantially, was asleep in the corner in his nest made of a faded merino shawl in a timber crate.

'Who would like to come down to the stream for a picnic tea and some yabbying?' Mamma asked with a warm smile. 'I think you all need some fresh spring sunshine to put the roses back in your cheeks.'

'*Me, me*,' chorused the children, hurriedly packing away their notebooks and pencils.

The girls scrambled to find gloves, shawls and bonnets. James dug out the bucket, net and yabby lines, and raced to the kitchen to beg Bridget for some finely cut meat to use for bait.

Louisa searched everywhere for her favourite doll, Lucy, to join the expedition. Samson joined in the excitement, wagging his whole body from side to side, pink tongue lolling as he ran back and forth between the schoolroom and the door. Emily carried Maugie, his eyes slowly blinking in the late afternoon light.

This expedition lay to the front of the house, through the formal flower garden with its neatly clipped hedges, and down the carriage drive towards the stream. Snowdrops, creamy jonquils and bluebells danced on their long green stems under the trees, filling the air with their delicate scent. White primula and pale-blue forget-me-nots provided a carpet of early colour under the bare rose bushes. The buds on the white lilies were fat and ripe, ready to burst into bloom.

The children skipped and joked, delighting in the unexpected expedition. Louisa, brown ringlets bouncing, ran to and fro, chattering non-stop. James kicked a ball along, zigzagging down the path.

Down at the rivulet, the sun glinted on the water. Ducks waddled and quacked along the mossy banks, demanding to be fed. Blue-and-black dragonflies and silvery midges danced above the surface of the still water. Behind them, Oldbury House glowed in the warmth of the late afternoon light, looking as majestic and magical as a fairy palace.

James tucked his ball under his arm and ran ahead to the waterhole with the rods and bucket.

'I'll bait all the rods,' he offered, pushing his fringe out of his eyes. 'If you don't tie the knots properly the yabbies pull them loose.'

'I know how to bait a yabby rod, James,' Charlotte reproved, throwing down the blanket. 'Remember that beauty I caught last time? It was massive.'

'You can bait mine, James,' offered Emily. 'I'll help Mamma set up the picnic.'

'Lucy wants to catch yabbies too,' said Louisa, holding up her doll. 'But Lucy doesn't like yabbies for supper.' She grimaced, scrunching up her grey eyes and revealing the gap between her teeth.

'That's all right, my poppet,' Emily replied, carefully spreading the blanket out on the grass. 'We can help Lucy with her rod, and then we can share her yabbies.'

'Lucy could *try* eating yabbies,' suggested Mamma, straightening Louisa's bonnet. 'She might find they are delicious with my lemon, butter and parsley sauce.'

'My favourite,' agreed Charlotte, gathering twigs into a pile. 'The thought of it is making my stomach rumble.'

At the water's edge, James became very serious, tightly tying a strip of raw meat to the end of a length of string, which in turn was knotted to the wooden rod. Samson sat beside him, eyeing the bait longingly. Louisa stood on the bank and threw scraps of bread to the squabbling ducks.

'Louisa,' James objected, waving her away. 'Do that over there or you'll frighten away all the yabbies.'

Charlotte and Emily gathered twigs and branches and built a small campfire to boil the billy for tea. Mamma sat on a wooden bench under one of the elm trees, unpacking the picnic basket beside her. This was her favourite place to sew, or draw, or read when all the many chores were done.

Emily helped Mamma make up slabs of freshly baked bread smothered in creamy yellow butter, topped with pale-pink ham and a smear of mustard.

When the billy boiled, Charlotte made cups of sweet, milky tea for everyone, which they drank out of tin mugs, while Mamma handed around slices of bread and ham. James stood sentinel on the bank, watching the lines of five makeshift rods carefully to see if one of them twitched.

'Mmmm,' said Charlotte, feeding a scrap of ham to Samson. 'Why is it that everything tastes better out in the open air? This is the best ham I have ever tasted!'

'Tea tastes completely different out of a tin mug,' added Emily. 'It has an exotic smoky flavour, as though it has travelled thousands of miles on camelback.'

'I wish we could live out of doors always,' added Louisa. 'Then we would never have to do chores or study or practise the piano.'

Louisa fed her doll a crusty crumb and a teensy sip of tea.

'Being outside is the best place to learn, poppet,' replied Mamma, gesturing at the creek, the paddocks and the graceful trees. 'Surrounded by the beauties of nature. Out here, you are learning without even realising it.'

One of the yabby lines dragged taut. James dropped his bread, where it was quickly gobbled up by Samson, and grabbed the net.

Slowly, slowly he inched the line in and gradually pulled it up to reveal a plump crustacean clinging to the strip of bait. In an instant, James had the net under the yabby so that when the creature realised it was out of the water, it dropped off and was captured safely.

'I caught one,' James cried. 'We are having boiled yabbies for supper tonight.'

'Boiled *yabby*,' corrected Charlotte, her hand on her hip. 'At this rate we will have barely a quarter of a teaspoon each!'

A second string tugged. James smiled triumphantly at Charlotte and dropped his first catch into an iron bucket of pond water. Charlotte and Emily raced down to the water-hole to help, trying not to slip on the mossy, muddy bank.

In a moment, another rod twitched sharply, then another.

'Come on, Louisa,' called Emily. 'That one is for us to land.'

Louisa skipped down to help hold the rod while Emily scooped the net. The bucket soon held four plump yabbies.

'That's one for Mamma, one for me, one for Louisa and one for Emily,' James said, tying a new strip of meat onto his string. 'Looks like you might be going hungry tonight, Charlotte.'

Charlotte tossed her head, flicking back her long black hair. 'With all this racket you are making, it's a wonder we have caught any yabbies at all,' she retorted. James poked out his tongue.

Mamma had been sitting quietly, mending some of James's torn breeches and sipping on her tea. She rubbed her forehead as though it ached.

'My darlings, there is something I must talk to you about,' Mamma began, putting aside the sewing. She slipped her hand inside her pocket and took out a small, red-brown pebble, which she rubbed between her finger-tips. 'It is something of grave importance . . .'

Emily stopped tidying up the bread scraps and sat down quietly, her head to one side and her hazel eyes gazing steadily at her mother. James safely landed a fifth yabby in the bucket while Louisa continued to feed her doll.

Charlotte felt her stomach knot. *What does Mamma want to talk to us about? Why does she look so worried? Is it something to do with that letter?*

'I have been corresponding with the executors,' Mamma announced. She took a deep breath and smoothed out a crease in her skirt.

Charlotte glanced at Emily. Louisa put her doll down.

'The executors have decided that it is not in your interests for us to live here at Oldbury anymore,' Mamma announced, her eyes on the yabby lines. 'They plan to sell all the sheep, cattle and horses, and lease out Oldbury for the next seven years.'

Charlotte sucked in her breath. Emily leant forward and clasped her mother's skirts. James frowned and put down his net. Louisa picked up her doll and began to play again, rearranging the petticoats and velvet pelisse.

'Not in our *interests*?' asked Charlotte, her voice rising.

'But this is our home! You and Papa built Oldbury when I was a baby — we've always lived here.'

James stood up, the yabby lines forgotten. He ran his hand through his thick brown hair, mussing it up on end. 'They can't do that,' he said firmly. 'Papa left Oldbury to me. I'm the boy — it's mine and I want to live here with you and the girls.'

'It must be some kind of mistake,' suggested Emily, her face hopeful. 'We just need to explain that we are happy here. We belong here.'

Mamma slipped the pebble back in her pocket and rubbed her eyes, blinking rapidly. 'Darlings, I know it is difficult, but we don't have any choice. The executors control all the money and how it should be spent until you come of age. They have appointed an auctioneer to sell everything except the property itself so that they can hold all the money in trust for when you are older. The property has already been advertised in the newspapers.'

Emily's eyes filled with tears. James walked over and kicked over the remaining yabby lines, his lip pouted.

'I don't like the executors,' said Louisa. 'They are horrid.'

'How can they do this, Mamma?' asked Charlotte, her voice trembling. 'This is our home. Papa meant for us to live here forever. How can they sell our sheep? Our cattle? Our horses? They can't mean to take Ophelia and Clarie! Where would we go?'

Mamma held out her arms to the children, her face pale with grief. 'I do not know,' she confessed. 'I do not know. I have written and begged and pleaded, but nothing I say will deter them. I do not know what else I can do.'

Emily fell into Mamma's arms, followed by Louisa and then James.

Charlotte knelt on the rug all alone, her mind churning. *There must be something Mamma can do? Surely it is not possible for total strangers to turn our lives upside down on a whim? Surely the men far away in Sydney Town cannot dictate how our lives should be lived? Why did Papa have to die? Why did Mamma have to marry Mr Barton?*

'It's *him*, isn't it?' accused Charlotte, glaring at Mamma. 'It's all *his* fault we have to leave Oldbury. If he didn't steal our money and sell our livestock, the executors would not be doing this.'

Mamma bit her lip. 'Charlotte, my dearest . . .'

Charlotte stood up, her body trembling with rage, and cried, 'They can't make us go. I simply refuse.'

'Charlotte —'

Charlotte turned and ran, her eyes blinded by tears. She ran through the gardens, in the front door and upstairs to her bedroom. She lay on the bed, her face buried in her pillow, and became lost in thought. *There must be something we can do? There must be something that will change the executors' decision?*

5

Mr Barton

The table in the breakfast room was set with floral china and bone-handled silverware. A bowl of pale-pink cabbage roses stood in the centre. Bridget carried in a basket of hot, steaming rolls straight from the oven, their warm, yeasty scent making Charlotte's mouth water. Mamma poured out cups of milky tea from the polished silver teapot into delicate china cups.

'Today, Mamma, can we go searching for tree frogs down in the swamp?' asked James, spooning some strawberry jam onto his plate. 'I want to catch some to keep in the terrarium.'

'Not today, dearest,' Mamma replied with a fond smile. 'You all need to do some arithmetic, then we are going to study the North American Esquimaux. They are a truly fascinating people. Then I need to talk to the superintendent about the sheep. The ewes will be starting to lamb.'

James pulled a disgusted face, his fringe flopping over one eye.

'No, Mamma — please no arithmetic,' Charlotte wheedled, putting down her bread roll smothered in marmalade. 'Why don't we do a composition, or perhaps we could just ride up to the mountain and sketch?'

Mamma smiled again. 'Definitely arithmetic this morning, but possibly we can go for a wander after lunch and sketch down by the rivulet?'

'That would be heavenly,' agreed Emily, the peacemaker. 'Perhaps we could catch some frogs for James and sketch those?'

Mamma brushed Emily's forehead with her fingertips. 'I think that would be an excellent compromise, dearest.'

Suddenly a loud crash came from the back of the house, near the kitchen.

'Mrs Barton — woman!' yelled a loud male voice.

Mamma stiffened and went pale. 'Quickly, children,' she urged, standing up with a small, forced smile. 'Finish your breakfast and then go to the schoolroom and start your arithmetic. I'll come in shortly to see how you are progressing.'

Mamma hurried from the room, back straight, her full skirts swishing.

'It's Mr Barton,' Charlotte announced gloomily. 'He's back.'

Emily dropped her crust, no longer hungry. James stood, clutching his butterknife smeared with strawberry jam. Louisa's bottom lip trembled.

'Oh, there you are, woman,' yelled the rough voice from the back verandah. 'You bother to welcome your husband home then?'

'Where have you been?' their mother asked.

'Oh, I've been away on business.' His voice sounded slurred. 'Not that it's any business of yours what your husband chooses to do.'

'Business at the tavern by the sound of you,' replied Mamma, sounding bitter. 'You have been gone for a week. Perhaps you could tell me why the silver dinner service has disappeared? Plus all the money I had hidden in the tea caddy— the whole quarter's allowance is gone. I do not suppose you know what may have happened to that?'

There was another loud crash, either of something being thrown or someone falling. Charlotte felt her neck muscles clench with anxiety.

'Nagging, nagging — always nagging,' shouted Mr Barton. 'I swear I don't know what I did to deserve such a shrew for a wife. Spare a man from a wicked tongue.'

Charlotte glanced at her siblings. Louisa stared at the door with wide, frightened eyes. James picked up his butterknife again and clutched it firmly. Emily, her eyes swimming with tears, bit her fingernails.

'Come on,' Charlotte whispered, gesturing to the others. 'Mamma wished us to start our schoolwork.'

'I wish I could kill him,' whispered James, jabbing his butterknife into his bread roll. 'He is an evil man.'

'Shush, James,' replied Emily in horror. 'You don't mean that.'

'I do,' James insisted, lifting up the butterknife like a sword. 'I wish I was older, then I would cut out his wicked heart.'

Charlotte pushed away her half-eaten breakfast.

'I know he's difficult, but he's our stepfather,' Charlotte reminded her younger siblings. 'It would grieve Mamma if we were to vex him.'

'He's a thief and a villain,' insisted James, his voice rising. 'He steals from us and from Mamma, the things that Papa worked and paid for. He gets drunk and does nothing to help Mamma with the farms. He would be better off dead.'

'Hush, James,' repeated Charlotte, glancing nervously towards the door. 'He'll hear you and then we'll all be in trouble.'

There was a loud clang from the verandah, the sound of some heavy metal object hitting the stone wall. Mamma stifled a shriek.

'Blast you and blast your impertinent brats,' screamed Mr Barton. 'It's more than a man can stand to see your long face over the dinner table. Do you wonder that I'd rather spend my time at the Three Legs of Man Inn? I don't know why I slave to feed you and those spoiled brats. You think you are all so superior, but you are no better than me.'

There was the sound of Mamma's voice, low and soothing.

'Don't talk to me like I'm an imbecilic child,' roared Mr Barton. 'Of course I don't need to go to bed.'

Charlotte looked around at her brother and sisters. She tried to smile brightly. 'Come on, Louisa,' she urged. 'Time to do some arithmetic! Let's go the schoolroom.'

The children rose from the table reluctantly. Someone stumbled in the hallway outside. The door flew open and their stepfather staggered into the room.

'Well, brats — did you leave me some breakfast?' asked Mr Barton.

Their mother followed closely behind, a strange false smile on her face. 'Come along now, children,' she said. 'Time to start your schoolwork. Mr Barton would like to eat his breakfast in peace.'

Charlotte noticed an angry red streak on her mother's cheek that had not been there before. Charlotte and Emily hurried away obediently. James glared at the tablecloth. Louisa started to sob.

Mr Barton swore and clutched his forehead. 'My poor head! For goodness' sake, get that wailing brat out of here,' he demanded, swaying on his feet. 'Before I do it myself.' Louisa ran to Mamma and buried her face in her skirts.

Mamma kissed her head and stroked her ringlets. 'Charlotte, my dear, be so good as to take Louisa for me,' she suggested, her voice tight and high. 'I'll be there very shortly.'

Charlotte glanced at Mamma then at her detested stepfather. 'Come on, James. Come on, Louisa,' she urged, trying to take her sister's hand. Louisa clung to Mamma's skirts more tightly, her sobs rising to a howl.

'I said shut that brat up,' shouted Mr Barton, cuffing Mamma on the shoulder. 'I can't stand that blasted noise.'

Louisa screamed once more before her cries subsided and she raised her tear-filled eyes to her mother. Mamma compressed her lips.

'Don't you dare hit my mother!' Charlotte shrieked, leaping forward. 'Don't you dare touch her with your filthy hands!'

'No, Charlotte,' Mamma warned, holding out her arms.

Mr Barton whacked Charlotte with the back of his arm, sending her flying across the room. She squealed, slid across the floorboards and banged her head on the skirting board. Samson bailed up Mr Barton and growled menacingly, the hackles on the back of his neck raised.

'No!' Mamma shouted, darting forward to kneel beside Charlotte. 'My dearest, are you hurt?' Charlotte was shocked and angry but not badly hurt. She sat up, shaking her head and blinking back tears, and glared at Mr Barton and Mamma. 'Are you sure you are all right?' her mother asked.

Mamma stroked Charlotte's forehead, gazing into her pupils to check for signs of concussion. Charlotte nodded and rubbed the side of her head.

Mamma stood and faced her husband. 'You will not strike my children.'

'She deserved it,' snarled Mr Barton. 'She needs to learn respect for her elders.'

'You will not lay a finger on any of my children,' Mamma reiterated. 'I will not tolerate it.'

Mamma was much shorter than Mr Barton, but she looked so fierce that Mr Barton stepped backwards.

'I will not be treated like this in my own house,' screamed Mr Barton, spit foaming at the corner of his lips. '*I* am the master. *You* are my wife and I have total dominion here. I will not be thwarted in my own breakfast room.'

Mamma took a deep breath and raised her chin. 'Children, please go the schoolroom and start your work for the day,' she repeated calmly. 'I will come to check on you shortly.'

The four children edged slowly, cautiously towards their mother. Mr Barton glared at them, his bloodshot eyes daring them to speak.

'Come on, Samson,' ordered Charlotte. 'You had better come with us.'

Samson stood firm, growling at Mr Barton, who lashed out and kicked the dog in the belly. Samson whimpered in pain.

'*Now*, Samson!' Charlotte insisted urgently, grasping the dog by the collar. Together, the dog and the four children slunk from the room.

Charlotte looked back at her diminutive mother swathed in voluminous skirts. *She looks so vulnerable. Can Mamma protect us from him? Can she keep us safe?* The four children scuttled into the schoolroom and sat at the long table. James picked up a pencil and hurled it across the room. Samson curled up by the fire, his tail wrapped around his body and his eyes alert for trouble. Charlotte handed out the arithmetic exercises, her hands trembling and her head throbbing.

They could hear the heavy tread of their stepfather as he mounted the stairs and headed to his bedchamber. There was the sound of a key grinding in a lock, followed soon afterwards by muffled snoring that seemed to shake the stone foundations of the house.

'I hate him,' Emily cried. 'Why did Papa have to die? Why did Mamma have to marry such a good-for-nothing spendthrift?'

'I don't know,' Charlotte replied, her shoulders slumped. 'I truly don't know.'

Mamma came in a few minutes later, her eyes rimmed

red, with a cold compress and some lavender water. She hugged Charlotte close and kissed the top of her head. Charlotte stiffened initially then relaxed against her mother, breathing in her soft scent.

'I am so sorry, Charlotte,' whispered Mamma. 'I am so, so sorry.'

6

The Sheep Wash

October, 1839

Dandy Jack arrived at the kitchen door, his blue shirt wet and muddy. He took his hat off and smiled at Bridget, who was scrubbing a pot at the stone sink, soap suds up to her elbows.

'Excuse me, ma'am,' he said to Mamma, slicking his hair back with one hand. 'Mister Ash sent me up to fetch the food for the men. We're all hungry and parched.'

'Thank you, Jack,' replied Mamma, beckoning him into the kitchen. 'It is all here ready for you. You may carry the basket with the beef, if you please? Bridget, can you manage the puddings?'

Three large joints of meat had been roasted, wrapped in cloth and deposited in a basket, along with a cutting board and some long, sharp carving knives. A smaller basket held two massive plum puddings that had been steaming in their bowls for hours.

Bridget nodded, wiping her hands on a cloth and hefting the basket onto her hip. 'Yes, o' course, ma'am.'

'Is Mr Barton coming down to inspect the washing, ma'am?' asked Dandy Jack, flashing a grin at Bridget. 'It's nearly midday.'

More than 2000 sheep had been mustered in from all over the main estate and their sheep stations in the surrounding area. Washing the wool prior to the annual shearing was vital to ensure the best possible price for the clip. The washing and the subsequent shearing were two of the biggest events on the Oldbury farming calendar.

'No,' Mamma replied, tucking a pot of mustard in with the beef. 'Regrettably, Mr Barton is indisposed today. I went down early this morning to check on the progress and will come again now that the food is ready. Is everything going smoothly?'

'Hard, backbreaking work, as usual,' complained Dandy Jack. 'I'll be glad when it's finished.'

Mamma frowned and rubbed her forehead. 'Well, better hard work than starving,' she replied. 'Emily, would you fetch the bread from the pantry, if you please?'

The girls carried flat cane baskets filled with loaves of bread, slabs of butter and knives. Louisa was entrusted with the canvas bag containing the tin mugs for tea and a small sack of sugar.

They could hear the deafening sounds of the washing long before they could see it. Hundreds of sheep bleated plaintively to their lambs. Men yelled and called instructions. Water sloshed and splashed. Dogs barked.

The men had set up temporary pens that were filled with unwashed sheep, their heavy fleeces matted with muck. The creek at this point had steep, rocky sides. A rough dam of boulders and soil had been constructed to capture the winter rains, forming a wide waterhole warmed by the spring sunshine.

Mamma directed the girls to set the baskets down in the shade with Bridget to mind them, then she led them to the half-full pen to inspect the sheep.

James was helping Charley tend to a campfire with a huge kettle suspended over the coals. When he saw them, James ran over. His clothes were soaked to the skin, his hair was sticking out from under his hat, and his face was flushed. He had been down helping the men since dawn. It was the first year he was old enough to join in.

'Mamma, come and see the sheep,' called James. 'We have washed hundreds and hundreds of them, and John was knocked over by a big ram who escaped before he was washed, and we had to chase after him. The dogs were so clever and brought the ram back, meek as a lamb. And Mr Ash said I did a fine job.'

'Hello, James,' called Mamma, ruffling his damp hair. 'It sounds like you are having a wonderful time. Have you minded everything Mr Ash has told you?'

'It has been so much fun,' James said. 'I've been helping herd the sheep down into the water and running errands and washing some of the smaller ewes.'

Mr Ash, the superintendent, came over to greet Mamma, raising his cabbage tree hat. 'Master James has been a good young stock hand this morning, ma'am,' he assured her with a grin. 'We'll make a good farmer out of him yet.'

'I hope he will be, just like his father,' confessed Mamma with a fond glance at her son.

'May I wash our pet lambs too, please, Mamma?' asked Louisa, looking up with excitement. 'They look so pretty, all fresh and white.'

'It's a little rough down in the sheep wash today, Miss Louisa,' explained Mr Ash. 'But perhaps you can wash the lambs in the yards tomorrow. I'll get one of the men to carry up some buckets of water for you.'

'I can use our lavender soap and they'll smell beautiful,' Louisa decided, bouncing from one foot to another.

'Charlotte and I will help you, poppet,' said Emily with a smile. 'Then we can walk them around the orchard on leads made of ribbon while their coats dry.'

Mr Ash grinned at the image. 'I'm glad we don't have to give the whole flock that kind of special treatment,' he joked. 'It would take us months to get the job done.'

'How is the washing proceeding?' asked Mamma, her brow creased.

The two leant on the rails of the stock pen, checking the milling ewes and rams. Charlotte and James climbed up on the rail, their legs hanging down inside the pen. A shepherd was using a long timber crook and his dog to separate out individual beasts and send them down the race towards the water.

'When this pen is empty, we will have washed four hundred sheep,' said Mr Ash. 'We should finish another three hundred this afternoon, so it should take us three days to do them all.'

Mamma nodded, gazing out over the crowded pens. 'How does the wool look so far?' she asked, feeling the dirty fleece of an unwashed ewe pressed against the railing.

'It looks excellent,'. replied Mr Ash. 'We should get a good yield.'

'Well, let's pray the wool prices improve,' said Mamma with a frown. 'The prices in Sydney so far this year have been dreadful. Our agent says if they do not improve soon it will not be worth shipping the wool to England.'

'It's much worse out west where the drought is really bad,' said Mr Ash. 'At least we've had rain. Things must improve soon.'

Mamma bit her lip and pushed away from the railing.

'How are the men?' Mamma asked briskly. 'Are they managing tolerably?'

'They are tired and hungry, so I hope you have loads of food for us!'

'Enough to feed an entire army, I assure you,' Mamma replied.

'I'm starving,' chipped in James, looking at the baskets with hungry eyes.

'It's not time for the meal break yet, dearest,' Mamma reproved. James looked crestfallen. 'But here is a little morsel to keep you going.' She tore off a crust of bread and handed it to James, who gobbled it down. 'There is beef and mustard and plum pudding to go with that when the job is done.'

'We'll just finish this pen of sheep and then we'll break for dinner,' said Mr Ash. 'There's a nice shady spot under that tree where you'll get a good view without being in the way.'

'Thank you, Mr Ash,' said Mamma.

'Come, on Master James,' said Mr Ash. 'Time to get back to work.'

James ran back to join Charley at the fire.

The girls spread a blanket under the shade of one of the trees and watched the action in the waterhole below. One by one the sheep were urged down a timber race towards the creek. Once in the water, all the air in the fleece made the sheep float.

The men stood thigh-deep in water in a line across the waterhole, swinging each sheep from hand to hand and vigorously rubbing their woolly coats to wash away the dirt and muck. On the other side of the creek, two burly shepherds pulled the drenched sheep from the water and squeezed the excess water from the fleece with their hands.

It was hot, exhausting work as the unwilling sheep struggled and the sodden coats made them even heavier. Once the sheep had been rubbed down, they were reunited with their lambs on the other side and released into the grassy paddock to dry in the sunshine.

The girls watched until the pen was empty and the last sheep was released. Then they helped Mamma and Bridget serve the midday meal for the men, carrying around the baskets of bread and platters of roast beef.

Charlotte overheard Dandy Jack talking to one of the convict stock hands sitting on a rock overlooking the waterhole.

'Another two days of this, a week to dry them off, then shearing starts next week,' complained Dandy Jack. 'I'll be glad when the whole lot is sold off.'

'We'll just be consigned to someone else when the

stock is gone,' replied the other. 'I hope the lawyers find someone decent to lease the property and they keep us on.'

'I heard the sheep were passed in at the auction in Sydney last week,' retorted Dandy Jack. 'No one bid on the sheep or the leasehold on the property. They didn't think the stock could be much good with Barton in charge.'

Charlotte stiffened, her heart lifting with excitement. *The sheep haven't been sold. Perhaps if no one buys the sheep, they can stay here and we can stay too.*

'Humph,' snorted the stock hand. 'As if he's in charge. He hasn't come out to see the stock in months. He's only interested in hunting and drinking.'

'It's better when he stays away,' said Dandy Jack. 'He's a harsh man.'

The two stockmen started puffing on their pipes, and Charlotte returned to join her family under the tree.

On Saturday afternoon it was supply day. Shepherds and stockmen, farm labourers and sawyers had ridden to the homestead from the huts on the estate and the far-flung outstations to collect their rations and gossip for the week. Some of the men had ridden a full day for their week's supply of flour, sugar, tea, salt beef and tobacco.

The estate employed dozens of people — both convicts and free labourers — to herd the large flocks of sheep, cattle and horses, and to tend and harvest the crops of wheat, barley, oats, turnips, hay and peas. In addition, there were sawyers, carpenters, stonemasons, blacksmiths and brick-layers, whose jobs were to cut timber, clear paddocks, build fences, mend tools and construct outbuildings. Many of these men lived isolated lives in huts and camps out in the bush, while others lived in the workers' huts along the creek.

Mr Ash had unlocked the storehouse — one of the out-buildings behind the main house — and was supervising the weighing of flour, sugar and tea into smaller calico sacks with the help of Charley. The crowded, dim room was stacked to the rafters with casks, kegs, sacks, crates and barrels brought down from Sydney by dray. Motes of dust danced in the shaft of sunlight that streamed through the open doorway.

The storehouse had a counter with weights and measures like a shop. In addition to the basic food rations they received from the estate, the men were also able to purchase other foodstuffs with their wages, such as currants, sardines, pickles and jam.

Charlotte had been sent to fetch a bag of tea for the kitchen pantry, but she dawdled about the chore, enjoying the escape from the baking in the kitchen. She waited outside in the warm spring sunshine, petting one of the orphan wallabies and lazily letting the sights and sounds wash over her. Dandy Jack and O'Brien the sawyer were standing just inside the door, chatting and smoking their pipes.

'Did you hear another shepherd's been murdered by the blacks down south at Hume River?' said Dandy Jack. 'Speared.'

'Poor blighter,' replied the sawyer, stroking his thick, bushy beard. 'The natives move quiet as ghosts. He never had a chance.'

'They say they found the blacks and wiped out the whole camp,' Dandy Jack continued. 'Men, women and children.'

'That's what they should do here — wipe out the whole danged lot of them.'

'Missus wouldn't stand for that,' retorted Dandy Jack. 'She's given strict orders that none of the natives are to be touched.'

The sawyer spat in the dust. 'All right for her, safe in the big house,' he complained. 'What about us living out in the bush? The natives keep spearing the bullocks.'

'If it's not the natives spearing the stock, then it's the bushrangers shooting them, or the neighbours moonlighting — it's all the same to me.'

John the dairyman came and joined the group, calling out greetings. 'Did you hear another dray was held up by bushrangers last night just up the road?' he asked. 'It was the dray owned by Mr Moses with supplies for his store on its way down from Sydney.'

Charlotte stopped patting the wallaby and pressed against the wall, listening intently.

'A tempting target then,' said Dandy Jack, chewing on the stem of his pipe.

'The driver set up camp last night where the creek crosses the Southern Road,' explained John the dairyman, pointing upstream. 'A group of seven men with black crepe hiding their faces rode up and threatened the passengers with fowling-pieces.'

'Oh, the cheek of them,' said O'Brien the sawyer. 'Was anyone hurt?'

'The bullock driver was asleep under the dray,' John

explained. 'But there was an emigrant called Sanders travelling with his wife and child on their way to start work at Mr Moses's store.

'Sanders tried to hold off the robbers, but his pistol appears to have been faulty and misfired. Mrs Sanders threw herself in front of her husband, begging the bushrangers not to harm any of them. The leader of the ruffians had her dragged away and shot Sanders in the belly.'

'Did he live?' asked Dandy Jack, blowing a puff of smoke in the air.

'Yeah, but he's not expected to survive long,' replied the dairyman. 'The bullocky didn't go for help till this morning.'

'We'll have the place crawling with constables,' said O'Brien.

'The bushrangers'll take to the hills,' said Dandy Jack with confidence. 'They'll never find them in that scrub — they never do. I've heard they have a hide-out in the caves that is as protected as a fortress.'

A group of workers left the store, carrying bags of dry goods to be loaded onto their pack horses tethered in the shade. Charlotte bent and patted the wallaby again, her mind whirling. *Another bushranger attack so close. Do they have no morals at all?*

'Come on, Dandy,' called Mr Ash from inside the store. 'We haven't got all day. Take your rations and be off with you.'

Dandy Jack whispered something to his companions, who all guffawed.

'Nice jacket, Dandy,' said Mr Ash. 'Is it new?'

'Aw, no,' said Dandy Jack. 'Just felt like a change

today. My old one was torn and I haven't been bothered to mend it yet.'

Charlotte didn't really feel like going inside the store, but if she didn't Mamma would be cross that she had taken so long and returned without the tea. She took a deep breath and entered the dim store. She breathed in the throat-tickling scent of tobacco smoke, tea and dust.

'Good afternoon, Mr Ash,' greeted Charlotte. 'Mamma sent me to fetch some tea, please.'

'Of course, Miss Charlotte,' replied Mr Ash. 'Charley can fetch it for you at once.' Charley grinned at Charlotte. He scooped tea leaves out of a large sack, into a calico bag which he placed on the counter.

Charlotte took the bag, her mind buzzing with gossip. *Where could the bushrangers be?*

7

The Chief Constable

The constables arrived the following day just as the family was sitting down to dinner. On Sundays, Mamma ordered a special meal that was eaten with great ceremony around the long dining room table, which was covered with a starched, white damask tablecloth.

The spacious, formal dining room was at the front of the house, overlooking the garden. A fire roared in the fireplace to ward off the chill spring air. A collection of Mamma's landscape paintings hung on the rich-green walls. She had painted some of them in England, but most were of the surrounding countryside in soft, silvery greens and ochres.

Mr Barton sat at the head of the table, nursing a tumbler of brandy. Charlotte and James sat on either side of him, dressed in their Sunday best, while Louisa and Emily sat on either side of Mamma at the other end.

Mamma was standing, carving the roast beef, while the children passed around the side dishes of roast potatoes, peas and beans, baked onions and the gravy boat. The silver gravy boat had disappeared, so they had to make do with the china one from the kitchen. Likewise, the massive silver soup tureen was missing from the cedar sideboard.

Bridget entered the dining room and bobbed a curtsy, looking flushed and flurried.

'Mr Chalkley, the chief constable, would like to see you in the office, sir,' explained Bridget to Mr Barton.

'Danged if I'll see him,' swore Mr Barton. 'It's the middle of dinner. Tell him to go away and come back next week.'

Bridget glanced at Mamma. Mamma put down the carving knife and straightened her lace cap. 'I will see him, Bridget,' she said, frowning. 'You may start dinner without me.'

Mr Barton drained his tumbler of brandy and banged it down on the table. 'No, you won't see him,' he shouted. 'He didn't ask to see you. He asked to see me — I'm the master of the house.'

Charlotte froze in the middle of passing the potatoes to Emily. Her stomach clenched with nerves.

'It will not take a moment,' replied Mamma soothingly. 'He may have some news of those missing cattle. Mr Ash thinks that they may have been moonlighted by one of the local farmers.'

Bridget stood stationary by the open door, not sure whether to obey the master or the mistress.

'You won't,' insisted Mr Barton, pouring himself another tumbler of brandy. 'You'll serve my dinner. The bleeding constable can go hang himself.'

The chief constable appeared in the doorway, hat in hand.

'My apologies for intruding, ma'am,' said the policeman, inclining his head. 'I'm sorry to arrive at the dinner hour, but I need to speak with Mr Barton about a certain matter. Could we perhaps retire to the office?'

Mr Barton glowered at the constable then at his wife. 'No need — we can talk here while I eat,' he decided, his voice more civil.

'Would you like to join us, Mr Chalkley?' invited Mamma. 'May I pour you a glass of wine?'

'Get the man a brandy,' Mr Barton demanded.

'Thank you, ma'am,' replied the constable. 'A brandy would be appreciated.'

'Bridget, could you fetch Mr Chalkley a glass, if you please?'

Bridget hurried to obey, relieved to have the decision made. Mr Chalkley sat down between Charlotte and Emily. Mamma continued carving the roast beef, and everyone helped themselves to meat, gravy and vegetables.

Mamma said grace and everyone began to eat.

'Now what is it you want to tell me?" asked Mr Barton, picking up his knife and fork.

Mr Chalkley glanced around at the children, who were quietly eating, their eyes on their plates. Mealtime was uncharacteristically quiet when their stepfather was present. He firmly believed that children should be seen and not heard — but preferably not seen, either. Any childish chatter was likely to be met with a roar and a slap.

'Well?' said Mr Barton.

'It is about the robbery of the dray from Sydney on Friday night on the main road,' began Mr Chalkley. 'The victim, Mr Sanders, died yesterday but was able to dictate a complete account of the attack.'

Charlotte leant forward, a crowd of questions on her tongue begging to be asked.

'The poor, unfortunate man,' replied Mamma, putting down her cutlery. 'May his soul rest in peace.'

'What's that to do with me?' asked Mr Barton. 'I've never heard of him.'

Mr Chalkley turned to Mr Barton. 'No, but yesterday we discovered a young man by the name of Knight, who says he is employed by you. We apprehended him on his way back to Oldbury, laden with goods that correspond with items stolen from the dray.'

'Oh, I don't know anything about that,' said Mr Barton.

'Today another two of your convict labourers were apprehended by Mr Loveby the innkeeper for attempting to sell stolen goods at The Three Legs of Man,' continued Mr Chalkley. 'A number of the goods seem to have been stolen from the dray, yet they also offered several items from this house that they said you had instructed them to sell.'

Mr Barton flashed a guilty look at Mamma, shrugged nonchalantly, then speared a potato and thrust it in his mouth.

'They're now being escorted to the Berrima lockup,' advised Mr Chalkley. 'The goods have been impounded as evidence.'

'Oh, my goodness,' said Mamma, her hand to her throat. Charlotte kneaded her hands together under the table.

'After questioning them, it seems that most of the robbers were employed on Oldbury Estate. We have just apprehended two more of your convicts — Jack Ellis and William Barnes.'

'Dandy Jack?' whispered Charlotte.

'I always thought that Dandy Jack was a rogue,' said Mr Barton, pouring himself another brandy.

'These Oldbury men shot an innocent man?' asked Mamma.

'Yes, murdered him quite callously in front of his wife and child,' said Mr Chalkley. 'Apparently the bullock driver, who pretended to be asleep during the attack, was actually an accomplice. He refused to ride for medical help until he had finished his breakfast that morning. We've arrested him too.'

Louisa slid out of her chair and crept to her mother's side, twisting a curl around her finger. Mamma cuddled her close.

'That poor woman,' Mamma said. 'I wish she and her child had come here for help — perhaps we could have saved her husband.'

'I don't believe it would have helped, ma'am,' replied the constable. 'He was shot in the abdomen — a slow and painful way to die.'

'Where are they now?' asked Mamma. 'Can we be of assistance to the unfortunate woman and her child?'

'Thank you, ma'am, however they are taking the mail coach back to Sydney tomorrow,' replied Mr Chalkley.

Mr Barton suddenly shoved his chair back. 'I know who's behind it all,' he announced, eyes blazing. 'It's that murdering convict bushranger John Lynch. I know he's escaped and is hiding out there in the bush, just waiting to take a shot at me. It's John Lynch who put them up to it.'

Mr Chalkley stared at Mr Barton then glanced at Mamma.

'Next he'll be coming for *me*, and you constables will do nothing about it,' Mr Barton shouted. 'You sit here at my table eating my food, drinking my brandy and letting that murderous Lynch skulk about my farm, waiting to kill me!'

Mamma stood up and straightened her skirts, attempting to smile reassuringly at everyone. 'Children, perhaps it's time . . .?'

'Why aren't you searching for Lynch?' interrupted Mr Barton, waving his arms.

'I believe the convict Lynch has been transferred to a road gang down south,' began Mr Chalkley, wiping his moustache with the damask napkin. 'There is no evidence —'

'Evidence be danged!' shouted Mr Barton. 'I tell you he's out there.'

Mamma beckoned urgently to the children, signalling them to leave the room.

'Excuse me, sir,' whispered Charlotte as she pushed back her chair and hurried to the door, along with Emily, James and Louisa.

A thunderous smash filled the air. The children spun around.

The crystal decanter lay in shattered pieces on the carpet and amber liquid dripped down the pale-green wallpaper. One of Mamma's watercolour paintings had fallen to the floor and lay face down in a puddle of liquor, its gilt frame snapped.

It seemed Mr Barton had just thrown a half-full brandy decanter at the chief constable's head. Fortunately, he'd missed. Mamma's eyes widened in shock. Mr Chalkley jumped to his feet, his hand on his pistol.

'Oh, Mr Chalkley, I do apologise profusely,' cried Mamma breathlessly. 'Emily, take Louisa upstairs and read her a story. James, run and get Bridget to clean up that mess. Charlotte, can you get Mr Ash as fast as you can — I may need his help.'

The children ran to do as their mother ordered. Charlotte's mind reeled with all that she had seen and heard: the murderous bushrangers were actually Oldbury servants she saw every day; Mr Barton had thrown a crystal decanter at the chief constable; Mr Barton thought a murderer was hiding on Oldbury waiting to kill him.

Charlotte found Mr Ash at his cottage and explained the situation. By the time she returned, Bridget had mopped up the broken glass, the ruined painting had been thrown out with the rubbish and Mr Barton was resting in the drawing room in an armchair in front of the fire, his booted feet up on an ottoman.

Emily was reading to James and Louisa upstairs, so Charlotte helped Bridget clear away the ruined meal, which was now cold and congealed on the plates. Samson looked delighted as Charlotte fed him some of the scraps.

Afterwards, as Charlotte was creeping along the passage to go upstairs to her room, she heard a muffled sound coming from the study. It was the sound of deep, desperate grief. She cautiously opened the door. Mamma was collapsed on the floor, her face buried in the wide circle of her grey skirts. Her back and shoulders shuddered as distraught sobs escaped her.

'Mamma?' whispered Charlotte. 'Mamma — are you all right? Does something ail you?'

Mamma sat up and wiped her face on a sodden handkerchief. 'No, my dearest. Do not concern yourself,' she insisted, sniffing. She twisted the handkerchief between her fingers.

Charlotte dropped to her knees and hugged her mother's narrow shoulders. 'Mamma?'

Her mother dropped a letter onto her lap. 'The sheep have been sold,' she croaked. 'It was the finest flock in the colony. It took your father years to build it up, and now they have been sold for a mere sixteen shillings each. The Oldbury cattle have been sold also. The Budgong cattle will be next — even our flour mill has been sold.'

Charlotte gulped in shock. *It is happening. It is really happening.*

'Oh, Mamma, that's dreadful news!' exclaimed Charlotte, patting her mother on the back.

'The executors wish to take legal action against Mr Barton for the property that he sold that belongs to you four children,' continued Mamma. 'Mr Barton has apparently made arrangements to send a large quantity of our finest furniture to Sydney to be sold at auction. He has said the most unspeakable things about me to anyone who will listen.'

Mamma began to sob again, scrunching the handkerchief in her palm. 'Oh, Charlotte, I do not know what to do,' she cried. 'Nothing I say will sway him. I think he has gone completely insane.'

Mamma stood up and began pacing back and forth across the floor, leaving the letter on the floor. Charlotte glanced down at it. Among the florid handwriting she read:

Nothing that he may do will surprise me after what he has said of yourself — I consider him ready to deprive you and the children of their last morsel . . .

She wrenched her eyes away.

'I have no money,' Mamma continued, frowning fiercely. 'This is our home. It was built for me by your papa as a wedding present. I cannot bear the thought of strangers living here.' Charlotte shook her head vehemently. 'If only your stepfather would stop interfering, I could run the farm and make an income for us. He thwarts me at every turn, countermanding my orders and alienating the workers.'

'But I don't understand,' said Charlotte. 'Why can't you just tell the executors what to do? Oldbury is *ours*. Mr Barton and the executors have no right to it!'

Mamma pulled Charlotte to her feet and gazed steadily into her eyes. 'Charlotte, they have every right,' she said bitterly. 'I have written to my lawyers. I have tried everything. But as a woman I *have* no rights. My husband owns all my property — not me. Mr Barton is my husband. He can do what he likes and I can do nothing.'

A shiver of revulsion ran up Charlotte's spine. *I hate him. I wish he would go away and leave us alone. I wish John Lynch would shoot him.*

Mamma straightened her back and hugged Charlotte. 'I am sorry, my dearest. I should not have troubled you with all this. I do not want you to worry. There must be something I can do.'

Mamma slipped her hand into her pocket and ran her fingers over the pebble hidden there.

8

Stealing the Furniture

Oldbury, Summer 1839

On Tuesday Mamma rode into Berrima early to see Mr Chalkley about retrieving the items that the convicts had been trying to sell and to warn the businesses in town that they were not to buy any property that Mr Barton should try to sell them.

As she came downstairs, Charlotte was surprised to see Mr Barton dressed and emerging from the breakfast room, a cup of coffee in one hand. He usually slept most of the morning.

'Good morning, Charlotte,' said Mr Barton jovially. 'Has your mother left already?'

'Yes, sir. She left a few minutes ago to ride to Berrima,' replied Charlotte.

Mr Barton smiled at Charlotte. 'Good girl, and when do you think she'll be back?' he asked.

Charlotte frowned. 'She said not to expect her until teatime this afternoon.'

'Excellent,' replied Mr Barton, taking a large swig of coffee. 'Now, I have a lot to do this morning, so I don't want any of you children in my way. Understood? I'm sure you are responsible enough to take care of your siblings while your mother is away?'

Charlotte swallowed. 'Yes, Mr Barton. I'll make sure they don't bother you.'

'Good. I have some sweets here that you can have if you keep them well away.' Mr Barton handed her a paper bag of red-and-green boiled lollies.

Charlotte took them reluctantly. She didn't feel like accepting sweets from her stepfather, so she hid them in the kitchen where Louisa or James couldn't see them. She didn't think they'd be so scrupulous about accepting bribes from him.

Charlotte rounded up her siblings, their bonnets and shawls, Samson the dog, Maugie the koala and took them all for a walk. First they visited the cool, dim dairy to beg more milk from John the dairyman. He obliged, giving them an iron bucket filled with foaming, creamy milk.

Charlotte dipped her fingers in the milk for Maugie to lick. They headed through the courtyard, past the stables, carriage house, store and vegetable gardens. Charley waved to them from the stable, where he was pushing a wheelbarrow piled high with manure and straw.

The wallabies hopped along behind the children, just in case the bucket held hay or grain. Charlotte felt troubled. *What is Mr Barton up to? There's something he's trying to hide.*

Well behind the house was a large orchard of about eight acres, planted with many different types of fruit trees. Wide paths were mown between the trees, with the rounded domes of beehives placed along the fence. Five orphan lambs came running, their long tails twitching at the sight of the bucket.

Mr Ash had given them the lambs to raise by hand when their mothers had died. Louisa and James took turns to let the lambs drink from the bucket, while Emily tried to stop Louisa from being knocked over by the exuberant orphans.

James ran up and down the grassy avenue with Samson chasing him and barking loudly. Charlotte picked some long grass and plaited it. Emily sat down in the grass under an apple tree and began picking tiny daisies and weaving them into a crown for Louisa.

'A crown fit for a fairy princess,' said Emily, taking off Louisa's bonnet and setting the crown on her head.

Louisa grinned with her gap-toothed smile and stroked her ringlets back behind her ears. 'I'm a fairy princess,' she told Charlotte.

Charlotte nodded absent-mindedly.

'Can you make me wings?' Louisa asked Emily.

Emily frowned and looked around. 'Perhaps back at the house I could make some, poppet,' she replied, weaving a necklace out of daisies.

Louisa jumped up. 'Well, come on, then. Let's go back and make some wings.'

Emily glanced at Charlotte, who pulled Louisa into her lap and said, 'We cannot go back to the house now, poppet. Mr Barton would be cross.'

'But I want fairy wings, *now*,' Louisa insisted, her lip pouting.

'I know,' said Emily. 'Why don't we make you some wings from the bonnets?'

Emily took Louisa's discarded white bonnet and tied the ribbons around one shoulder, leaving the headpiece as a frilled white wing. Charlotte pulled off her own bonnet, which Emily tied to the other, then draped over the other shoulder to make the right wing.

'Pretty wings for a princess,' soothed Emily. 'Now how about a bracelet?'

Charlotte glanced back towards the house, which was out of sight behind the outbuildings and trees. 'Are you hungry?' she asked James as he raced past.

James, who was always starving, stopped and grinned with anticipation. 'I'm famished.'

'Yes,' added Louisa. 'When is Mamma back?'

'Later,' said Emily. 'When she has finished all her business in town.'

Charlotte pulled Louisa's chin gently so she was looking at her. 'I'm going to creep back to the house on a secret mission to fetch us some food,' she explained. 'But it's really important that you stay here with Emily. Don't follow me, or Mr Barton will be annoyed.'

Louisa's eyes widened. She knew what Mr Barton was like when he was angry.

'We can play fairies and witches,' suggested Emily. 'You can be the fairy princess Titania, and I'll be the evil witch Malevolence, who has captured and imprisoned you in the tower.'

Charlotte smiled at Emily in thanks.

'I'll come with you, Charlotte,' offered James.

'Thank you, James, but it might be best if you stay here,' Charlotte suggested.

'We need you to be the brave knight Sir Lancelot to vanquish Malevolence,' Emily reminded him.

James picked up two apple tree branches that had fallen to the ground. 'Quick, Louisa — you climb into your tower,' he ordered, handing Emily one of the branches. Louisa obediently scrambled up the trunk of the apple tree, her daisy crown slightly askew and her wings lopsided.

'*En garde*, foul witch,' James declared, raising his weapon in salute. 'I am here to rescue fair Princess Titania.'

Emily grinned, threw off her bonnet and adopted a fencing pose, brandishing her branch.

'Prepare to die an ignoble death, you insolent mortal,' retorted Emily. 'No man can defeat the supernatural power of Malevolence.'

The witch and the knight began fighting, James with his left arm tucked behind his back, Emily with her skirts hitched up in one hand. It looked like Malevolence had the upper hand as Sir Lancelot was beaten back under the strength of her attack.

'Save me, Sir Lancelot,' squealed Louisa, her legs dangling from the branch above. 'You can't let the witch win.'

Charlotte grinned then raced downhill towards the back of the house.

Outside the stable, Charlotte was surprised to see a team of bullocks harnessed to a dray with John the bullock driver standing at their heads. The dray usually took the wool and wheat to the markets in Sydney and returned with sacks of supplies to last for months. Sometimes it transported sacks of grain and vegetables to market in Berrima or the surrounding towns. This time, the dray was being loaded with furniture – Oldbury furniture. The long, red cedar table was up-ended on the dray bed and wrapped in blankets. The dining room chairs were lashed on top. The elegant sideboard was set in the middle of the courtyard, beside Mamma's favourite armchair.

A loud shouting came from the back verandah. Charlotte started, then ducked out of sight inside the stable. She peered through a crack in the stable wall. Through it she could see Mr Barton coercing two farm labourers who were struggling to remove Mamma's large oak desk from the office.

'He bad man,' came a whisper from the stall beside her. Charlotte peered around to find Charley lying in the straw.

'Charley, he's stealing all our furniture!' whispered Charlotte.

'Yes, missus gone to town.'

'Can you help me, please, Charley?' asked Charlotte. 'I have to ride to town to find my mother. If Mr Barton sees me he'll be furious.'

Charley thought carefully. He also knew what a terrible temper Mr Barton had when he was crossed. 'Yes, Miss Charlotte. What can we do?'

Charlotte paused. 'Could you help me catch Ophelia and saddle her up?'

Charley sprang to his feet. 'We need grain,' he suggested, taking down a halter and lead.

Charlotte filled a bucket with some grain and the two slipped out the back. It took precious minutes to coax

Ophelia into being caught and still more time to saddle her up. Charley pulled the girth firmly.

Charlotte peered through the spy-hole in the stable wall. The cedar sideboard, desk and armchair had been lashed to the dray and draped with blankets. The two men were now struggling through the back door under the weight of the sofa from the drawing room.

'Thank you so much, Charley,' said Charlotte. 'I am very grateful. If anyone asks, tell them I went for a ride up to Gingenbullen. Could you please tell my sisters and brother not to go near the house for anything, and perhaps take them some food. Tell Bridget I asked you to fetch some.'

Charley nodded and flashed a wide smile, bright white in his dark face.

'Don't worry, Miss Charlotte,' said Charley. 'I look after them.'

Charlotte led Ophelia to the fence and used a rail to help her mount into the side-saddle. Charlotte paused beside the stable, watching the proceedings anxiously.

It's important that he doesn't know that I know, thought Charlotte. *I'll creep away silently, then ride like the wind to Berrima to find Mamma.*

The men went back inside to fetch more furniture. The bullocks twitched and fretted, swishing away flies with their tails. The sun beat down on the laden dray. Charlotte urged Ophelia forward into a walk. The horse pranced and cavorted nervously, sensing Charlotte's anxiety. Charlotte skirted around the house, avoiding the formal gardens in front that could be seen from the drawing and dining room windows.

She splashed across the rivulet, the water rising to her horse's knees, and forced her way through a hedge and onto the carriageway. Once there, she risked a slow trot, heading north-west, hoping the hoof beats could not be heard back at the house.

Around the bend the dirt track stretched before her, bordered by thick hedgerows. Charlotte kicked her heel into Ophelia's sides and the mare broke into a canter. Charlotte leant forward, urging her to gallop faster. The driveway to Oldbury curved then straightened, flanked by a formal avenue of elms and poplars. Ophelia stretched her neck, enjoying the gallop, her hooves kicking up clods of red earth.

At the end, Charlotte turned right onto the main South Road. She had never ridden this way by herself before. This part of the road, just a couple of miles from Berrima village, was a common haunt of highwaymen and bushrangers. To the left was Mereworth Estate, owned by her father's brother, Uncle John Atkinson. Mereworth was now home to the Three Legs of Man Inn, which was frequented by the local labourers, Berrima soldiers and infamous bushrangers — and, of course, Mr Barton. It had more than once been implicated in a local murder or robbery, just like Oldbury itself.

A labourer on Mereworth called out to her, but Charlotte ignored him and galloped on. When Ophelia tired, Charlotte let her slow into a trot, then after a few minutes kicked her back into a steady canter. Within half an hour Charlotte was cantering across the sandstone bridge and down the rutted main road of dusty Berrima.

She slowed Ophelia into a trot as they entered the rectangle of the village green, which was surrounded by inns and houses built of sandstone and red brick. Outside the Victoria Inn, Charlotte recognised a brickmaker named James Welling. He usually worked at Oldbury but Mr Barton had set him to work building a couple of cottages on land that he had recently purchased in Berrima.

'Mr Welling, have you seen my mother?' asked Charlotte. 'I need to find her as a matter of urgency.'

The brickmaker shook his head. 'No, but you might try the store near the Surveyor General Inn. She often has business there,' he suggested, gesturing further north with his hand.

Charlotte called out her thanks as she cantered up the street. Near the store, Charlotte recognised her mother's bay mare, with its distinctive white blaze, tied to the hitching post. Charlotte tethered Ophelia beside her and ran inside the store. It was crowded with ladies poring over ribbon and feathers, men testing harnesses and small children jostling over the sweets display.

'Excuse me, Mrs Mason, have you seen my mother by any chance?' asked Charlotte of a woman whom she recognised.

Mrs Mason peered down her nose at Charlotte. 'Your mother?' said Mrs Mason, looking as though she had accidently sucked on a slice of lemon. 'I believe I saw Mrs Barton walking to the courthouse.'

Mrs Mason looked Charlotte up and down with a disapproving glare before continuing. 'You should know better than to ride into town with no hat or bonnet on your head, with your hair hanging down your back like a complete hoyden.' She sniffed. 'There is never a reason why a lady should be in an unseemly haste. You are not all

93

alone? I am surprised your mother let you leave the house like that. But then, perhaps she does not realise how young ladies are expected to conduct themselves. My daughters would never —'

'Thank you, ma'am,' replied Charlotte, backing away. 'I'm sorry but I need to go. My mother is expecting me urgently.'

'Well,' complained Mrs Mason. 'Such rudeness. But what would you expect with a mother like that?'

Charlotte turned and ran out of the store towards the courthouse a few doors up. Mamma was there, wearing her best clothes for town: grey gloves, cream silk shawl and a dark-blue bonnet.

'Mamma, Mamma,' Charlotte called desperately. 'I need you to come home.'

'Dearest, what's wrong?' demanded Mamma, her voice rising in panic. 'Has something happened to Louisa or James? Is Emily all right? Don't tell me one of them has been thrown from a horse? And why have you ridden for me? Why didn't you send Mr Ash or one of the men?'

'Don't fret,' Charlotte said. 'Everyone is fine, Mamma. It's the furniture. Mr Barton is emptying the house of all the finest furniture and packing it on a dray.'

Mamma's hand flew to her mouth; then she frowned fiercely. 'That man will be the death of me. I was just on my way to visit Mr Chalkley about the impounded goods. Perhaps he will be able to help us.'

Fortunately it only took a few minutes to find the chief constable in his office at the gaolhouse. After Mamma had explained the situation, he agreed to escort them back to

Oldbury, together with two of his constables. They all rode at a gallop, and at every bend Charlotte expected to see the bullock dray, dragging away their belongings.

The five horses eventually thundered up the carriage-way and around the back of the house, where the two labourers and the bullock driver were lashing down a canvas tarpaulin over the furniture. Mr Barton came out the back door brandishing a loaded pistol. A moment later, Emily, James and Louisa charged down from the orchard to see what the commotion was.

Mr Barton stared at Mamma, then at Charlotte, and a look of fury washed across his face. Then he took in the three mounted constables with their own pistols drawn.

'Good morning, Mrs Barton, my dear,' said Mr Barton, replacing his own weapon in his belt. 'How are you this morning? Good morning, officers.'

'What are you doing?' demanded Mamma, sitting ramrod straight in the saddle, pointing with her riding crop. 'Why is all the furniture packed on a dray?'

Mr Barton flashed a glance at the constables. 'Don't you remember, my dear?' asked Mr Barton. 'We discussed this. I am having the furniture removed to Sydney . . . for *storage*.'

'We did not discuss this and I do not wish our furniture removed to Sydney for storage,' Mamma contradicted. Mr Barton scowled.

'You are not planning on selling this load of furniture, I hope, Mr Barton?' asked Mr Chalkley. 'The furniture is part of the estate of the late James Atkinson, and therefore was bequeathed to his four children. If you were to sell the furniture, that would be a felony.'

Mr Barton glared at Mamma and Charlotte again, still mounted on their horses. Mr Chalkley indicated to his two constables to dismount.

'No,' Mr Barton replied. 'I beg your pardon. It must have slipped my mind to mention it to my wife. But as the estate is soon to be let, we will not be requiring this quantity of furniture. We will move into one of my new cottages in Berrima, where our needs will be much simpler.'

Mamma frowned. Charlotte's heart sank. The thought of living in a little cottage in the village with Mr Barton was intolerable.

'I wish we could help you, ma'am,' said Mr Chalkley. 'But if the furniture is just being moved, we can't stop him.'

Mamma paused before dismounting. She was tiny compared to the tall, brawny bullock driver and the other men. 'Thank you, Mr Chalkley,' replied Mamma. 'I appreciate your kindness, but my husband is correct. If we are to move from our home, we will not require such a quantity of grand furniture.'

Mr Barton smirked with satisfaction. Charlotte's eyes filled with bitter tears. *How can Mamma give in like this? How can she let Mr Barton triumph?*

Mamma turned to one of the labourers. 'Samuel, I will need you to ride for Sydney at once with a message for my lawyers,' she ordered sternly. 'I will write them a letter directing them to organise storage for the furniture in a suitable warehouse until further notice from myself. Once you have delivered the letter and received your instructions, you are to ride back to Brickfield Hill and await the dray so you can direct them to the warehouse.'

Mr Barton started forward, his face red with fury. 'Now just a moment . . .'

Mamma ignored him, turning to the bullock driver and the other labourer. 'John, you are to take this load as swiftly as possible to meet Samuel at Brickfield Hill and ensure it is stored safely in the designated warehouse. Paddy will accompany you as a guard.'

The three men glanced at Mr Barton for confirmation.

'That's unnecessary, my dear,' interrupted Mr Barton, his face sweating. 'I'll go to Sydney and organise the furniture.'

'Thank you, that is very kind, Mr Barton,' Mamma said sweetly. 'However, my lawyers would be more than happy to ensure that my children's inheritance is secure. I would not wish to put you to any trouble.'

Mr Chalkley grinned to himself at the exchange.

'Perhaps we could be of assistance, ma'am?' suggested Mr Chalkley to Mamma. 'My two constables would be happy to escort the dray as far as Nattai to see it safely on its way.'

'Thank you, Mr Chalkley. That would be most kind of you. I would hate anything untoward to happen to the dray on the journey.'

Mr Chalkley turned to the labourers. 'I must remind you that if anything were to happen to the belongings of the Atkinson children, it would also be a felony, and I would have to pursue the culprits with the full extent of the law.'

The labourers shuffled and squirmed, glancing between Mr Barton, Mamma and Mr Chalkley.

'Yes, sir,' replied John the bullock driver. 'We understand.'

Mamma smiled. 'Samuel, would you be so good as to unsaddle our horses and saddle up a fresh one for yourself while I compose a letter to the laywers?'

'Yes ma'am,' agreed Samuel, taking both horses by the reins.

Mamma turned to the two bullockies and gave them their final instructions. 'Farewell and take care.'

John and Paddy turned the big team of bullocks in the confined space with some difficulty and set off on the road to Berrima with much whip-cracking and yelling, accompanied by the three constables.

Charlotte followed Mamma inside, where she scribbled off a note to the lawyers on the kitchen table and saw to it that the message was safely on its way with Samuel.

9

Decision

Charlotte, Emily, James and Louisa wandered around the echoing rooms of the forlorn house. Louisa began to sob. Emily and Charlotte did their best to comfort her, but their eyes were brimming too. James kicked a stool that had been knocked over.

The dining and breakfast rooms were empty; only Mamma's paintings were left on the wall. The drawing room held nothing but Mr Barton's favourite armchair and a small side table with a decanter of rum. The schoolroom was untouched but the study was ransacked — the desk and chair gone, papers all over the floor, many of Papa's books taken.

The children heard Mr Barton coming up from the cellar, carrying a small flagon of rum. He yelled at Bridget to bring him a glass and retreated to the drawing room. The children, each one lost in his or her thoughts, hid in the schoolroom — the only downstairs room that seemed normal.

Soon they heard Mamma and Bridget next door in the study, tidying up the shambles.

'Let's play a game,' suggested Emily, trying to cheer them up. 'We could play knuckles?' James looked at Emily witheringly. 'Or toy soldiers?'

Not even this could tempt James to play. Louisa cuddled up next to Emily, thumb in mouth, twirling a ringlet around one finger.

Charlotte strode up and down the room, thinking. *What is going to happen? Are we really going to leave our beautiful home and move into a little cottage in Berrima with Mr Barton? How could we bear it!*

Through the closed double doors, Charlotte heard a crash and loud swearing from the drawing room next door, then the sound of Mr Barton staggering out into the entrance hall. A glass smashed on the floor.

Loud shouting came from the study. Bridget screamed. There was another loud crash.

Charlotte ran into the passage, followed by the other children and Samson, who was barking loudly. The study door was flung open. Bridget cowered against the bookshelves, her hands over her head.

Mamma was sprawled on the floor, her face smeared with crimson from her bleeding nose. Mr Barton stood over her screaming, his eyes bloodshot and spit flying from his mouth.

'You think you can make a fool of me, you insolent woman?' he bellowed. 'I won't be made a fool by you or that pack of brats!'

He struck Mamma again, sending her reeling. Charlotte flew across the room like a dart and sprang on her stepfather's back, her arms around his neck.

'Leave her alone,' yelled Charlotte, her rage bubbling over. 'Don't hurt her, you monster.'

Mr Barton swung around, throwing Charlotte off like a discarded cloak. Charlotte thudded into the bookcases, knocking the wind from her.

Mamma leapt to her feet, her face alight with horror.

Mr Barton pulled Charlotte to her feet and shook her like a limp rag doll. 'Don't speak to me like that, girlie,' he hissed. 'I'll do whatever I wish to your mother. And I'll do whatever I wish to you. I'm the master of this house, and don't you forget it!'

'Put her down,' ordered Mamma.

'You're not my master,' retorted Charlotte, her face flushing with anger. 'You're just a pathetic bully.'

Mr Barton's eyes bulged and he grabbed Charlotte by the throat and slammed her against the wall. Charlotte kicked and struggled, but her strength was no match for him. He dangled her by the throat, her feet no longer touching the floor.

'It was *you* who fetched your mother and the constables,' he spat. 'I told you to keep your nose out of my business.'

Charlotte choked for air, tears filling her eyes. *I can't breathe. I can't breathe.*

'Put her down!' screamed Mamma, beating at his arms. 'Put her down — you're strangling her!'

Emily sobbed, Louisa whimpered. Mr Barton squeezed tighter, his bloodshot eyes gleaming with a fanatical light. Charlotte felt her throat burning, her head swimming. Her body felt limp and cold.

Mamma pulled at his arms beseechingly. James ran

and kicked Mr Barton's shins. Samson darted inside and lunged, his teeth sinking into Mr Barton's calves.

Mr Barton yelled and kicked Samson and James across the room. Mamma let go and ran towards her desk. Charlotte felt the blood pounding in her ears and the world slipping away. She thought she was fainting. She thought she was dying.

There was a loud click.

'Put my daughter down or I will shoot you,' said Mamma, her voice low and steady.

All the children turned to look. Mamma had a pistol trained squarely at Mr Barton's chest.

'You wouldn't dare,' chuckled Mr Barton, shaking Charlotte. Charlotte could smell his sour, stale breath hot on her face.

'Put her down,' said Mamma.

Mr Barton stared at Mamma, smiling uncertainly. 'You joke, madam.'

'I do not jest with my children's lives. Release her *now* or I *will* pull the trigger.'

Mamma tightened her finger on the trigger, the muzzle still pointed directly at Mr Barton's torso. Mr Barton slumped, slackening the pressure on Charlotte's throat. Charlotte sucked in air deeply as she slid down the wall.

'I was only disciplining her,' whined Mr Barton. 'She is wilful and unruly, like her mother. She needs to be taught to be docile and obedient. She needs to be taught that I am the master of this house.'

'You are *not* the master of this house,' spat Mamma. 'You are a raving lunatic. This house was built by my beloved husband and left in trust for his children. It is *their* house. You do nothing but swig rum, laze around and steal our very bread. You do not deserve their respect — or any man's. You are a good-for-nothing wastrel.'

Samson stood firm, growling. Charlotte staggered to her feet, ready to fly at her stepfather again. Mamma stopped her with a sharp gesture.

'Charlotte, will you please take the children and Samson safely up to your room and lock the door,' instructed Mamma, still staring down the sights of her weapon. 'Do not open it unless I tell you to.'

Charlotte nodded and grasped the dog by his leather collar. Samson refused to be led away, his eyes darting between Mamma and Mr Barton.

'Bridget, would you be so good as to fetch a pitcher of water and some food, and place them in Mr Barton's bed-chamber, if you please?' asked Mamma. Bridget nodded and hurried from the room.

'Come now, Samson,' Charlotte insisted urgently. Together the dog and four children slunk from the room. Charlotte looked back at her diminutive mother, swathed in her flowing skirts, holding off that madman on her own.

I think he meant to kill me, thought Charlotte, touching her bruised throat. *I think he nearly strangled me.* She looked back at her mother with fear. *Will she be all right? Will he harm her again?*

Her throat constricted in fear. Mamma stood firm, her back straight, her aim steady.

'I think I might just take myself to bed,' moaned Mr Barton from behind them. 'I'm feeling a little weary.'

He staggered from the room — his cheeks flushed and veined, his nose glowing — and headed down the cellar stairs. He returned a few minutes later with another flagon of rum under one arm. Mamma followed him, the gun aimed at his back.

Charlotte urged all the children up the stairs. On the upper level were eight bedrooms off the central hallway — three large bedrooms at the front of the house and five smaller ones with sloping ceilings across the back. The front bedrooms were occupied by Mr Barton, then James in the middle room and Mamma on the southern corner with Louisa. Charlotte and Emily shared one of the smaller bedrooms at the back.

After a few minutes, Mamma knocked on the door. 'Let me in please, Charlotte,' she whispered.

Mamma came in, putting the pistol down on the dresser. The four children were huddled on Charlotte's bed, seeking comfort from each other's closeness.

'I am so sorry, my dearests,' she said, hugging each one in turn. 'Are you injured, Charlotte?'

Charlotte felt her throat. It was sore, but not as sore as her heart.

Mamma kissed her in the centre of her forehead. 'Do not worry, dearest,' she murmured. 'I will make sure he never hurts you again.'

How can Mamma make that promise? How can she stop him from ruining our lives?

Mamma took a deep breath. 'Now, my loves, we have some work to do,' she announced. The four children stared at her in surprise. 'I want you to pack a bag of clothes and your most important treasures. You will not be able to take very much. Charlotte and Emily, I need you to help the younger ones as Bridget will have much to do to help me.'

Charlotte and Emily glanced at each other with worried faces.

'When you have packed your clothes,' Mamma continued, 'I want you to pack a box with sketchbooks, pencils, paints and brushes. You will also need your schoolwork and your favourite books.'

'Why are we packing, Mamma?' asked Charlotte, feeling sick in the stomach.

Mamma looked over her shoulder towards the door, biting her thumbnail. 'We are leaving Oldbury.' Her face furrowed with grief. 'We are going somewhere far away, where we will be safe.'

'We can't leave Oldbury,' insisted James, jumping to his feet.

Louisa scowled. 'I don't want to go.' Mamma scooped her up in her lap and held her close.

Where could we possibly be safe? Charlotte wondered, pinching folds of her white skirt between her fingers.

'My dears, we must leave,' Mamma assured them. 'We have to escape from Mr Barton and go to the only place I can think of where he will not follow us.'

'Where would that be?' asked Emily calmly.

Mamma smiled at the children. 'Budgong,' she said. 'We are going to the outstation at Budgong.'

Charlotte caught her breath. Budgong was a cattle run that their father had established in the middle of the almost impenetrable wilderness on the coast near the Shoalhaven River. It was many miles from the nearest settlement.

There was nothing there but two stockmen's slab huts and some cattle yards.

'Budgong?' asked Emily, wrinkling her nose.

'How do you know Mr Barton won't find us?' asked James. 'He might follow us with a gun and make us come back.'

Mamma sighed. 'Mr Barton will not follow us to Budgong because he is too afraid.'

'Afraid?' asked Emily, looking pale. 'Why would he be afraid of going to Budgong?'

Mamma took Emily's hand and stroked it. 'Do not fret, my dearest. We do not need to be anxious. You know I ride to Budgong to check on the cattle every three months and have always returned safely.' Emily nodded, her hazel eyes wide. 'You see, Mr Barton is scared that the bushranger John Lynch will find him and murder him if he rides out in the wild country. That is why he has never gone there to check on the cattle, and why I must go instead.'

The four children looked at each other.

'Well, I am certainly not afraid,' declared James, putting his hand on Mamma's shoulder.

'Neither am I,' said Emily, raising her chin.

Louisa continued sucking her thumb and twirling a ringlet around her finger.

'It will be an adventure,' added Charlotte. 'Won't it, poppet?'

Mamma smiled reassuringly. 'I knew you would be brave, my dearests,' she said. 'Now we need to pack quickly and quietly. I would prefer it if your stepfather did not realise what we were planning. We will need to take many of our household goods as there is absolutely nothing there but the stockmen's huts.'

Charlotte nodded her understanding. 'When do we go, Mamma?'

'At first light tomorrow,' she replied, standing decisively. 'It will take us most of the afternoon to prepare everything.'

So soon? Charlotte thought. 'What about Mr Barton? He will surely try to stop us from leaving.'

Mamma nodded. 'He is sleeping, so I locked his bedroom door. I will leave the key with John the dairyman and he can let him out tomorrow after we have left. Hopefully he will sleep half the day away — by then we will be long gone.'

Mamma gave each of the children a carpetbag and a couple of canvas sacks that they could fill with clothes and treasures. Emily had to coax and cajole Louisa to be practical since she insisted on filling her bag with dolls.

Charlotte lay all her clothes out on her bed to decide what to take, folding neat piles of linen drawers, lace-edged petticoats, fine chemises, cotton and woollen dresses, white stockings, merino shawls, gloves, coloured pinafores, nightcaps and nightgowns, bonnets and shoes, which she then carefully packed in her carpetbag. The bag filled far too quickly and many of her clothes had to go back in the drawers.

Next door, James had thrown all of his clothes on the floor and was surrounded by a pile of white shirts, brown trousers, cravats and blue jackets all jumbled together. Charlotte sighed and helped him fold and sort them.

Down in the kitchen, Bridget was packing up hampers

of crockery, cutlery and cooking implements. Mamma tackled books, papers and food supplies. When the children went to bed after a picnic supper, Charlotte's ears strained in the darkness listening for any telltale sounds. Much later, when Charlotte finally fell asleep, Mamma had still not come upstairs to bed.

10

Flight

'Charlotte, dearest,' whispered Mamma, shaking her gently on the shoulder. 'Charlotte, wake up.'

Mamma stood over her bed, black hair hanging down her back and a shawl thrown over her white nightgown. Mamma's face looked pale and drawn in the flickering light of the candle. Charlotte glanced over to the other bed where Emily was still asleep, her nightcap tied tightly under her chin.

'I am sorry to wake you,' apologised Mamma. 'But we must get ready to go. I need you and Emily to dress and help me. We can leave Louisa and James asleep until the very last moment.'

Charlotte yawned and nodded reluctantly, not wanting to leave her warm bed.

Mamma woke Emily quietly and lit a candle for them to dress by.

Charlotte shivered in the cold early morning air as she

climbed out of bed and grabbed her shawl. The floorboards felt icy under her bare feet. The rest of the house was dark and quiet, except for the long, rumbling snores that came from Mr Barton's room at the opposite end of the hall.

The girls splashed their faces in the washbasin and dressed hurriedly in chemises, petticoats, dark riding habits, stockings and boots.

Together, Mamma and the girls carried down the trunks to the rear courtyard. Charley and Mr Ash had saddled up a number of horses, including Ophelia and Clarie, and they were tethered outside the stable, stamping their hooves and jingling their bits. Charlotte worried that the noise might wake Mr Barton. Fortunately, his bedroom faced the front of the house. Charlotte shivered and wrapped her woollen shawl more tightly around her shoulders.

Mr Ash, Charley and Bill the bullocky were now loading the trunks onto three red Devon bullocks by the light of several lanterns. The track to Budgong was too narrow and precipitous to drive a vehicle. The bullocks would be driven on foot by Bill and one of the convicts.

Mamma flitted to and fro anxiously in the darkness, glancing back to the house, giving the men directions and checking that all was packed to her satisfaction. The men loaded sacks of flour, potatoes, sugar and tea from the storehouse. The first two bullocks had already been loaded up with tents, bedding, Mamma's medical chest and food-stuffs. Bridget carried a wicker hamper of provisions from the kitchen.

Charley had captured a number of chickens, which were now imprisoned in a wicker hamper, squawking with disgust. The bullock at the rear bellowed mournfully.

Samson ran among the bullocks and men, barking with excitement.

It was impossible that Mr Barton had not heard the commotion.

'Run and fetch Maugie, if you please, Emily,' asked Mamma. 'I have a pannier here for him. He'll be snug in a nest of old clothes.'

Emily ran to obey, her brown ringlets tangled and tousled.

'Charlotte, my dear, would you be so good as to wake Louisa and James and help them dress?' asked Mamma. 'We must get away as soon as possible. It is nearly dawn.'

The horizon to the east was streaked with a glimmer of crimson. The men fumbled with buckles and straps on the packsaddles in the dim light. A cock crowed.

Charlotte ran upstairs, her heart thumping. The house seemed bare and cold and her footsteps echoed on the timber floorboards. In the middle bedroom, she woke James first, urging him to be quick and quiet. Then she went to Mamma's room next door. Louisa was fast asleep in Mamma's wide four-poster bed, tangled in the damp sheets, her thumb in her mouth.

Charlotte leant over her youngest sister and breathed in the warm, milky scent of her skin.

'Louisa,' whispered Charlotte. 'Poppet? It is time to wake up.' Louisa rolled over and burrowed deeper into the blankets, her back to Charlotte. 'Come on, poppet. We are going on a wonderful adventure today. You get to ride your pony all day long. Won't that be lovely?'

Louisa moaned and her eyelids fluttered open. Charlotte lifted her gently out of the sheets and sat her on the side of the bed. Using a wet cloth, she quickly sponged her face and hands, then dressed her sister like a limp doll. Louisa was too sleepy to either help or complain.

Picking Louisa up, Charlotte piggybacked her into James's room. James was up and dressed, wearing his fawn trousers, white shirt, a blue jacket and boots – his hair standing on end. He was standing by the fireplace, penknife in hand.

'What are you doing, James?' Charlotte demanded.

James started and guiltily hid the knife behind his back. He had carved some letters on the mantelpiece.

'I'm carving my name,' he confessed, shamefaced. 'Just in case we never come back. I wanted to leave my name as a record that we belong here and Oldbury belongs to us.'

Charlotte nodded, a lump in her throat. 'Then you had better finish it,' she suggested. 'I'll wait for you.'

When Charlotte, James and Louisa came downstairs, the men were loading Maugie's basket on top of a bullock, opposite Mamma's portable writing desk and a large hamper of earthenware crockery. Maugie roared with indignation.

It was this roar that finally roused Mr Barton. He began banging on the locked door, yelling and swearing at the top of his voice.

'We must make haste,' Mamma urged the men.

A loud crash came from upstairs. The children glanced back towards the house in fear.

'Hurry up,' whispered Charlotte, jiggling up and down.

At last, the final parcel was strapped onto the rear bullock's packsaddle. Bill the bullocky swung his long-handled whip over his head, cracking it sharply over the bullocks' backs.

'Walk on, boys,' called Bill. The three bullocks started forward slowly in unison, directed by Bill's verbal instructions and whip cracks.

'We will be right behind you, Bill,' said Mamma.

'Right you are, ma'am,' he replied, lifting his cabbage tree hat.

As the bullocks moved out of the yard, the two men walking along their left side, Mamma hurried the children and Bridget towards the horses.

Another loud crash came from the house. This one sounded closer.

Louisa had just been lifted onto her grey pony and James mounted on his gelding when Mr Barton staggered onto the verandah, carrying a pistol.

'I outwitted you, woman,' jeered Mr Barton. 'I smashed the door off its hinges.'

Mr Ash started forward but Mamma gestured to him to stay back. She grasped Samson by the collar, holding him by her side.

'Mount your horses, girls,' whispered Mamma, holding Ophelia and Clarie by the reins with her other hand.

Charlotte and Emily scrambled up into their side-saddles as quickly as they could, their eyes trained on their stepfather and his gun. Mr Ash helped Bridget into her saddle with more difficulty, as she was not used to riding on horseback.

'What d'you think you're doing?' bellowed Mr Barton, waving the pistol in the air.

'We are leaving, George,' explained Mamma gently. 'You have succeeded in driving us from our home.'

'You can't leave,' he shouted. 'You can't leave me here alone.'

In answer, Mamma lifted her skirt in one gloved hand, stepped on the mounting block and swung into the saddle.

'We are going away to a place where you cannot harm my children ever again,' said Mamma, pulling the reins.

Mr Ash and Charley mounted their own horses.

Mr Barton raised the pistol and took aim at Mamma, squeezing the trigger — nothing sounded but an empty click. He tried again. Mamma ignored him and twitched her horse's neck with her riding crop. The cavalcade of horses and riders moved forward.

Mr Barton sank to his knees and sobbed. 'I'm sorry. Don't go. Don't leave me alone, I beg you.'

'Farewell, George,' replied Mamma. 'I pray you find peace away from here.'

Mr Barton leapt to his feet and threw the unloaded pistol after them.

'I'll show you,' he shouted. 'I'll burn the place down. I'll ruin your reputation so that no decent person will ever speak to you. I'll make sure you and your brats never get a penny from this place ever again.'

Louisa whimpered. James wheeled his pony to charge back at his stepfather.

'Keep riding, dearest,' Mamma insisted. 'We cannot do anything more for him.'

'Mamma, how did you know that Mr Barton couldn't shoot you?' asked James, his brow furrowed as he nudged his pony towards the others.

Mamma smiled at him reassuringly. 'Of course he could

not — I hid the lead shot and dampened the powder of all the guns myself.'

The horses turned right onto the carriageway and trotted away to the east, away from the home where the children had lived their entire lives. Charlotte felt a huge lump in her throat that made it difficult to breathe. Her eyes swam with tears so the road ahead was a blur of green and ochre.

She was determined not to look back. She was determined not to cry.

The road, still deep in shadows, twisted and rose up the hill. Samson followed behind, his pink tongue lolling as he panted, running to keep up.

To Charlotte's right was the tall, prickly hawthorn hedge, which blocked the view towards the estate. Then came a small break in the vegetation, offering a glimpse back to Oldbury. Charlotte couldn't resist. Through it she could see the house of golden stone, its windows dark and empty, surrounded by trees. Beyond that she could see the graceful elm, with the empty bench seat where they loved to sit and read and sketch. Further still she could see the waterhole, where she imagined the dragonflies dancing above the shadowy water with shimmering wings. And then, a moment later, Ophelia passed the gap and it was gone.

Charlotte glanced at Emily to see that her sister's face, like her own, was slick with tears. They rode on in silence, except for the drumming of the horses' hooves and the jingling of the tin mugs and pannikins tied to the saddles.

The road crested the hill and beyond that, as far as they could see, lay a dense, green forest bathed in the rosy glow of the rising sun. A narrow, twisting track led to the horizon.

It's a beautiful day, thought Charlotte. *A beautiful day for an adventure.*

After about three miles they reached Sutton Forest, a village consisting of a small schoolhouse, several bark-and-slab huts, a store and three inns, all huddled around a wooden chapel. Just outside the village, they overtook the two servants and the trio of bullocks, plodding steadily along with all their possessions.

Mamma directed Mr Ash, Charley and Bridget to wait for them at the Talbot Inn while she took the children into the cemetery, fringed with weeping willows. Mamma led them to a sandstone tablet that marked a burial vault, carved with the name of James Atkinson.

'I wanted to come and say goodbye to your dear papa,' said Mamma, her voice shaky. 'He was a good man — kind and just.'

Charlotte breathed in. Her mother rarely spoke of their father.

Charlotte's memories of him were hazy — a man with soft brown hair and a gentle voice, who would swing her up in the air and make her laugh. Her father, strong and safe, holding her in his arms on the front of his saddle, way up high on his thoroughbred stallion. Her father gently handing her Samson as a wriggling, chubby puppy and telling her that Samson would protect her with his life. She cherished these memories because she knew the other children could barely remember him at all.

'He was taken from us far too early,' Mamma contin-ued. 'Louisa was just a babe of two months. He died of a lingering illness after drinking impure water on top of Razorback Mountain on his way back from a trip to Sydney. He loved you all very much.'

'Did he know me?' asked Louisa, pouting.

'I carried you into his bedroom, and you began to cry,' said Mamma. 'He saw you for just a moment, but then I had to take you away. The crying was too much for him in his delirious state.'

Mamma closed her eyes then pulled out the golden oval locket that she always wore. She opened it to reveal a plaited curl of hair, twisted from six strands of hair — two black and four brown.

'Rest in peace, my love,' she murmured, touching the thin wisp of hair, then snapping the locket closed.

Over against the fence, at the edge of the bushland, some native wildflowers grew. Charlotte ran over and picked a bunch of creamy flannel flowers and gently laid them on the grave.

'We'll be back, Papa,' whispered Charlotte.

At the Talbot Inn, they said a reluctant farewell to Bridget, who was travelling to Sydney to seek another job. Mamma had no money left to pay her. They paused for a few minutes while Mamma wrote a hasty letter to the executors to explain that the family had left Oldbury and Mr Barton and were fleeing to Budgong. She begged for the quarterly allowance to be sent to them there.

Charlotte kept glancing back down the road, expecting to see Mr Barton chasing after them at any moment. It was a great relief to ride out again.

Once they left Sutton Forest, Mamma began to tell them stories to pass the time, pointing out native plants and animals and teaching them the Latin, Aboriginal and common names for many of the plants and wildflowers they passed. The dusty, rutted road continued north-east towards Bong Bong. Along the way they passed several bullock-drawn drays plying north to Sydney and south to Goulburn, and the odd neighbour on horseback.

'This land belongs to Charles Throsby,' Mamma commented, gesturing with her riding crop at the surrounding vale. 'He was a great friend of your father's. His sister Mary was my cabin companion when I came out to the colony aboard the *Cumberland*.

'Charles Throsby's uncle explored all this country about twenty years ago and recommended it be opened for settlement. His property, Throsby Park, was the first farm established south of Camden. Shortly afterwards, your father was granted the land that he named Oldbury, after his birthplace in Kent.'

Charlotte remembered visiting the grand homestead at Throsby Park when she was younger, before her father died, for picnics and race days and family parties. They were long, sunny days filled with laughter, music and good food — much like the parties, ploughing competitions and dinners they used to have at Oldbury. But that was all a long time ago.

Now, whenever they saw the Throsbys at church or in the village, Mr Throsby would tip his hat and make polite conversation. Mrs Throsby would nod and smile sympathetically, but she wouldn't say much at all. It was just the same with Papa's brother, Uncle John Atkinson, and his wife, Aunt Jane, who lived at the property next door, Mereworth. They had four sons and three daughters, and when they were younger the cousins were always playing together, but now they rarely saw the Atkinsons, and Aunt Jane was decidedly distant with Mamma.

Soon afterwards, they caught up with the trio of bullocks again and rode along in front. The procession took a narrower side road, heading east past the odd sawyer's or shepherd's hut, and then another track winding southwards, which was narrower still. Gradually all signs of civilisation disappeared.

11

A Perilous Journey

For three hours, they rode in single file along a narrow stock track just wide enough for a laden bullock to pass. Mr Ash led the way, with the children following in age order. Mamma and the bullock team brought up the rear. Conversation was difficult, so each rider was left alone to observe the wild landscape, watch out for dangers and think melancholy thoughts.

On either side grew thick, impenetrable bushland with towering eucalypts and low scrub, flowering with a profusion of sweet-smelling bottlebrushes, acacia and gum blossom. Occasionally a tree trunk or branch would have fallen across the path, and the horses and bullocks would have to jump the obstacle. At other times, the vegetation had overgrown the path so thickly that they would have to force their way through, holding back branches to avoid their faces and clothes being ripped to shreds. All the while, the summer sun beat down upon them, making their clothes stick to their skin and sweat trickle down their spines.

Once Mr Ash yelled out as a long brown snake slithered off the path and into the undergrowth. A large goanna ran up a gum tree, causing Charlotte's horse, Ophelia, to shy and prance. The forest, which earlier had been noisy with the laughing of kookaburras and the warbling of magpies, was now heavy with an ominous silence, broken occasionally by the crack of Bill's stockwhip.

Charlotte felt mentally and physically exhausted. Her limbs were heavy and her head ached. She turned around to see Emily, her gentle face taut with tiredness.

At last they came to a creek where icy, clear water gushed and splashed over massive boulders and feathery ferns swathed the mossy banks. The horses eagerly jogged to the water to suck in deep, long draughts. Samson waded out to the centre of a shallow pool to cool off and have a drink.

'We will halt here for a little while,' Mamma decided, indicating a small clearing beside the waterhole. 'Let's build a campfire and brew some tea.'

Everyone dismounted thankfully, stretching their tired legs. Once the horses and bullocks had drunk their fill, the saddle girths were loosened and they were tethered in the shade to crop on some wispy, dry grass.

Charlotte and Emily squatted by the water's edge and filled their pannikins over and over again from a small waterfall to quench their thirst. James pulled off his boots and waded out up to his knees, splashing water over his head and face. Louisa was so weary she lay under the tree on a bed of leaves. Mamma tended to her, bringing over water in a tin mug and washing her face with a damp cloth.

Mr Ash and Charley gathered some branches and soon had a small fire burning, with a quart pot of water bubbling on the coals to make tea. Mamma dug a loaf of bread out of her saddlebag, and they ate it with cold bacon. Louisa was too tired to eat and lay with her eyes closed and head in Mamma's lap.

'Are we nearly there?' asked James as he swallowed a mouthful of bread.

Mamma laughed. 'No, unfortunately the hardest part of today's journey still lies ahead of us,' she warned, stroking Louisa's soft ringlets. 'Just beyond this far ridge is the Meryla Pass. The path is very steep, with steps cut into the cliffs leading from the escarpment down to the valley floor.'

Louisa's thumb stole into her mouth. Charlotte's heart sank.

'Oh dear,' said Emily, gripping her cup tightly in both hands. 'The hardest part is yet to come?'

'Indeed,' agreed Mr Ash, throwing the dregs of his tea away. 'We've some way to go yet.'

'Do not fret,' Mamma soothed. 'We will rest here for a while after lunch, then press on.'

James stood up and began skimming stones across the surface of the waterhole. Mr Ash and the bullock drivers lay down in the shade to snooze, their hats covering their faces.

'Look, dearests,' called Mamma, pointing to a striking crimson flower on the opposite bank. '*Telopea speciosissima*, commonly called the native lily. The latin name *telopea* means "seen from afar", and *speciosus* means "handsome" or "beautiful".'

'It is beautiful,' Emily agreed, settling her back against a tree trunk.

'This flower is highly regarded by the Aborigines,' continued Mamma. 'They call it a waratah and like to sip the sweet nectar from the bloom. One of the women told me a charming legend about the first waratah.'

Charlotte leant forward. She loved it when her mother told stories.

'Many years ago there was a comely young maiden who wore a red cloak of wallaby fur, with a headdress of pink gang-gang cockatoo feathers. She was deeply in love with a courageous warrior.

'One day, there was a fierce battle between the tribes and all the men went off to fight with their boomerangs and spears. Her beloved was killed in the battle, and when she heard the dreadful news, the maiden dropped dead with grief. In the spot where her body fell, there grew the first crimson waratah.'

'Oh, that is so romantic,' cried Emily, her eyes shining.

'No, it's so *tragic*,' said Charlotte. 'Do people really die of grief?'

Mamma sighed and swished a fly away with her gloved hand. 'I thought I might die of grief when your father died,' she confessed. 'But I had you four children to care for. You were all so young, so while I lost my beloved husband, I had my beloved children to live for. Slowly, slowly the wound heals a little. There is always hope.'

Charley had been sitting to the side, listening. 'There is another story my people tell about the waratah,' he said, smiling shyly. 'Once there was a female wonga pigeon that was attacked by a hawk. The hawk ripped her breast with its claws, but she escaped. The injured bird hid in a thick waratah bush among the white blooms. Later, the bird's husband returned from hunting and called for her. The pigeon struggled and tried to fly to him, but she died and her blood turned the blooms to red.'

Mamma nodded seriously.

'Another beautiful and sad story,' Emily said.

'So many of the Aboriginal stories are sad,' added Charlotte. 'About untimely death and blood and thwarted love.'

'I think perhaps the Aborigines have many reasons to be sad,' suggested Mamma. 'Did you know that when your father first came to Oldbury in 1820 there were about fifty Aborigines in the local Sutton Forest tribe? After I married him and moved here in 1827, there were only eighteen left — and now there is only a handful. Smallpox, influenza and rum have all taken their terrible toll.'

Charley hung his head and drew in the dirt with his finger.

James turned around. 'Don't forget about the massacres, like the ones last year, when the stockmen at Myall Creek and Waterloo Creek murdered dozens of Aboriginal men, women and children.'

Mamma frowned, placing a protective arm around Louisa. 'Those massacres were perpetrated by lawless men, who were reported to the Governor. Several convicts were tried and executed for their crimes,' she said. 'However, your father believed that it was possible for the English to live in harmony with this country's original inhabitants.'

Mamma sighed and gently lifted Louisa's head. 'Wake up, poppet. I know you are weary but we must be on our way. It would be even more treacherous to have to complete the descent in darkness.'

Charlotte sighed and stood up, stretching her stiff muscles. She didn't think she could pull herself back in the saddle. But there was no choice. The men and Charley prepared the animals, and then they were off.

At last they reached the edge of the escarpment overlooking the Meryla Valley. Before them was a magnificent view of hazy, rolling mountains swathed in thick, green forest, stretching as far as the eye could see. There was nothing that indicated humans had ever trod here, except the narrow, overgrown pathway twisting down the mountain side. In the steepest sections, rough steps had been cut into the pathway to help the animals keep their footing.

'We're going down *there*?' Charlotte asked in disbelief. 'That's impossible.'

'No – not impossible,' Mamma assured her with a tight smile. 'Although it will be somewhat difficult.'

The riders milled at the top of the descent. Ophelia's hoof dislodged a clod of mud that tumbled down the cliff and disappeared into freefall.

'Yes, it's straight down,' Mr Ash announced. 'It's slippery and narrow, so you must be very careful. That means you, Master James.'

James pushed his hair out of his eyes and nodded.

'It is too steep to ride, so we must dismount and lead the horses,' explained Mamma, her voice low and serious.

Emily peered over the cliff and pulled her horse back

away from the edge. Charlotte bit her lip and stroked Ophelia's neck.

'If your horse stumbles or slips towards the edge, you need to let it go,' warned Mr Ash. 'Don't try to save the horse or you may fall over yourself.'

Charlotte looked at Mr Ash in horror – she couldn't let Ophelia go if she fell. Obediently, everyone dismounted and took their horses by the reins on the left side of the bridle.

'Mr Ash will go first,' instructed Mamma. 'James, you will go next, but you must leave a large space between the horse in front and the horse behind. If anyone slips, we do not want them to collide with another horse and risk flinging them from the cliff. Do you all understand?'

Charlotte and Emily exchanged a quick glance of trepidation then nodded.

'I'll start,' Mr Ash said, leading his own horse and Mamma's down the trail.

The others followed slowly: James, Charlotte, Emily, Mamma holding Louisa's hand, Charley leading Louisa's pony then Samson bringing up the rear. The bullock train rested at the top to give them time and space to descend the steepest slope.

Ophelia was reluctant to step down the precipitous path and skittered nervously on the brink. Charlotte had to pull her firmly to urge her forward.

The horses' hooves slid. Charlotte's stomach was in knots and her heart felt like it was in her throat. The cliff plunged away on her left, with nothing between her and the valley floor hundreds of feet below.

A third of the way down the steepest slope, Ophelia

slipped and fell to her front knees. Charlotte was knocked over and sent sprawling on the path right near the dizzying drop. She grasped hold of a tuft of feathery ferns to stop herself from plummeting face-first down the cliff.

Emily screamed. Ophelia reared in fright, the edge of the path crumbling away beneath her back hooves.

'Stop, everyone!' Mamma shouted. 'Charlotte, are you all right?'

Charlotte cowered. A plunging hoof had caught her on the left shoulder and knocked the breath from her with its painful force. She whimpered, tears smarting her eyes. Ophelia shied, the reins dragging in the dirt.

Charlotte scrambled to her feet and caught the reins. Ophelia reared again, snorting and whinnying in panic, pulling away from Charlotte towards the cliff edge.

'Let her go, Miss Charlotte,' yelled Mr Ash. 'Let her go or she'll pull you over too.'

Charlotte glanced over the precipice. Nothing could survive a fall like that. Ophelia snorted, her eyes rolling in terror, and pulled again.

'Charlotte,' shrieked Mamma. 'Step away!'

Charlotte could hear Mamma calling, but she focused on breathing calmly and deeply. She stepped towards Ophelia and the crumbling cliff edge.

'There girl, easy girl,' murmured Charlotte, grasping Ophelia by the bridle. 'Walk on, Ophelia.'

The horse snorted and whinnied, then harrumphed with relief. She took one step forward, then another, and rubbed her nose against Charlotte's arm. Charlotte stroked Ophelia between the eyes, breathing deeply, her heart pounding with fear.

'I am fine,' called Charlotte, glancing back up the path towards her mother and sisters with a weak smile. 'Just a little muddy.'

Charlotte ruefully examined her soiled hands and the torn skirt of her blue riding habit. Her shoulder screamed with agony from where Ophelia had kicked her. She rubbed it gingerly.

'Are you all right to keep going?' asked Mr Ash. 'Or do you need a rest?'

Charlotte shuddered. The sooner they could get down this path the better. 'Let's keep going.'

Mr Ash nodded with relief.

The cavalcade continued, zigzagging down the cliff face. Louisa cried out as she slipped and stumbled. Mamma hauled her back by the hand, clumsy in her long riding habit.

'Come on, poppet,' urged Mamma. 'You are all right.'

The worst of the slope was eventually conquered, so they could walk faster. Lower down the mountain, where the track widened, Emily's horse, Clarie, collapsed and flopped down on her side, her belly heaving. Emily stumbled out of the way, still clutching the reins. The horse refused to rise, lying there wheezing and panting. Once again, the whole procession came to a halt.

'Come on, Clarie girl,' begged Emily, her voice choked. 'Please get up.'

Clarie whinnied and rocked, but couldn't rise to her feet.

'Charlotte, can you help her?' Mamma asked anxiously. 'I dare not leave Louisa – she has already fallen three times.'

Charlotte tethered Ophelia to a branch, stroking her neck for reassurance, and squeezed past to get to Emily.

Together they coaxed and cajoled until Clarie struggled to her feet, heaving and blowing.

'Well done, Miss Charlotte,' called Mr Ash. 'Let's keep moving forward, Master James.'

It took another hour until they reached the valley floor. Charlotte stared back the way they had come, her legs trembling. *We made it. I can't believe we are all safe at the bottom.*

'Well done, my dearests,' said Mamma, smiling with relief. 'I am proud of you.'

Louisa, her thin chest huffing with exhaustion, collapsed on the ground.

'It wasn't so difficult,' James boasted. 'Although *my* horse didn't collapse . . .'

'Ophelia didn't collapse — she slipped,' Charlotte explained.

James poked out his tongue then grinned. 'Glad you didn't let her go,' he said.

Charlotte grinned back and ruffled Ophelia's forelock. 'Me too.'

12

Light in the Darkness

At the bottom of the valley, in a shadowy gully, was a natural clearing with a small, sparkling stream surrounded by cabbage tree palms, thick tree ferns and soaring rainforest. Stockmen had built a series of timber yards to hold horses and cattle for the night.

'This is where we camp tonight,' Mamma announced, pulling off her gloves. There was a patch of ashy ground surrounded by a circle of rocks, where there had clearly been a campfire.

'Thank goodness,' Charlotte sighed, sinking to the ground. Her legs screamed with pain, her arms throbbed, and her knees trembled. She couldn't remember ever feeling this exhausted. Emily collapsed beside her and pinched the bridge of her nose as though she had a headache.

'Not so fast, young ladies,' reproved Mr Ash. 'First, we need to get these horses unsaddled, watered and rubbed down. Then we need to gather firewood for the fire.'

Charlotte closed her eyes in disbelief. *I can't get up. I simply can't.*

'Come on, my dearests,' Mamma encouraged. 'It will not take long if we all help. Poppet, you can lie here and watch out for the bullockies.'

Charlotte sighed but struggled obediently to her feet. Mr Ash and Charley unsaddled each of the horses in turn, stowing the saddles on the top bar of the stockyard fence while the girls rubbed them down with twisted handfuls of grass. After a long, deep drink at the creek, the horses rolled happily on the dusty ground of the yards, their backs slick with sweat. Grain for the night feed would come with the bullock train.

Mamma and James gathered a pile of timber and branches from the surrounding bush. King parrots swooped and shrieked through the trees. A swamp wallaby, startled by James, bounded away across the clearing.

Soon the campfire was roaring and everyone huddled around it, glad for its cheery flames in the cool dimness of the damp valley. With high mountains surrounding it on all sides, darkness fell quickly. Mr Ash threw a handful of tea into the bubbling water of the quart pot and crossed two eucalyptus twigs on top. He let it boil for a few minutes on its bed of glowing coal, then poured the black, steaming liquid into the tin mugs lined up beside the fire.

Samson slept by the fire, gently snoring.

'The bullocks should be here by now,' Mr Ash commented with a frown, handing Charlotte her mug of black tea.

'At least we know they can't be lost,' joked Charlotte,

stirring a teaspoon of sugar into her tea. 'There's only one way down.'

'Did you know your father became dreadfully lost in the Meryla Valley when he was exploring the Shoalhaven many years ago?' asked Mamma.

'Poor Papa,' Emily said, wriggling into a more comfortable position. 'What happened?'

'In the early 1820s he set off on a journey from Oldbury to explore the coastal region, guided by the Aboriginal chief of the Shoalhaven, Yarrawambie,' Mamma explained.

'Yarrawambie is a great man,' agreed Charley. 'He's my uncle.'

Mamma smiled and nodded. 'A great chief and a very good man. They spent several weeks exploring the mountain gullies and coastal flats, searching for suitable pasture land for cattle runs and harvesting red cedar.

'Yarrawambie guided James to the land at Budgong and showed him the way to the coast at Shoalhaven Heads. Papa had good friends — Mr Berry and Mr Wollstonecraft — whom he had known in England, and had settled there. Your papa was a very sociable man, with many friends.'

Mamma smiled fondly at the memory. 'However, on the return journey, once they had left Yarrawambie's traditional hunting grounds, they became lost in the gullies and endless forest of this mountain range. You see, while the Aborigines know their own land intimately, they rarely venture onto their neighbours' lands unless by invitation.'

Mamma gestured around them at the dark, impenetrable wilderness. Louisa shivered and cuddled closer to Mamma's side. Charlotte stroked Samson's back.

'After many days of wandering, the provisions ran out,' Mamma continued. 'Yarrawambie hunted a large goanna, which he roasted in the campfire coals. When that was finished, he discovered a bees' nest and took the honeycomb, which they carried in a bark basket. Yarrawambie refused to eat any of it, saying, "Master could not do so well as a blackfellow without food."'

Charley laughed and nodded, his dark eyes sparkling.

'Your father ate nothing but native honey for three days until they finally found their way to this track, which was then used only by the local Aborigines passing through the valleys to the highlands near us. All that time Yarrawambie took nothing but water. They were both very weak when they climbed this pass and made their way home. If it was not for Yarrawambie's care, your father would have perished in this valley, and none of you would have been born.'

Mamma smiled and sipped her tea.

'Thank goodness for your uncle Yarrawambie,' Emily said to Charley. 'I wish I could meet him and say thank you.'

'I am sure you will all meet him, Emily,' Mamma said. 'He is still the king of the Shoalhaven Aborigines, and I am sure he will come to see us at Budgong sooner or later.'

Mr Ash stood up and let out a loud cooee. 'I can't imagine what is keeping the bullockies. They should have been here long since. Those bullockies have done this track many times.'

'I'm hungry,' complained James. Charley nodded in agreement.

'All the provisions are in the bullock packs,' Mamma explained. 'They will be here very shortly.'

The group lapsed into silence, ears straining through the darkness to hear any sound of the missing men and pack animals. The fire burned low. Emily huddled closer to Charlotte.

'There they are,' called James, pointing into the bush. Moving among the trees was a small fiery light about two feet above the ground.

'Bill,' called Mr Ash. 'Is that you?'

There was no answer. The light disappeared.

'Who's there?' called Mamma, her voice high.

Samson rose and barked into the darkness. The light reappeared, moving closer to the camp.

'It's a devil-devil spirit,' Charley said, shrinking closer to the fire.

'Or a bushranger!' James exclaimed, jumping to his feet. 'That's the light of his pipe.'

Charlotte remembered Mr Barton, who was too frightened to ride to Budgong in case the bushranger John Lynch shot him. She grasped Emily's hand and held it tight. Louisa hid her face in Mamma's skirts.

'Nonsense, boys,' Mamma said sternly. 'What can it be?'

Mr Ash picked up a dead branch and threw it onto the campfire, causing the flames to blaze up.

'Look,' Charlotte shouted. 'It's just a beetle.'

They could see the light was flickering from the underside of a small brown beetle.

'It's a firefly,' said Mamma, laughing with relief. It was so ridiculous that everyone had just been terrified by a tiny insect no larger than a fingernail. Soon everyone was joining in, the hilarity ringing around the quiet gully.

Suddenly, another distant noise disturbed the night. Samson barked again in warning.

'Listen,' called Mr Ash. 'That must be them.'

A loud crashing sounded from the direction of the track. It was a large animal smashing through the undergrowth, dragging something heavy.

Everyone jumped to their feet. The bullocks were not meant to run.

'Something's gone wrong!' Charlotte said.

A bullock, dragging a trunk by a length of rope, thundered by in the darkness, straight through the creek and then stopped, panting and huffing at the gate to the yards. A second bullock followed, and then a third, all running loose and out of control. There was no sign of the two drivers.

'What has happened to the drivers?' Mamma said.

'Do you think they've been killed?' asked Emily, her voice trembling.

'Master James and Miss Charlotte, could you put the oxen in the yards?' suggested Mr Ash. 'Charley and I will go back up the track to see if we can find them.'

James and Charlotte shooed the bullocks into the yard, where the animals seemed relieved to be safe in the familiar enclosure. After a few minutes, the men returned. Charley carried Maugie the koala and Bill held a couple of baskets.

'We're quite safe,' called Bill.

'What happened?' asked Mamma.

'It seems Master Maugie did not enjoy his ride on a bullock's back,' said Mr Ash, grinning broadly.

Charlotte went to Charley and took Maugie in her arms, patting him and crooning.

'He's heavy,' Charley complained, shaking his arms.

'I think Maugie had a fright and stuck his claws through the wicker pannier and into the bullock's back,' Bill explained. 'The bullock bellowed, Maugie roared, and the bullock took off, galloping down the hill, shedding boxes and parcels along the way. The other two bullocks took off after him.'

'Maugie's pannier was thrown and he escaped up a tree,' Mr Ash said.

'Oh, no,' cried Emily, stroking the koala's furry ears. 'Poor Maugie.'

'Poor us,' Bill retorted. 'We had to chop down the tree and rescue him, because I didn't want to be the one to tell Miss Charlotte that we lost her precious pet bear.'

'Thank you, Bill,' replied Charlotte. 'We'd have been so sad to lose him.'

Maugie blinked around at the group and cuddled into Charlotte. The men laughed.

'I have to tell you, ma'am, most of the crockery was smashed,' confessed Bill. 'Only a few pieces survived.'

Mamma shrugged philosophically. 'Never mind. At least no one was hurt. You must all be famished. Let us unload the packs and I will prepare a meal.'

Everyone went to work setting up the tent and bedding, locating provisions and utensils. Louisa lay pale and listless, propped against a saddle and covered in a blanket.

Mr Ash made them a fine fireside sofa with a blanket on the ground and carpetbags to lean against.

Mamma fried slices of salt beef, which they ate with fresh, hot damper cooked on the coals. Louisa again couldn't eat and fell asleep with her head on Emily's lap.

Charlotte could barely keep her own eyes open but ate a small slice of damper before crawling off to bed.

The men and boys slept by the fire with a blanket and a saddle for a pillow. Mamma and the girls made beds under a rough canvas tent, using carpetbags for pillows. Samson slept beside Charlotte, one ear cocked to listen for danger.

As Charlotte lay under her rough blanket, she could hear the varied sounds of the bush — koalas roaring, possums crying, mosquitoes buzzing and the fire crackling. She thought the novelty of sleeping out of doors would keep her awake half the night. Instead, she fell asleep and slept more deeply than she had in months.

When Charlotte finally awoke, it was past dawn. The men had traipsed back up the mountain with the bullocks to collect some of their scattered belongings and were now repacking the loads. The horses were saddled, ready to go, and Mamma had made tea and damper for breakfast. Louisa ate something at last and looked a little better, a faint colour returning to her cheeks.

The ride was more pleasant than the previous day's. It was cooler in the shady gullies, and Charlotte no longer feared that a thundering of hooves behind them would bring Mr Barton, waving his flintlock pistol and shouting at them to return.

The track meandered downhill, then along the valley floor for an hour before coming to a wide river.

'These are the upper reaches of the Shoalhaven River,' Mamma explained as the horses stopped to drink. 'If we follow the river downstream for many more miles, it eventually wends its way to the sea.'

Charlotte twisted in the side-saddle, gazing down the gently flowing watercourse. She knew that she had been to Sydney when she was younger, and must have seen the sea there, but she had no memory of it. Once again, that was a memory from the distant time before Papa died.

'We cross the river here and then it is only another hour or so to Budgong,' Mamma said, pointing with her riding crop. 'We are nearly there, James.'

'Woohoo,' James cried, kicking his gelding into a canter, splashing through the water and up the other bank.

Charlotte was not to be outdone, so she urged Ophelia into a canter as well, chasing her brother across the wide river. The water surged up to her stirrup, wetting her lower boot and soaking her petticoats. A deep-blue sky soared overhead. A brown speckled eagle floated in the air, drifting on the currents, searching for prey.

Emily, with Mamma leading Louisa's pony, walked across at a more cautious pace, followed by the remainder of the cavalcade. Louisa squealed in delight, holding tightly onto her pony's pommel as the water rose up over her boots, drenching her skirts.

Samson paused reluctantly on the riverbank but refused to be left behind. He swam, swept sideways by the current, until he reached firm ground further downstream. He shook himself, sending a spray of water into the air, then raced to join his family.

The dog, tail wagging, looked so pleased with his cleverness that Charlotte and James laughed for joy.

'Who's a clever boy?' called Charlotte.

'James, you should have waited to find out how deep the river was,' Mamma mock-scolded, but her twinkling black eyes showed she was not really cross. 'You too, Charlotte — you might both have been swept away to the sea.'

'Mamma, I could see it wasn't dangerous,' James retorted. 'We're not frightened of a little water.'

'This is a wonderful adventure,' decided Charlotte. 'I wish we could keep riding forever.'

Mamma laughed, tipping her dark head back towards the sky. Charlotte thought her mother looked younger and less careworn than she had in a long time. She remembered back to the days when her mother was always laughing and joking. That was a long time ago.

'Come on,' James cried, waving his siblings on. 'Enough talking. Let's get there.'

The horses sensed the journey's end and picked up their pace, alternatively cantering and trotting up the trail.

The forest opened into a wide clearing. At the base of another mountain were two bark-and-slab huts, bleached grey by the sun. To the left was a series of timber stock-yards, and to the right a narrow mountain creek tumbled over grey boulders and mossy rocks on its way to join the river. In front was a wide, green clearing, nibbled into a lawn by the resident wombats.

'Budgong,' announced Mamma. 'Our sanctuary.'

13

Swanton

Present Day

Aunt Jessamine stopped talking and pulled her coat closer about her body.

Millie shivered. The shadows of the trees had grown long as the sun had moved to the west.

'Don't stop, please, Aunt Jessamine,' Millie begged. 'What happened next? Were they safe at Budgong? Did Mr Barton follow them? Did they ever go back to Oldbury?'

Aunt Jessamine laughed. 'I'm so glad you are enjoying my story,' she replied. 'But my poor old voice is getting tired and it's cold. Let's go back home for a very late lunch!'

'Ooh, yes please, I'm starving,' Bella agreed.

'Oh, Aunt Jessamine, I'm so sorry,' apologised Mum. 'We shouldn't have kept you out here so long.'

Millie felt so disappointed. She hated the spell to be broken. She didn't want to leave Oldbury.

'Could we come back again, please, Aunt Jessamine?' asked Millie. 'We haven't had a chance to explore the gardens or the back of the house. It's so beautiful here.'

Mum smiled at Millie's enthusiasm. Aunt Jessamine nodded seriously.

'Perhaps tomorrow morning,' she replied. 'I had thought we could go for a drive to some of the local historic villages, like Moss Vale and Berrima, or drive into Bowral for lunch?'

'I'd much rather come back here,' insisted Millie. 'We saw Berrima on the drive down. Please, please could we come back?'

Aunt Jessamine's face softened. She rose and pulled Millie up by the hand. The charm bracelet jingled. Millie saw Aunt Jessamine take in her short, rough fingernails and the red, torn quicks.

'Of course, Millie,' said Aunt Jessamine. 'Let's go and make sure everything is locked up securely.'

Millie remembered she was still wearing Aunt Jessamine's charm bracelet. Reluctantly she began to take it off. 'Here is your bracelet — thanks for letting me wear it. It's so beautiful and precious.'

Aunt Jessamine gazed at Millie for a moment. 'Why don't you wear it, just for the weekend,' she suggested. 'I know you will take good care of it.'

Millie beamed with pleasure. 'Thanks, I would love to.'

Mum and Aunt Jessamine walked behind while Bella and Millie ran ahead. Bella chatted excitedly, but Millie was lost in the stories of Oldbury long ago.

The afternoon was spent lazing around, reading books and exploring. Millie borrowed Aunt Jessamine's books, which included copies of sketches and paintings by the Atkinsons, particularly Louisa. She found a delightful sketch of two chubby possums and began to copy it, trying to reproduce its sense of mischievous playfulness.

As Millie was coming back from the bathroom, she overheard Mum and Aunt Jessamine chatting in the kitchen, preparing dinner. Millie could smell the mouth-watering aroma of garlic and onions sizzling in the pot.

'Millie seems to be quite a shy girl,' Aunt Jessamine commented as she chopped carrots. Millie froze. She hated it when people called her shy.

Mum sighed. 'I never think of her as shy at home,' she confessed, worry in her voice. 'But her teachers tell me she's quite withdrawn at school and doesn't like to join in class discussions. I think there's a lot of loud and very self-assured girls in her class, which shakes her confidence.'

Millie thought of the noisy girls at school as being like a flock of parrots – with their perfect plumage, raucous chatter, eye-rolling and sharp claws. They seemed to enjoy pecking and cawing at the other girls, fighting over who would be queen of the parrots.

'They do say that an empty vessel makes the most noise,' quipped Aunt Jessamine. 'Your Millie is obviously sensitive and thoughtful, and a talented artist. I think she will blossom into a very special and delightful young lady, who will leave the outspoken girls far behind. You should be proud of her.'

'I am,' Mum replied, sounding as though she had a lump in her throat. 'Very proud.'

Millie felt a sense of warmth and happiness flood through her. She turned away and went back to her drawing with renewed determination.

In the evening, after a simple meal of lasagne and salad, the girls cleared the table and washed up. When everything was dried and put away, they joined Mum and Aunt Jessamine in the sitting room in front of a cheery log fire. Bella curled up on the sofa while Millie sat on the rug with the two golden labradors.

'Could you tell us some more of the story, Aunt Jessamine?' asked Millie. 'Please? I'm dying to know what happened next.'

Aunt Jessamine nodded and took a sip of her herbal tea. 'Where were we?' she asked.

'They had just arrived at Budgong,' Millie reminded her. 'After fleeing Mr Barton and Oldbury.'

'Ahhh, yes,' said Aunt Jessamine. 'Their sanctuary . . .'

14

Sanctuary

Budgong, Summer 1839

Two grizzled stockmen wandered out from one of the huts, smoking short, black pipes, their faces covered in thick, long beards. They were accompanied by a group of several dogs — a mixture of cattle dogs and kangaroo-hunting dogs — who barked and growled at Samson until one of the stockmen ordered them back onto the verandah.

'Good morning, Jim,' called Mamma. 'Good morning, David.'

'G'day, ma'am,' they said, eyeing the large group of children and pets with some trepidation.

'We didn't expect you for another few weeks . . .' said David, who was usually called Bluey by the men. He removed his pipe from between his brown, chipped teeth.

'No,' Mamma admitted, 'but unfortunately circumstances changed and we have come here to live. I apologise that I did not have time to send you word.'

The men looked shocked. They were used to living in this remote clearing with little interference from the main estate. Someone would ride out regularly and bring back supplies by bullock, and Mamma would come once every three months to check on the cattle and the men, but otherwise they were left to their own devices — principally smoking pipes, hunting kangaroos and checking on the cattle. The mistress and her children living here was not what they had in mind.

'Well, look lively, lads,' called Mr Ash. 'Come and help unload.'

The men reluctantly started forward to help.

Mamma gave directions, one hand on her hip. The stockmen moved their own belongings out of the larger hut to make room for them. Jim scuttled to and fro. Bluey swaggered slowly, as though to prove he was no one's subordinate, especially not a woman's with four children in tow.

Charlotte pushed open the heavy plank door to their new home, and her heart sank to her boots. It was one large room, roughly built of sawn log slabs with a bark roof. The floor was packed dirt. The windows had no glass, merely timber shutters that could be opened to let in light and air. At one end was an open fireplace for cooking and warmth, with a mantle decorated with spurs, hobble chains, horseshoes and a coiled stockwhip.

All the furniture was rough-hewn bush carpentry, built from felled gum trees — a slab table and three timber platforms that doubled as beds and seats. The room smelled of pipe smoke, ash and rum.

'Oh,' said Emily, carrying a basket of provisions into the room. 'It is . . .' Words failed her.

'Dismal?' Charlotte dropped her load on the table.

Mamma followed behind with an armful of bedding, along with Louisa.

'Rough,' Mamma corrected her with a smile. 'However, we can make it a cozy little home.'

Mamma flung open all the shutters to let fresh air and sunlight into the room.

'Today we will make up some beds and rest a little after such a long journey,' suggested Mamma. 'Tomorrow, with lots of soap and elbow grease, you will not believe the transformation.'

The next few days were a hive of activity — scrubbing, removing rubbish, decorating, unpacking and arranging. Mamma had brought lengths of cream calico, which they tacked over the bare timber slab walls. Charlotte picked a big bunch of flannel flowers growing in the nearby bushland and set them in a jam jar of water on the kitchen table.

Emily set up all the books and sketchbooks on a shelf made by Mr Ash. Mamma arranged her portable writing desk in the corner. James helped Mr Ash and Charley build a henhouse and yard for the chickens to protect them from the dingoes and quolls.

On the bullock packs, Mamma had carefully packed some cuttings of scarlet geranium wrapped in wet newspaper to grow around the door of the hut. These had miraculously survived the chaos caused by Maugie and were tenderly planted and watered.

Mamma had even brought seeds and cuttings to plant a small, quick-growing vegetable patch of lettuce, spinach, radishes and herbs to add some green variety to their new diet of salt beef, bacon and damper.

On the third morning, the girls were given the job of planting the seeds in a patch of earth that had been dug over by the stockmen. The summer sun was already hot.

'I'm so tired, Emily,' complained Louisa grumpily, her ringlets damp with sweat. 'And it's hot. Can't we stop now?'

Emily straightened her aching back and smiled at her younger sister. 'Come on, poppet,' she encouraged her. 'Let's plant the seeds now and they can start growing while we rest.'

Charlotte smiled at her sister. Emily was always so gentle and kind. She never seemed to lose her patience or get cross.

'I'll fetch the water from the creek,' Charlotte offered, picking up the iron pail. 'Mamma says we will have green leaves to pick in less than a week if we water them every day.'

Louisa sighed but set to work with a will, dropping the seeds into the furrows and covering them with earth.

That night, after supper, the family sat around the fire. Mamma was sewing by lamplight, mending some clothes that had been torn on the journey through the under-brush. Emily read a book while James and Louisa played knuckles on the rug. Samson lay sprawled by the fire, and Maugie chewed on a pile of fresh eucalyptus shoots, his tiny eyes blinking. Charlotte was sketching a portrait of Ophelia with a pencil, although it was very difficult to get her head and body in proportion without a model.

'Mamma, can you tell us another story about Papa?' asked Louisa, looking up with her cheerful, gap-toothed smile.

Charlotte froze, her pencil suspended over the page. In recent years, since she had married Mr Barton, Mamma had rarely spoken about Papa. It was as though the memories were too painful, or the contrast between her first and second marriage was too stark to dwell on.

Mamma also paused, staring intently at her mending.

'Why don't I read you a story, poppet?' Emily suggested quickly. 'You can choose one of your favourites.'

'No — Mamma tells the best stories in the world,' complained James. 'They're much better than most of the ones in books.'

Mamma snipped the cotton thread with her scissors. She pulled out her golden locket and fiddled with it. She looked up and smiled. 'Very well then, poppet. Let me see . . .' Mamma picked up the mending again and kept sewing.

'It was September of the year 1826,' Mamma began. 'I had been working as a governess for a large, wealthy family on a beautiful country estate up in the far north of England when I became ill and had to resign. I went to stay for some months with my younger sister, Jane, and her husband in London to recuperate. When I had recovered, I saw a newspaper advertisement for a governess position that sounded simply too good to be true.

'I went to the interview at a fine, large house in London to find twenty-four other governesses had all applied for the job. But when they learned that the highly paid position would be on the other side of the world, in the faraway colony of New South Wales, they all withdrew their applications immediately in great horror.'

Charlotte laughed. She could imagine the twenty-four prim governesses with their high-necked gowns and button-up boots, all pursing their lips in distaste at the thought of living in the primitive wilds of the colony.

'The position, I learned, was to be governess for the three daughters of Mr Hannibal Macarthur, one of the leading families of the colony,' Mamma continued. 'I was interviewed by Mrs Harriet King, who was married to Mr Philip King, son of the former Governor and brother to Mrs Macarthur.

'My three sisters were appalled when I told them I planned to accept the position and begged me to stay with one or other of them. However, I was adamant that I must live an independent life. I had heard many fascinating stories of the colony and thought it would be a great adventure to travel so far.'

Charlotte smiled. *Of course Mamma was the only governess brave enough to tackle such an adventure. I wish I could have an adventure like that one day.*

'So I accepted and negotiated a one-year contract for the princely sum of one hundred pounds per year, plus first-class travel,' Mamma explained. 'Mrs King had chartered a ship, called the *Cumberland*, to bring out various members of her extended family — Kings, Macarthurs and Lethbridges — as well as some friends and various servants travelling in steerage.'

Emily nodded. All of the children had heard of these leading members of Sydney society.

'Most of the party was to come aboard at Plymouth,

but I joined the ship earlier at Gravesend.' Mamma smiled at the recollection. 'I boarded to find everything in chaos. The ship's deck was crowded with pens containing one-and-forty Saxon sheep, as well as hutches of twenty-three dozen turkeys, geese, fowls and ducks. A magnificent thoroughbred stallion was being loaded on board, as well as a massive bull.

'The stallion pranced and reared in fear at being loaded onto the unfamiliar vessel. Five black-and-white sheep-dogs were running about on deck, yapping and barking. Crates of plants were stacked on the quayside — dozens of fruit trees of every kind, cuttings of hops, wallflowers and even glass-topped boxes of delicate white lilies.

'I soon discovered the owner of all these beasts and flowers was a handsome young man called Mr James Atkinson.'

'Papa,' cried Charlotte, her heart swelling with pride.

Emily and Charlotte exchanged quick glances of delight. Louisa giggled. James sat up straighter, his game of knuckles forgotten.

'This dashing gentleman smiled at me and lifted his hat, and I felt my heart flutter,' Mamma confessed. 'We chatted on deck and later down in the cuddy, which is the small cabin where the first-class passengers would gather. James told me much about the colony, but especially about his beautiful estate that he called Oldbury and that the Aborigines called Gingenbullen. I could listen to his stories about this new land for hours.'

Papa told stories too, thought Charlotte. *I wish I could remember some.*

'James had come back to Europe to investigate the best

breeds of merino and Saxon sheep with his friend Charles Macarthur. It was during his time in England that James wrote his first book about the colony, because he said he became tired of answering the same questions over and over again.'

Their father had published several books and journal articles giving advice to settlers about farming practices in the colony. Mamma had kept them all neatly stacked together on the bookshelves in the study, and she had brought them to Budgong on the bullock packs.

'He was the most fascinating gentleman I had ever met.' Mamma's eyes lit up with memories. 'I wrote pages about him in my journal that night. Later, the captain's wife told me that James Atkinson was one of the most successful settlers in the colony and teased me about the attention he was giving me.'

Charlotte stroked Samson's black fur and felt a wave of sadness well through her.

'The ship was detained for a few days in Gravesend due to some damage caused during an accident, so those of us on board — James, Miss Throsby and myself — entertained ourselves as best we could, going for walks, joking, laughing and reading.

'When we finally set sail, a terrible gale blew up. Miss Throsby was dreadfully seasick and kept to her bed. The only passengers on board who were not overcome with nausea were James and me. The captain's wife, Mrs Carns, had given me some excellent advice before we sailed, suggesting that I stay up in the fresh air on deck as much as possible, as it is harder to be ill there than down in the stuffy confines of the cabins.

'I grew to love walking up on deck in the bracing wind, sitting on the poop deck gazing across the stormy seas or reading on my makeshift garden bench on top of the poultry hutches. One evening, James discovered me sitting up on the poop and insisted that I be wrapped in his warm, plaid cloak. James had a way of making me laugh.'

How romantic, thought Charlotte. *I hope one day a gentleman cares enough to wrap me in a cloak to keep me warm.*

'At Plymouth, the rest of the party came aboard and we said goodbye to England. All of us knew we might never see our homeland again.' Mamma looked wistful for a moment and then continued. 'Sailing into the Bay of Biscay, off the coast of France, the weather became increasingly wild and stormy. On Michaelmas Day we were sitting down to a festive dinner of roast goose when a huge wave washed into the cuddy, sweeping away our entire meal. I was thrown across the cabin by the full force of the wave and struggled to get up, held down underwater by the weight of my wet skirt and petticoats.'

Emily clutched Charlotte's hand, breathing in sharply. Charlotte could almost hear the wild wind howling and the waves smashing against the hull of the beleaguered ship.

'I thought I would drown. I could not get my head above the seawater, but James dragged me up,' Mamma exclaimed. 'I was saturated and shivering with shock, so once the waters receded, James wrapped me in his warm plaid cloak and made sure I was comforted.

'Then another huge wave crashed into the ship, shattering the stern windows and washing much of the cargo overboard. The sea again foamed right into the cuddy, carrying with it a coop of seventy chickens, which were strewn all about, squawking and flapping. The ladies were screaming and crying. The gentlemen were struck helpless with horror. The only one to exert himself was your father, who set to work bailing out the cuddy.'

Charlotte's heart surged with pride. *Of course practical, sensible Papa was the only one to keep his head.*

'The storm continued ferociously and none of us thought we would live through that dreadful voyage,' Mamma confessed. 'Finally, the gale blew itself out and only then did we know that we would survive. The next day, up on the poop deck, your papa took my hand, dropped down on one knee and asked me to marry him.'

'Oh!' exclaimed Emily.

Louisa clapped her hands. 'Clever Papa!'

'That is so romantic,' said Charlotte. 'Did you say yes at once?'

Mamma smiled. 'I thought about it for just a moment, and then I laughed out loud. After that terrible night, when I was sure we would all die, to find my world suddenly filled with so much joy was overwhelming. Many of the sailors saw what was happening and cheered and clapped.'

James crowed with delight.

'Mrs King was furious with me when I told her that we were engaged, as she had gone to so much trouble to find a suitable governess for the girls, but I insisted that I be mistress of my own actions,' Mamma said. 'So a year later, in September 1827, I married your papa in the little chapel at Sutton Forest and came to live at Oldbury.'

'Did you look after the little Macarthur girls?' asked Louisa.

'I did, and they were lovely girls — Elizabeth, Anna and Catherine. I taught them right up until my marriage, but then I hoped to have my own three beautiful little girls and a handsome son to love and teach.'

'And Papa built you Oldbury as a wedding present to remind you of England,' James added.

'Yes,' replied Mamma. 'We lived in a simple timber cottage on the farm for a couple of years while Papa built the big house. That's where my darling baby Charlotte Elizabeth was born.'

Mamma stroked Charlotte's forehead, then took up her sewing again. 'So that is the story of how I met your papa,' she finished.

'That was a fine story,' said James. 'Could you tell us another one? Can you tell us a story about cannibals or castaways?'

'Not tonight, James,' said Mamma, shaking her head with a warm smile. 'We will save the next story for tomorrow night.'

It was a perfect summer's morning under a vast blue sky, the air fresh with the tang of eucalyptus oil. After breakfast the girls lugged a basket of washing down to the creek, while James tagged along to collect wood for the voracious fire. Louisa carried a bucket with the soap. Mamma stayed behind to mix the dough for bread.

They had fallen into an easy routine. Chores, such as gardening, cooking, feeding the animals and cleaning, were done in the early morning before the heat set in. Later in the morning, Mamma set schoolwork around the kitchen table. In the late afternoon, when it was cooler, she took them on expeditions out into the bush on foot or on horse-back or by boat on the river, to study natural science and art.

'Good morning,' called Charlotte, waving to Mr Ash, Jim and Bluey, who were sitting on their verandah, sur-rounded by a pack of kangaroo dogs. The two stockmen nodded and tipped their hats. They were not very talk-ative, especially to females. Jim had been playing his tin whistle but stopped immediately once he saw the girls. He always looked particularly frightened around Mamma, as though he was terrified she'd bite his head off.

'Don't stop, Jim,' Charlotte said. 'You play very well.'

Jim blushed and stared intently at his boots, shoving the musical instrument in his pocket.

'Can I help you carry that, Miss Charlotte?' asked Mr Ash, standing up and jamming his hat on his head.

'We're fine, thanks, Mr Ash,' Charlotte replied, hefting the wicker basket higher.

Charley was sitting by himself on the steps, eating a crust of damper with salt beef.

'Charley, do you want to come and help me collect wood?' called James. Charley jumped up and ran over to join them, swallowing the last of his breakfast as he went.

The children chatted as they wandered down to the creek bank, where they paused to take off their boots and stockings so they could paddle barefoot in the water while they washed the clothes. Mamma always joked that the clothes they were wearing came back wetter than the clothes they had washed.

Charlotte began to sort the clothes, soaking some white pinafores in the bucket with the soap. Suddenly from the other side of the creek, Charlotte recognised the sound of a musical instrument.

'Shush,' whispered Emily. 'Someone is playing music.'

'Who could it be?' asked James, scanning the clearing on the other side.

'It sounds like Jim playing his tin whistle,' Charlotte answered. 'But how did he get in front of us?'

Charley laughed. 'It's not Jim. Look!' Charley pointed to a small brown bird that was scurrying across the clearing. The bird strutted up a small mound of earth, then held up his thistledown tail in a superb display, dipping and dancing to his unseen mate. The tune he sang was the unmistakable echo of Jim's tin whistle.

'Oh,' said Charlotte. 'It's a lyrebird mimicking the tune.'

'Isn't he beautiful?' Emily added. 'His mate must be hidden in the shrubbery.'

'I wish I had my sketchbook and pencils,' Charlotte complained. 'We could draw him, couldn't we, poppet?'

'I'll go back and get them,' Emily offered. 'Mamma might like to come and see him too.'

'No, I'll go,' Charlotte said. 'I'm the only one still wearing my boots.' Charlotte ran back to the hut. Mamma was now tipping the leftover washing-up water on the geraniums beside the steps. Charlotte explained about the lyrebird and raced inside to the shelf where the sketchbooks and pencils were stored, gathering them up.

As she turned she saw a letter in familiar handwriting on Mamma's portable writing desk. It must have come in yesterday when David brought the mail in from Berrima.

Mamma hadn't mentioned the letter, but it seemed to be a response to her latest urgent request for the executors to allow her access to her allowance. The words jumped out at Charlotte:

Mr Humphery has returned from Oldbury — he found Barton alone — in charge of the farm, confined to his room and semi-insane — he however refuses to give up the sheep that are running about the place without anyone to look after them . . . Under these circumstances I see no chance of having one shilling for the children's property unless we send someone to take possession of the sheep . . .

Charlotte averted her eyes. She didn't want to read Mamma's private mail — it was never good news. She took the sketchbook and pencils down to the creek, but the lyrebird had fled, frightened by James's noisy chatter.

'Never mind, dearest,' Mamma soothed. 'This afternoon we will ride along the river towards the coast, and I am sure we will discover an abundance of subjects for our pencils.'

15

Dance of Death

L ate one afternoon, the family returned from a horse-back expedition to gather fossilised shells embedded in the shale and limestone cliffs of one of the river gorges for their museum collection, which they kept on the verandah. James's saddlebag bulged with rocks, shells and other marine fossils, while Emily and Louisa had dug up some wildflowers that they hoped to transplant into their native garden.

As they rode back towards the huts, they noticed a great deal of activity in the grassy clearing. Dozens of Aborigines were building gunyahs made of bark and tree branches. Others were just arriving, carrying their spears, shields and other belongings with them. Gaunt dingoes howled a loud warning at the family's arrival.

'It looks like we will have lots of company tonight,' Charlotte said. 'I've never seen so many Aborigines before.'

'There are a hundred or more!' James added. 'Do you think they are here for a battle?'

Mamma had told them the story of a bloody battle at Oldbury several years before, when a number of local clans had fought against each other with spears and woomeras to settle a dispute over hunting rights on the bordering territory.

'It must be a gathering of the local tribes,' said Mamma as they rode closer. 'They do not look as though they are here to settle a quarrel. Over there is Yarrawambie, the chief of the Shoalhaven, the man who saved your father many years ago! And there is Errombee, the chief of the Sutton Forest tribe.'

The two elders were conferring in the centre of the camp, surrounded by various men of their clan. Women were sitting in groups around campfires, roasting whole possums and goannas in the coals for their evening meal. Several of them stood when they noticed the riders and came over, waving and smiling in welcome.

Mamma dismounted just outside the camp, followed by the four children.

A group of about twelve Aborigines clustered around them, chatting and calling in both English and their Gandangara language. Both men and women wore cloaks made of possum skins, which they wrapped under one arm and pinned to the other shoulder. Children ran around, wearing nothing but a possum yarn belt, shrieking with laughter.

'Good afternoon, Errombee,' called Mamma. 'Hello, Woomby, hello Nemmett.'

Errombee was an old warrior, tall and proud. He was an elder of the Gandangara people who lived on the land that stretched from Budgong to Sutton Forest and Oldbury.

He smiled in welcome, revealing a gap where his tooth had been knocked out; his beard and long hair were grey and grizzled.

'What are you doing here, missus?' asked Errombee. 'Why are you living here and not in your big house? Where have all your jumbucks gone?'

Mamma sighed, her smile touched with sorrow. 'We had to leave, Errombee,' she explained. 'The sheep have been sold by the men who should be looking after my children's interests, but I think they are not truly concerned for us, only looking after their own affairs. They said we could not live at Oldbury anymore. They plan to let strangers live there instead.'

The gathered Aborigines looked affronted.

Errombee lifted his spear menacingly, making a stabbing, downward motion. 'You tell us where to find these men, missus, and we'll spear them for you,' he insisted. 'We'll help you.'

Mamma looked horrified and caught Errombee's spear hand.

'Thank you, Errombee, but you must not harm them,' Mamma assured him. 'That would cause too much trouble for you with the Governor. We will be all right.'

Charlotte looked around at the Aborigines crowding around them. They looked so striking with their ochre markings, scars and tattoos. The women had kangaroo teeth woven into their black curly hair, necklaces made of golden-yellow reeds looped around their necks and woven net headbands. The men each had one front tooth missing, which Mamma explained had been knocked out in adolescence by a boomerang in a male coming-of-age ceremony.

There could not have been a greater contrast between the near-nakedness of the dark-skinned Aborigines and the white-skinned Atkinson family — the girls swathed in layers of petticoats, skirts, bonnets and tight-laced bodices. Yet there was a real bond of affection between the two groups, linked by their love of the land.

Yarrawambie, the Shoalhaven elder, came over with Charley beside him. Charley was no longer wearing his scarlet serge shirt and blue trousers, but was like the other children, clad only in a possum skin belt. He suddenly looked older and taller. Charlotte glanced away in shock and confusion. She was used to seeing the young Aborigines with very few clothes on, but not Charley, who always wore European clothes.

Yarrawambie solemnly greeted Mamma. Mamma introduced each of the children.

Emily looked up at Yarrawambie and smiled shyly. 'Thank you for saving my father. Mamma says he never would have survived if you hadn't fed him and found the way home.'

A smile momentarily washed over the great elder's serious face, then he looked concerned once more. 'We won't speak of it,' he said.

Charlotte remembered that the Aborigines would never again mention the name of someone who had died.

'Tonight we have invited the other tribes for a big corroboree,' explained Errombee. 'Would you like to come to watch?'

'Thank you, Errombee,' said Mamma gravely. 'That would be an honour.'

One young Aboriginal mother, Ginny, turned around

and smiled shyly at them. She had her baby slung on her hip and wore a woven net bag across her back that carried her belongings, including the white charmed pebble that all the women hid in their bags. In her hand she carried a seed pod, which was slowly smouldering. This pod had been lit from the coals of the old campsite fire, and the burning ember was carried to the next camp to start the new home fire.

'You can sit with us, missus,' Ginny invited. She was one of the few Aboriginal women who could speak much English, as she had often worked for some of the neighbouring farmers around Sutton Forest, including the Atkinsons at Oldbury from time to time. Unlike many of the older women, she did not wear a bone pierced through her nose.

'Thank you, Ginny,' said Mamma. 'I see you have had a beautiful baby since we last saw you. Is he well?'

'Yes,' she replied, jiggling the baby in her arms. 'I called him Georgie.'

The baby's skin was much lighter than his mother's, and he stared at them with solemn, wide eyes.

'He's gorgeous,' cooed Charlotte, taking his tiny, starfish hand. 'Hello, Georgie.'

'Does he have an Aboriginal name as well, Ginny?' asked Mamma.

'Yes, but it will be easier for him to have an English name,' Ginny said. 'The white people can't say the old names.'

Charley laughed and nodded in agreement.

Charlotte remembered the day that Charley had come to live with them two years ago. His father had appeared in the doorway of the kitchen in his possum skin cloak with Charley looking frightened and small beside him. He had told Mamma that he wanted his son to learn the customs and language of the white people.

Mamma had promised to look after the young Aboriginal boy and teach him English. She had named him Charley and given him European clothes and boots. She paid him in provisions, which he shared with his family.

'Are you joining in the corroboree too, Charley?' Charlotte asked.

'No,' he replied, shaking his head. 'I can't yet. But I am going back with my family.'

'Oh no, Charley,' Mamma said. 'Are you leaving us? I thought you were happy.'

Charley smiled cheekily. 'It's time for me to go back,' he explained. 'I miss living free. I miss the bush. All you white people are slaves to work. It's a hard life sometimes in the bush, but we live free and happy.'

Mamma nodded in understanding. 'I'm sorry to lose you, Charley. Come up to the hut tomorrow and I'll give you some stores to take with you.'

Charlotte wondered that Charley would prefer to live in a bark gunyah in the bush, hunting wild animals, than on a 'civilised' farm. *Then again, none of us are living on a civilised farm anymore and Charley must be looking forward to going back to his family*, thought Charlotte. *I couldn't imagine anything worse than being separated from my family. It doesn't matter where we are living as long as we are together.*

That evening, when it was dark, the family walked down to the camp carrying a lantern. Dozens of bark gunyahs had been set up in family groups, separated by a wider space to form an avenue between each camp. Each gunyah faced onto the back of the one in front to give the occupants privacy. Campfires smouldered by the entrances.

Several rotund wombats waddled across the clearing, nibbling the grass as they went. Chubby possums swung between the branches of the trees, their tails curled up to form question marks. There was no moon overhead, and the black sky was spangled with thousands of sparkling stars.

Some of the children, accompanied by skinny, red-gold dingoes, came to greet them and lead them further on to another clearing closer to the river. A group of women were sitting near a small fire, chattering with great excitement. On their laps, each one had a possum skin cloak folded fur-side in to form a thick pad.

'Come sit here,' offered Ginny, gesturing them to come and sit down with the women.

'Thank you, Ginny,' replied Mamma. 'We have brought some tea for you to share.'

The women exclaimed over the precious gift. Mamma spread a blanket on the ground for them to sit on.

'Ginny, could we play with Georgie?' asked Emily.

Emily and Charlotte cooed over Ginny's baby, tickling his tummy. James ran around with the other boys, who were throwing sticks and chasing each other.

'Missus, have you got some white medicine for Nanny?' asked Ginny, pointing to an old woman in the group. 'She cut her foot on an axe.'

Mamma gently examined the badly lacerated foot, which was crusted with blood and dirt. It had been treated with a poultice made of crushed tea tree leaves.

'Tell Nanny to come with me up to our hut,' Mamma suggested. 'I will wash it with soap and warm water, and bandage it with wet cloths to keep the wound clean and moist. I have some medicine for her too.'

Ginny translated for Nanny, who gesticulated wildly, shaking her head and replying in her own language.

'She will come tomorrow,' Ginny explained. 'She doesn't want to miss the corroboree.'

As if on cue, there was a shout in the darkness. The women fell silent. Out of the shadows jumped dozens of men from behind trees where they had been hiding. The men carried flaming torches of burning leaves and twigs, which lit up their bodies, painted with white and yellow ochre to represent skeletons. The skeletons stamped and sang, twisting and twirling in the fiery light of the torches.

The women pounded on their possum skin drums and chanted, their voices rising and falling in rhythm to the dance. The singing sounded strange and unearthly to Charlotte's ears. She shivered as the rhythm soaked into her bones.

The other children sat in silence, mesmerised by the beauty of the scene. With their dark skin melting into the backdrop of night and the luminescent ochre markings, it almost looked as if the clearing was full of dancing, leaping skeletons, risen from the dead.

The dancers moved in perfect time, forming a large circle. They leaned forward as one and at an angle that seemed impossible for the human body to sustain. Then, at some unseen signal, they all leant back the other way in a graceful display of highly rehearsed athleticism.

Afterwards, the dancers presented more contemporary stories, featuring local animals, such as kangaroos, emus and cheeky kookaburras, their images painted on large sheets of bark. Charlotte wished she knew the stories that were being represented in the dances.

It was very late when the Atkinsons said their thank-yous and good-nights and wandered home to bed under the blazing, starlit sky. Louisa stumbled along, almost asleep.

Charlotte felt exhilarated and curious. 'What do you think the dance of the skeletons was meant to signify?' she asked. 'It was eerie and strange, but also beautiful.'

Mamma sighed and picked up Louisa. 'It seemed to be a lament for the dead,' she guessed. 'Sadly, so many Aborigines have died in recent years from disease and violence and drinking the white man's rum. I fear the Aborigines have suffered much since the English have settled here.'

16

Letters

Budgong, Autumn 1840

A call of 'cooee!' rang out through the valley. The four children were sitting on the verandah in the late afternoon, reading books, and looked up to see the familiar figure of Mr Ash galloping up the green slope, followed by two packhorses on lead reins.

'Mamma,' James called through the open hut door. 'Mr Ash has returned.'

Mr Ash had ridden to Berrima several days ago to fetch the post and supplies. Mamma had written to the executors again, begging them to pay her the allowance from the estate and asking if they could return to Oldbury now that Mr Barton had finally been prevailed upon to leave. Mamma had asked Mr Ash to stay in Berrima until he received a reply.

Everyone ran to greet him with great excitement. They

had run out of tea and sugar many days ago and were almost out of flour. Worse than that, they were starved of news from the big world outside their tiny valley.

Mr Ash rode up with a grin, lifting his hat and calling out greetings to them all.

Mamma ran out of the hut, drying her hands on her apron. Mr Ash was no sooner out of the saddle than Mamma had grabbed the pile of letters he offered her.

'Thank you, Mr Ash.' Mamma collapsed into a chair on the verandah, flipping eagerly through the letters. 'Charlotte, Mr Ash must be parched. Could you make us all a cup of tea from the new supplies, if you please? Emily, could you cut some bread and butter for us?'

Emily and Charlotte went inside as they were told. Through the open door, the girls could hear Mamma chattering to James and Louisa about the content of the letters.

'This one is from my sister Jane in London. She has sent me some sketches of Queen Victoria. Apparently the Queen married her cousin, Prince Albert of Saxe-Coburg, in February. Is she not beautiful? Jane says they are deeply in love and much respected by the people.'

Charlotte and Emily popped their head around the door, curious to see. Mamma brandished some sketches that had been cut from a London newspaper several months ago with news of the Queen's engagement. The diminutive young Queen was shown dressed in an array of riding habits, day dresses and evening gowns that she had worn during the Prince's state visit. Of course, the letter was sent when the wedding was still months off.

'Oh, I love that white satin dress,' Emily said, peering

over Mamma's shoulder. 'It says it is trimmed with a wide, blue velvet ribbon and Honiton lace.'

James was more interested in the sketch of the Prince in his ceremonial German uniform, with its gold braid and dress sword.

Mamma checked the next letter. 'There's also a letter from Elizabeth Macarthur, one of the lovely girls to whom I was governess before my marriage. I will read that one later.'

Charlotte carried out the tea tray. Mr Ash had unsaddled the horses and unpacked the new supplies, placing them in the small storeroom at the back of the hut.

'I'm sorry, ma'am, but I couldn't get everything you asked for,' Mr Ash apologised.

'No?' Mamma said with a frown. 'Was the store in Berrima out of stock of something?'

'Not exactly,' replied Mr Ash, looking discomfited. 'The store would not let me have anything more on credit. He said the last bill is still unpaid. I could get neither the new boots for Master James nor the dress material you wanted. I decided it was best to buy food supplies.'

'Oh,' Mamma replied, not looking at Mr Ash. 'I see. Well, thank you — I am sure you did your best.'

Mr Ash took his cup of tea and wandered out of earshot to give Mamma privacy. Mamma opened the last letter with a worried expression. She scanned the page then crumpled it up and threw it across the verandah floor in vexation.

'*Oh,*' she harrumphed. 'I cannot believe it.'

'Is everything all right, Mamma?' Charlotte asked, pouring a cup of tea for James.

'It is the *executors*,' Mamma explained, her voice emphasising her disgust. 'They still will not pay me any allowance. How am I supposed to feed you and clothe you with absolutely no money? They say that due to my "peculiar circumstances" and rash flight from my "lawful husband", they cannot see fit to pay me my own money!'

Mamma's voice rose with anger and frustration. Charlotte's heart sank. The dreaded executors always made Mamma furious. 'When we were at Oldbury, they were constantly writing to me, telling me to protect you from Mr Barton's improvidence and idleness,' she cried. 'Now that we have fled from him, they accuse me of rashness and indecorum. I suppose they would rather I maintained my respectability but risked our very lives by living with a raving lunatic?'

Mamma picked up the crumpled, offending letter and flung it in the fire. She watched the paper curl and burst into flame and took a deep breath.

'They also condescend to inform me that Oldbury has been let to a Mr Thomas Bott Humphery and his family,' Mamma added in a low voice. 'Apparently he has negotiated a lower rent for the estate, due to the uncertain financial climate. The executors tell me that the current economic depression in the colony has made our financial situation even more difficult. The tenant, Mr Humphery, has taken possession of the house and land. We cannot go back to Oldbury.'

The four children looked at each other with concern.

It is done, Charlotte thought. *Our home is inhabited by strangers. There is no going back.*

That evening, they sat down to their usual Budgong meal of salt beef, damper, salad and tea. Charlotte didn't feel hungry and pushed her food around with her knife and fork. Mamma was still fuming, her forehead furrowed. She suddenly noticed that Charlotte had not eaten.

'Are you not well, Charlotte?' asked Mamma. 'You are not eating.'

'I'm not very hungry,' Charlotte confessed, her stomach knotted with tension.

'You must eat!' snapped Mamma, her voice unusually harsh. 'I know that our meals here are not as fine and varied as the baked fowl and roast pork we ate at Oldbury, but at least we *do* have food to eat. We have hens for eggs, we have cattle for beef and milk and butter, we grow a few vegetables, and for the moment we have flour. Do not sneer at the bread I put on our table — at least that *is* something.'

'But Mamma,' Charlotte began, her voice raised defensively, 'I'm not sneering. I just —'

Mamma started to cry, burying her face in her apron. Louisa climbed onto her lap, thumb in mouth. Emily jumped up and hugged Mamma around the shoulders. James glared at Charlotte.

'I am so sorry, Charlotte,' Mamma apologised, wiping her eyes. 'I should not have snapped at you. It is just that I do not know what we are to do . . .'

'It is all right, Mamma,' Charlotte replied soothingly. 'I am sorry too.'

Charlotte forced herself to eat the salty, preserved beef, each morsel sticking in her throat. *It is not fair*, she thought. *What did we do to deserve this?*

The next day Mamma woke them early with a cup of hot tea and a slice of buttered honey toast.

'Today we are going to muster the cattle,' she announced with forced cheer. 'The executors informed me in the letter yesterday that the Budgong cattle have been sold. They have given instructions that Mr Ash and the stockmen are to drive the cattle to Goulburn to their new owner.'

'They've sold our cattle?' Charlotte repeated sleepily. 'Can they do that?'

'They have already done so,' Mamma replied. 'Come on. It will do us all the world of good to get out in the bush for a good gallop.'

The children ate their breakfast, dressed hurriedly and went out into the chilly dawn. The stockmen were already awake and the horses saddled. The cattle dogs were milling around, snuffling the air with excitement. Samson joined them, woofing with delight as he saw the stockwhips being coiled and tied to the pommels.

Mr Ash pointed up into the thick scrub on the mountain-side. Massive spotted gums and grey gums soared overhead, their feathery foliage brushing the sky.

'I saw a big mob of cattle up there yesterday as I was riding through,' he said. 'We'll ride up there and flush them out first.'

Bluey nodded, his eyes squinting against the glare as his gelding pranced skittishly beneath him.

'The cattle are pretty wild,' Mr Ash warned the children. 'They are not like the tame beasts we had at Oldbury. Be careful not to get too close because those horns can be lethal to a human or horse. And try not to get in the way if they stampede.'

Charlotte checked Ophelia's girth to make sure it was tightly buckled then swung up into the side-saddle. The skirts of her riding habit cascaded down Ophelia's flank.

'Louisa, you are to ride close to me at all times,' Mamma reminded her. 'We will observe from a distance.' James was already in the saddle and cantering his horse around the clearing, cracking his small stockwhip above his head.

They rode up through the thick bushland, wallabies jumping out of their way. Jim the stockman yelled out as he spied a small herd of red-and-cream cattle hiding in the scrub.

'Jimmy and Bluey, you take the right side,' called Mr Ash, spurring his gelding into a gallop. 'I'll take the left.'

The dogs looked up for their orders then responded to the men's whistles and calls, sprinting low to the ground to round up the cattle.

Charlotte galloped after Mr Ash, swinging her own stockwhip above her head. Mr Ash had plaited it for her from greenhide as a Christmas present. She had practised for hours and could now make the whip sound with a resounding crack. James came up the middle, while Mamma and Louisa trotted along in their wake.

Charlotte charged to the left, jumping Ophelia over a fallen log. The cattle skittered, nervous at the unaccustomed disturbance. A small section of the herd split off, heading for the hills.

'See if you can head them off, Miss Charlotte,' called Mr Ash. 'I'll keep these ones with the main herd. If you lose them, don't worry — Jim and Bluey can help bring them in later.'

Charlotte was determined not to lose her small group of four cows and their calves. She let Ophelia have her head and raced after the cattle, swinging her stockwhip above her head, the crack echoing through the gully. She felt Ophelia's hooves thunder over the dry, bare ground.

The dominant cow was dashing for the ridge, the others racing behind. For a moment Charlotte thought she had lost them. She leant low over Ophelia's neck, urging her to go faster. The lead cow hesitated as Ophelia gained ground. She dropped her head, horns up, preparing to charge. Charlotte cracked her stockwhip loudly, the tip flicking the ground in a puff of dust.

'Back you go, girls,' yelled Charlotte at the cattle. 'Back to the herd.'

The front cow started at the loud noise, changed her mind and twisted her calf at her heels. Once the leader had turned, the others followed obediently. The leader tried to make another break for the hills, but Charlotte was there in a moment, cracking her whip and yelling, so the rebels surrendered and trotted meekly down the hill.

'Woohoo!' Charlotte cried, elation pumping through her body. 'I did it!'

Mr Ash nodded and grinned as he saw her trotting back, the cows looking uncharacteristically docile as they rejoined the group. 'Took your time, didn't you, Miss Charlotte,' he quipped. 'What have you been doing?'

'Just admiring the scenery,' Charlotte retorted, rolling her whip onto her saddle. 'The mountains are going to be lonely with no cattle.'

'Yes, but orders are orders, Miss Charlotte,' replied Mr Ash. 'Let's get these beasts into the yards.'

The next morning, Bluey, Jim and Mr Ash set off to deliver the cattle to Goulburn. Only Mr Ash would be returning.

17

Croup

Budgong, Winter 1840

In July, the little hut was bitterly cold. The winds swept up from the Snowy Mountains to the south and whistled through the cracks in the slab walls. At night-time, Mamma warmed stones in the fire to put in their beds and added a rug sewn of sun-dried possum skins on top of their bedding.

One bitter night, Charlotte was woken by a barking cough. Emily was asleep beside her, tucked into a tight ball like an echidna. By the flickering firelight, Charlotte could see Mamma moving around the hut, adding timber to the fire and rummaging through her medical chest.

'Mamma?' asked Charlotte, yawning.

'Hush, my dearest,' whispered Mamma. 'Go back to sleep.'

The barking, racking cough came again, and Charlotte realised it was Louisa, who was tossing and turning in the tangled sheets of Mamma's bed. Her hair, damp with perspiration, stuck to her neck in curled tendrils. Mamma felt her fiery forehead with her hand, frowning at its warmth.

'Louisa is ill,' Mamma confessed. 'She's burning up with a fever.'

Charlotte bit her lip. Louisa had been delicate from birth and was prone to terrible croup, which more than once had been life threatening.

'Is it bad?' asked Charlotte.

'I pray not,' Mamma replied. 'I hope that if we can treat it swiftly, it will not progress.'

Mamma filled a bowl from a pitcher of warm water and added a few drops of lavender oil. She began to bathe Louisa gently, wringing out the wet cloths. The fresh scent of lavender filled the room, banishing the stuffy smells of the night. Louisa moaned and coughed.

The comforting scent helped Charlotte drift back to sleep again, but her dreams were haunted by the hacking barks that continued all night.

When she awoke again, it was the dreary half-light before dawn. Mamma was sitting up, fully dressed and wrapped in shawls, in a chair beside the sleeping Louisa. Her face was pale and furrowed with concern.

'Are you awake, Charlotte?' whispered Mamma. Charlotte nodded sleepily. 'I need you to help me — I dare not leave Louisa. She is worse. Will you get dressed and fetch Mr Ash from the other hut for me, please? Ask him to come as quickly as he can.'

Charlotte moaned inwardly. It was freezing. The tip of her nose, sticking outside the warm nest of the blankets and furs, felt like ice. Emily rolled over and burrowed deeper under the covers. Louisa coughed again and cried out deliriously. Charlotte sighed and wriggled out of the warm blankets. Her bare feet touched the dirt floor and she recoiled in dismay, shivering. She quickly reached for her petticoats, stockings, dress and shawl. She found her boots by the door and slipped them on.

Outside was even colder. Frost crusted the grass with an icy sheen. Wraiths of mist swirled around the huts and huddled in the creek bed. Charlotte crunched across the grass to the other hut and knocked on the rough-hewn door.

'Mr Ash?' called Charlotte. 'Mamma has asked me to fetch you quickly. Louisa is ill.'

There was a grumbling noise from inside, but soon Mr Ash appeared at the doorway, hurriedly dressed with his coat and cabbage tree hat in his hands.

Inside their own hut, Mamma was bending over Louisa again, bathing her burning skin with cool, wet cloths.

'Is Miss Louisa unwell?' asked Mr Ash. 'Can I do something?'

Mamma stood, and squared her shoulders.

'She is very ill with croup,' Mamma said. 'I have never seen her as bad as this. I was hoping, Mr Ash, that you might be able to ride for a doctor?'

Mr Ash baulked. 'The nearest doctor is a two-day ride away,' he protested.

Mamma glanced at Louisa, who was struggling to breathe, the veins on her neck protruding with the effort. When she coughed, her whole body was racked, then she collapsed back on the pillow, exhausted.

'Please, Mr Ash,' begged Mamma, her voice cracking. 'We need a doctor as quickly as we can. Four days may be too late.'

'I will do my best, ma'am,' Mr Ash promised. 'I pray I can fetch the doctor in time.'

Everyone looked at Louisa, lying there so crumpled and small. Charlotte felt a wave of panic surge through her. *Is she dying? Is my baby sister dying? Children die of croup all the time. But please, God, don't let it be Louisa.*

'I'll go and saddle a horse,' said Mr Ash.

'Charlotte, help me prepare a pack of food for Mr Ash, please,' asked Mamma.

Mamma and Charlotte packed up a loaf of damper, salt beef, tea and flour, which Charlotte took to Mr Ash. He stowed the provisions in his saddlebag, touched his whip to his hat and galloped out of the clearing, heading towards the track that wound over the mountains towards the sea.

Slowly, sadly, Charlotte walked back. Mamma was bustling around the house now. She had even woken Emily and James, who were dressed and ready to help.

'We need firewood, lots of wood,' Mamma ordered. 'And buckets of water.'

Mamma had dragged a tin hipbath in front of the fire and was boiling up the kettle to fill it with hot water. James scoured the forest for fallen timber, dragging it back to the hut to keep the fire roaring. Emily and Charlotte lugged buckets of water back from the stream to be boiled up for the bath.

When the bath was full of steaming water, Mamma added eucalyptus oil. Louisa, her breathing laboured, was carried over in her nightgown and slowly lowered in up to her throat. She moaned and wheezed, her dark head lolling back against the side of the bath.

Louisa's breathing became a little easier in the fragrant steam. Mamma kept topping up the bath with hot water. When Louisa was breathing more easily, and the bath was getting cold, Mamma sent James to fetch more firewood.

'Emily, you watch Louisa and make sure she does not sink below the water,' Mamma ordered. 'Charlotte, help me change the sheets on the bed.'

When the bed was freshly made, Mamma and Charlotte lifted Louisa from the bath, wrapped her in sheets and changed her into a fresh nightgown before tucking her back under the blankets. Mamma carefully spooned some water down Louisa's throat along with a concoction made of honey and vinegar.

Mamma hardly left Louisa's side, leaving Charlotte to take on the role of looking after the family. Charlotte and Emily washed the damp sheets and nightgown, wrung them out by hand and hung them in the wintry sunshine to dry. Charlotte then made tea and damper, which no one could eat.

'Mamma?' Charlotte whispered. 'She will be all right, won't she? She won't . . . die?'

Mamma breathed deeply, shaking her head. 'Shush, dearest.' Her eyes darted to the shrunken body in the big bed. 'I pray she will recover quickly. We are doing every-thing we can.'

That night, Charlotte was kept awake by Louisa's coughing and tossing, and Mamma moving around the hut, administering tea and water, sponging Louisa down. Mamma eventually collapsed back in the chair and Charlotte could hear the sound of muffled sobbing.

Charlotte crept from her bed and knelt beside Mamma, hugging her legs and burying her head in her mother's lap. 'Don't cry, Mamma,' she begged. 'She'll be all right.'

Mamma hugged Charlotte, huddling over her and stroking her hair. 'You need to sleep, Charlotte,' said Mamma finally. 'I need you to be strong to help me tomorrow.'

Charlotte reluctantly went back to bed.

The next day's treatment followed much like the day before: hot steam baths, medicine and sips of water. On the third day, Louisa seemed a little better – she even smiled wanly at Mamma. Charlotte and Emily took turns to read to their sister and watch over her while Mamma snatched a quick sleep.

In the late afternoon, Mr Ash cantered into the clearing, followed by a stout, whiskered older man on a dappled grey gelding. The horses were foaming at the mouth and dark with sweat.

Mamma rushed from the hut. 'Mr Ash,' she called. 'Thank goodness, you have come at last.'

'This is Dr Mackenzie from Nerriga,' explained Mr Ash, his face white with exhaustion.

'Thank you for coming, Dr Mackenzie,' said Mamma. 'My little girl is in here.'

Dr Mackenzie smiled reassuringly. 'We'll know soon enough whether I will be able to help or not.'

Dr Mackenzie bustled into the hut carrying his leather medical bag. He examined Louisa, listening to her laboured breathing, taking her pulse and feeling her skin. Charlotte, Emily and James stood back in the shadows, away from the bed, observing with bated breath.

'She has croup,' the doctor confirmed. 'The medical treatment is bleeding, followed by an emetic to induce vomiting, then blistering to remove the toxins.' The doctor removed a glass jar full of wriggling, worm-like creatures from his bag. 'Leeches would be best, I think.'

'Are you certain, doctor?' asked Mamma, her voice trembling. 'She is already very weak.'

'Undoubtedly,' he replied. 'Bloodletting is essential to reduce the body's toxins and rebalance the bodily fluids.'

Louisa struggled to breathe, her eyes wide with fright. Mamma took the child's hand and stroked her dry, hot skin.

First, the doctor washed Louisa's neck with a wet, soapy cloth. Using tweezers, the doctor placed one, then another leech on Louisa's neck.

Louisa's breathing became faster and shallower. 'No,' she begged, her voice croaky and desperate. 'Please, no.'

Charlotte felt her eyes fill with hot tears. Emily clutched Charlotte's hand and squeezed it till the bones crunched. Samson came to the doctor's side and growled, deep and low. James had to drag him away.

Through blurry eyes, Charlotte could see the repulsive black leeches twisting and writhing on Louisa's pale skin.

'They are not attaching,' the doctor complained, drawing out a scalpel. 'I will need to make a small incision to draw the blood. A taste of blood will help the leeches to attach.'

Charlotte looked away — she could not bear to watch. Louisa gave a muffled scream, then there was silence.

'She's fainted,' Mamma cried, her voice breaking. 'She's barely breathing!'

'That is a blessing,' replied the doctor calmly. 'Children do get very anxious when we have to bleed them.'

There was silence while the doctor watched the leeches sucking on Louisa's neck. At last, one by one, they dropped off, sated. The doctor returned the bloated creatures to his glass jar.

'Now, we need to administer the emetic to induce vomiting,' Doctor Mackenzie explained, taking a small bottle from his bag. 'Calomel will do the job. Fetch me a bowl.'

The doctor woke Louisa with cold water and smelling salts. She began to sob softly. Charlotte took the doctor a bowl because Mamma was holding fast to Louisa's hand. The doctor administered the syrup, and then in moments Louisa was vomiting violently, hunched over the bowl.

Charlotte and Emily clutched each other in horror. James ran from the room to wait out in the darkness on the verandah. At last, Louisa was finished and lay weak and limp.

'Now we need to blister her,' the doctor continued calmly. 'I will apply the blister powder to her throat.'

'Surely, doctor, that is enough,' begged Mamma, her voice strong. 'The poor child is fading away.'

'Madam, I assure you that medical science has proved the complete efficacy of purging the body,' reproved the doctor. 'I understand that, as a woman and mother, your nerves are fragile and you don't wish to see your child suffer. But I assure you that if you don't follow my recommendations to the letter, this malaise will surely prove fatal.'

He liberally sprinkled a caustic powder on a bandage, which he then applied to Louisa's throat. She moaned and whimpered as the chemical burned her skin, causing it to bubble and blister.

'Mamma,' Louisa begged. 'Mamma, take it away.'

Mamma bent over Louisa, stroking the child's hair back from her forehead. 'My brave, brave poppet,' she murmured.

'The blisters will draw out the toxins from the skin,' the doctor assured her.

Finally, when he had broken the blisters and cleaned away the seeping fluid, he dressed the wound with linen bandages spread with lard. Louisa was limp and motionless after these administrations. Mamma tucked her under the coverings and kissed her forehead.

'There we are,' the doctor pronounced, packing up his medical bag. 'All finished. Now I shall write up my bill, as I must leave to return home at first light.'

Mamma stood up straight and proud. 'Thank you, doctor, for coming,' she replied. 'I must confess that I may be a little tardy paying the bill. I have not yet received my allowance for the quarter. I could give you a piece of jewellery to cover your time and trouble?'

Mamma pulled out the gold locket that she always wore, the one that held a locket of all their hair, and began to unclasp it.

'No, Mamma,' cried James. 'Papa gave you that locket.'

The doctor smiled kindly. 'Not to worry, my dear lady. I do understand your situation. Please pay me when you are able.'

The doctor sat down at the table and wrote out the bill, which he left propped up on the mantelpiece.

'Lastly, madam, I should suggest that if your daughter does survive, that this primitive hut is not the ideal place to raise such a delicate child,' advised Doctor Mackenzie. 'She needs nourishing food, warmth and bracing sea air. If it is possible to remove her to a healthier location, I would do so as soon as possible.'

Mamma nodded.

'Goodnight, madam,' the doctor said, putting his hat on. 'I wish you luck.'

When the doctor had left to spend the night with Mr Ash in the other hut, Mamma gathered the children around Louisa's bed, where their sister lay still, barely breathing.

'She seemed a little better today,' said Emily, her voice choked.

'Louisa, wake up,' begged James. 'Don't just lie there. Please move.'

The terrible scene of the doctor's visit played over and over again in Charlotte's mind. *Did he help her? Did he make her worse? Will our darling poppet survive the night?*

'All we can do now is pray,' suggested Mamma.

James, Emily, Charlotte and Mamma knelt alongside the bed and prayed desperately. No one could eat. No one could talk. Mamma sat up beside Louisa's bed through the night, watching and praying over her. Louisa didn't stir.

Charlotte and Emily couldn't imagine they would ever sleep but, curled up together to keep warm, they eventually fell into a doze. It was a long, bitter night.

Miraculously, Louisa was still alive in the morning. She hovered between life and death for days. When the fever finally broke, she shivered convulsively. The children spent much of each day scouring the bushland for fallen branches to keep the fire roaring.

Mamma sent Charlotte to ask Mr Ash to kill a chicken, which Charlotte then had to pluck and boil up with herbs, onions and potatoes to make a broth. Mamma dribbled tiny sips of the broth down Louisa's throat. The hut smelt sour with illness, tinged with the aroma of eucalyptus oil.

A week later, Charlotte awoke to find the hut ice-cold. The fire had gone out. Wind whistled through the cracks in the slabs and scattered grey ash in swirling eddies. Charlotte crawled out of bed and wrapped a blanket around her shoulders.

Where is Mamma? Charlotte discovered her sprawled asleep on the fur rug beside Louisa's bed. Charlotte stepped over her mother to the bed where Louisa lay buried under the mound of coverings. She held her breath, heart pounding.

Slowly, tentatively, Charlotte reached out to touch Louisa's cold, pale face.

Louisa's eyelashes fluttered. Her eyes opened and she smiled weakly. 'Charlotte?' she croaked. 'Where's Mamma?'

'Poppet,' Charlotte breathed in relief, grasping Louisa's tiny, frozen hand. 'Mamma's right here — but she's sleeping. She hasn't slept for days. Are you all right? How do you feel?'

'Tired,' Louisa admitted. She closed her eyes again, then strained to open them and lift her head.

'Charlotte, I dreamt I saw Papa,' Louisa confided. 'I ran to him and he hugged me and lifted me onto his knee. I was so happy to see him, but then he sent me away. He said I couldn't stay with him because Mamma needed me here. He looked so sad and lonely that I begged to stay there with him, to keep him company. But he said it would break Mamma's heart if I left her.'

Louisa fell back against the pillow, exhausted.

'Papa was right, poppet,' Charlotte replied slowly. 'It would break Mamma's heart if you left her.' Charlotte stroked Louisa's damp curls. 'What can I get you, poppet? Can I make you a cup of tea?'

'Yes, please, Charlotte,' Louisa whispered, her eyes closing again.

By the time Charlotte had relit the fire, filled the kettle with water, boiled it and made the tea, Louisa was again fast asleep. But this time Charlotte felt that it was a good, healing sleep.

Still dressed in her nightgown, her long hair tumbling loosely down her back, Charlotte took her hot cup of tea outside on the verandah. She sat on an armchair wrapped in her blanket, Samson at her feet. The sun was peeping over the eastern horizon in a wash of apricot and rose. The sky was a vast, deep-blue dome overhead, while thick shrouds of mist wafted in the hollows. A wombat waddled slowly across the clearing.

A spider web, spun between the verandah posts, glittered with dewdrops that hung like dozens of sparkling diamonds. Charlotte buried her bare toes in Samson's thick black coat and warmed her fingers on the hot teacup. She took a sip. Louisa would be all right, she was sure of it.

18

Mount Gingenbullen

Present Day

Bella yawned. The fire had died down to a pile of glowing coals.

Mum looked at her watch. 'Oh, look at the time,' she said. 'You girls should really be in bed. It's very late.'

'Oh, no, Mum, please,' Millie begged. 'Just a little bit longer.'

'Poor Aunt Jessamine must be exhausted,' said Mum, pushing herself up out of the armchair. 'We can hear more of the story tomorrow.'

Millie and Bella tried to argue but Mum was adamant, so they reluctantly said goodnight and left the waning warmth of the embers to get ready for bed. Mum had popped two hot water bottles into the big double bed while they cleaned their teeth and changed into flannelette pyjamas.

Mum kissed them both goodnight and pulled up the extra blanket. Millie cuddled up to her hot water bottle. She fell asleep and dreamt of girls with dark ringlets and white petticoats, riding horses through the bush. She dreamt she rode alongside them, galloping on a shining black mare, her hair tangled by the wind.

In the morning after breakfast, Aunt Jessamine suggested that they take the dogs for a walk along the top of Mount Gingenbullen and down through the paddocks behind Oldbury.

'Yes, please,' Millie said. 'That would be lovely.'

The girls pulled on their coats and boots and whistled for the dogs. Once again they all set off down the road towards Oldbury, but this time they unlocked a farm gate further up the hill and walked through the paddocks. A black cow lowed and lumbered away.

'If we walk up to the ridge,' Aunt Jessamine suggested, 'we will have a glorious view back out over the valley.'

The way was steep, with no pathway, so no one spoke, concentrating instead on not tripping on the dewy tussocks of grass. At the top of the hill they paused and looked out to the west, over the valley. A strong southerly wind blustered. Down below, wisps of mist hovered in the hollows and along the waterholes. The house and outbuildings nestled among hedges and gardens, sheltered from the cold wind.

'The old Aboriginal burial mound must have been around here somewhere,' said Aunt Jessamine. 'The one Louisa sketched, with its carved tree trunks.'

'There's no sign of it now,' said Mum, looking around. 'It has completely disappeared.'

Millie wondered if the ancient mound might be buried somewhere under their very feet. She moved away.

'Brrr,' Bella complained, burying her hands deep in her pockets. 'It's freezing.'

'It will be warmer in the valley,' promised Aunt Jessamine, heading downhill once more.

'Why do you think the executors forced the Atkinson family to leave?' asked Millie as they descended. 'Why didn't they just let them stay?'

Aunt Jessamine shook her head. 'I think the executors were well meaning,' she explained. 'However, they were conservative men who thought a widow was incapable of managing her own affairs, and I'm sure they were right in thinking that George Barton would try to strip the estate of every last penny.'

Mum opened a gate, leading from the paddock into the gardens behind the house.

'He was a scoundrel,' said Mum. 'What a terrible mistake she made in marrying him.'

'By all accounts, George Barton was completely useless,' Aunt Jessamine agreed. 'But in those days divorce was not an option, and it was not considered respectable for a woman to leave her husband. In the eyes of society and the executors, Charlotte's duty was to stay with George Barton, which of course she refused to do.'

'The executors thought Charlotte Atkinson was difficult because she stood up to them and insisted that she was capable of managing her own affairs,' added Mum. 'They didn't like that.'

By this time, the group had wandered down around the back of the house, past the freestanding kitchen and around to the front. Eventually, they reached the rivulet and the timber garden seat under the old tree.

Aunt Jessamine sank down on the bench, which was now bathed in warm sunlight.

'What happened after Louisa's illness?' asked Millie. 'She did get better, didn't she? Did they stay at Budgong?'

19

The Fishing Village

Double Bay, Spring 1840

The sun sparkled down on the wide, blue waters of Sydney Harbour. Sailing boats with their white sails scudded across the water, plying back and forth between the northern and southern shores. Several gaily painted fishing boats were trailing their nets offshore.

The bay horse pulling the buckboard trotted along the dirt track, his tail high. Mamma drove the buckboard, a long-handled whip in one hand and the reins in the other. Charlotte and Emily sat beside her, their bonnets neatly tied, while James, Louisa and Samson sat in the back surrounded by trunks, carpetbags and Mamma's writing desk.

It had been a tedious journey of several days. Firstly, it took two days on horseback to retrace the treacherous track to Oldbury. The family couldn't rest there, as the house was now filled with boisterous strangers, so they paused just long enough to gather some belongings and switch to the horsedrawn buckboard wagon. They all cried when they had to leave Maugie behind in his favourite blue gum tree, but Mamma insisted that Sydney Town was no place for a pet koala. Another two long days driving, staying in crowded, dirty inns along the way, brought them to Sydney. Now they were on the final stage, their bodies numb with tiredness.

'We are nearly there,' Mamma encouraged them. Despite her weariness, Charlotte felt a surge of excitement as they clopped along the track.

The scattered gum trees gave way, opening up to lush, green fields of neatly tilled market gardens, with several farmers hoeing and weeding in fields. In the distance stood a small fishing village of modest red brick and timber homes.

On their left was a white, crescent-shaped beach. Fishing nets were hanging up to dry in the sun on timber racks, beside a pile of tattered wicker baskets. Two boats were laying hull-side-up on the sand, awaiting repairs. A group of Aborigines — men, women and children dressed in crimson or blue shirts — sat cross-legged underneath a gum tree, around a small campfire.

A timber plank bridge crossed over a small, sparkling stream leading into the main square. Mamma pulled the horse up outside a brick cottage — a front door in the middle, a shuttered window on either side and a stone flagged verandah.

'This is the village of Double Bay,' Mamma announced. 'And this is our new home.'

Mamma had written to her lawyers, requesting that

they find her a modest house to rent cheaply. Sydney Town itself was beyond their means, so the lawyer had suggested this small fishing village on the harbour just over two miles from the centre of town. It was mostly inhabited by fishermen, market gardeners and a handful of Aborigines.

The carriers had already moved in their heavy furniture from Oldbury, which had been in storage all this time.

Mamma opened the front door and the children raced in to explore, followed by Samson, his tail wagging with excitement.

On either side of the front door were two small bedrooms, each with a fireplace. One had Mamma's big four-poster bed and dressing table, while the other held three narrow beds — one for each of the girls — and a big chest of drawers. There was barely room to squeeze between the beds.

Charlotte flung open the shutters to let sunlight flood into the room. Through the window she could see the glinting blue harbour, the white sand and the fishing boats.

'My bed is the one near the window,' said Charlotte, throwing her bonnet and gloves on the quilt to claim it.

'I'm in the middle,' said Louisa, bouncing up and down on the side of the bed to test the springiness of the mattress.

'So this must be mine,' replied Emily, setting her carpetbag down next to the bed beside the fireplace.

Down the hall was a small parlour that held the round breakfast table and four armchairs grouped around the fireplace. James's tiny bedroom was next to this.

At the back of the house was a stone flagged kitchen with a large wood stove and the familiar scrubbed-pine table. This led to the overgrown garden with its broken-down hen coop, weed-infested vegetable beds and sagging washing lines.

At the very back of the block was the washhouse with its copper and burner, the water closet, the stable and carriage house, shaded by a tall gum tree. Compared to Oldbury, it was modest, but compared to the stockmen's slab hut at Budgong, it was luxurious.

It was strange to see the well-loved furniture from Oldbury in these unfamiliar, poky rooms.

'Where's the rest of the furniture?' asked Emily, looking around the crowded parlour. 'Will we keep it in storage until we need it?'

'No, my love,' Mamma replied, taking off her straw bonnet. 'I had to sell much of the furniture to pay for the first quarter's rent on this house. It is lucky the house is small, so we do not need quite so much.'

'Oh,' said Emily. 'But not the piano?'

Mamma stroked Emily's cheek. 'I am sorry . . . Unfortunately the piano had to go as well. There is no room in the sitting room. Perhaps we can buy a small spinet if we move to a larger house.'

Emily looked down at the floor, struggling to hide her distress.

'So no more piano practice?' asked Louisa with approval.

Mamma stooped and kissed the top of her curls. 'Not for a little while, poppet, just until we get some money.'

Mamma stood up and frowned. 'James, perhaps you would be so kind as to help me unharness the horse and stow the buckboard in the carriage house? Girls, you need to help carry in the bags and trunks.'

A dreadful thought suddenly crossed Charlotte's mind. 'There's only one stable here, Mamma?' she asked. 'Where are we going to keep Ophelia and Clarie? Is there a paddock out the back?'

Mamma sighed and took Charlotte's hand. 'Dearest, I am sorry but we simply cannot afford to keep the horses. I do not know how I am going to feed my children as it is. They are to be sold next week.'

Charlotte turned away, her face wooden. Ophelia was *her* horse. She had ridden her, groomed her, fed her and loved her for years. She could not bear to lose her.

Mamma took Charlotte's face in her gloved hand and turned it towards her. 'I know this is difficult for all of us, Charlotte,' she said. 'But I need you to be strong. I have not received one penny from the executors for nearly a year. I have debts owing to storekeepers, doctors, lawyers and carriers. I have been consulting my lawyers so I can fight the executors through the courts and get the allowance from the estate to which we are entitled.'

Charlotte shook her head, her throat thick with unshed tears.

'Mamma, where is your locket?' asked Emily suddenly. Everyone turned to look. The locket was gone.

'I had to sell that too,' said Mamma, turning away abruptly.

'But you never took it off,' said James.

'I had no money for food,' replied Mamma sternly. 'Now that buckboard will not unpack itself, so let us get busy, if you please.'

'At least we have each other,' murmured Emily.

Mamma paused and nodded, then gathered all her

children together in a hug. 'Everything will be all right,' she swore fervently. 'I promise you.'

After the remoteness of Budgong, everything in Double Bay was exciting and new. There were walks to take along the beach, through the fields and to the surrounding bays and peninsulas. Mamma decided to keep the harness horse and buckboard, as she needed to travel frequently to visit her lawyers' offices in Sydney to prepare for the legal case.

She loaned the horse out to the neighbouring fishermen and farmers on occasion, in return for fish and vegetables. The family worked to make a comfortable home, as they had in Budgong — weeding and tilling the garden to grow vegetables and planting flowers around the front steps to make it pretty. James ran errands for some of the local men in return for fish or a bag of potatoes.

Mamma took them on excursions to Bondi Beach to walk, sketch and collect specimens. The most exciting excursions, though, were into town. The streets were crowded with people, hackney cabs and carriages. There was no money for shopping, but it was fun to look inside the shop windows.

Their days fell into a regular pattern of chores and schoolwork done at the kitchen table in the morning, then in the afternoon walks or excursions in the buckboard to sketch, collect oysters or mussels from the rocks, or dig for pipis in the sand. Every evening they gathered around the fire in the parlour to draw and talk, and Mamma would tell them stories while she did the mending.

Mamma seemed to have lost her appetite and ate less and less, becoming thinner and thinner.

A few weeks after their arrival in Sydney, the children were sitting around the kitchen table. On a tray were numerous pink, cream, light brown and white shells that they had collected from a trip to Bondi the day before. Mamma was helping them to identify the different shells they had found.

'This one is a small conch shell,' said Mamma, showing them a brown-and-white shell on the palm of her hand. 'Conch shells can grow up to a foot long. On some Pacific islands, they blow on the conch shell like a horn, especially in times of war. It makes a harsh, powerful noise that is also reputed to frighten away evil spirits.'

James picked up the conch shell and tried to blow it, but only succeeded in making a rather rude noise. James laughed out loud and repeated the noise even louder. Charlotte tossed her head with impatience and took the shell away.

'These ones are pretty,' said Louisa, fingering some delicate spotted shells.

'Yes — that one is an Arab cowry shell, while this one is called a milk-spotted cowry,' Mamma explained. 'The spots are designed to help camouflage the creature in its habitat.'

Samson barked to warn them that the postman was delivering the mail.

'James, could you run and fetch the post for me, please?' Mamma asked with a smile.

James returned with a number of letters.

'Bills, bills and more bills,' said Mamma, trying to crack

a joke as she flipped through the pile. 'And more correspondence from the lawyers . . .'

Mamma used a knife to slit open the letter and began to
read. 'Oh my goodness,' she cried, her hand to her mouth.
Mamma had gone as pale as milk. She swayed on her chair
as though she were going to faint.

'What is it, Mamma?' Charlotte said with alarm.

'It cannot be possible . . .' Mamma stammered. 'They
cannot really mean it.'

Emily jumped up and rubbed Mamma's thin shoulders.

A terrible feeling of foreboding overcame Charlotte.
'Mamma, what is it?'

'It is the executors,' Mamma said, struggling for breath.
'They have made a claim that I am "not a fit and proper
person to be the guardian" of my own children. They recommend that you children be taken away from me.'

Charlotte exchanged a glance of horror with Emily and
James. 'Why would they say that?' she asked.

'Don't they know that you are the best, most loving
mother in the world?' demanded Emily.

Mamma waved the letter in the air. 'They claim that my
conduct is imprudent because I am living separately from
my husband, George Bruce Barton,' she stated in disbelief.
'They claim that you are not being properly educated, and
that I am not providing properly for you.'

'But how could they possibly know how we are being
educated?' demanded Charlotte.

'The executors dare to recommend that you would
be much better educated if they were to send you away
to a boarding school run by a Mrs Harvey at Liverpool,'
Mamma fumed. 'She is probably some milksop school

mistress who will teach you nothing but a smidgen of piano and how to simper and flirt.'

'Go away to boarding school?' repeated Emily, stunned.

'They want to appoint a "responsible" guardian who will look to "the benefit and advantages of the children",' said Mamma scathingly. 'Tell me, who on *earth* would look after the benefits of my children more than I would!'

Mamma stormed up and down in the kitchen, her skirts swishing. 'I swear I would scratch someone's eyes out before I would let them take away my children.'

Mamma sat down suddenly and lay her head on the table, her eyes closed.

'Mamma, it will be all right,' Emily soothed. She rose and took off her mother's lace cap, loosening her tightly pinned hair. The long, black hair, with a thin streak of grey at the temple, tumbled down Mamma's back. Emily took up a hairbrush from the dresser and began to run it through her mother's hair.

When did Mamma get that streak of grey? Charlotte wondered. *I don't remember seeing her with grey hair before. Boarding school? How can they possibly think it would be better for us to be apart from our family and sent to boarding school?*

Charlotte went to the sink and filled the kettle with water. She added some timber kindling to the fire to stoke up the heat and placed the kettle on the hob. 'Who would like a cup of tea?' she asked brightly. No one really felt like it, but somehow it made them all feel a little better.

They sat sipping on their tea around the kitchen table in silence, everyone thinking over the contents of the letter.

Eventually Mamma began to speak, her voice taking on the tone she used when she told them stories.

'My mother, Elizabeth, died when I was twenty months old,' said Mamma. 'She was only twenty-eight and she died giving birth to my younger sister Jane. According to my father, she was a tiny woman of exquisite beauty. I inherited her height but sadly not her exquisite beauty!'

Mamma laughed and pulled a face of self-mockery. The show of merriment softened the lines and angles, making her eyes bright. She looked youthful again, especially with her hair falling around her face instead of bound in its usual severe bun.

'Mamma, of course you are beautiful,' Emily cried. 'You are the most beautiful Mamma in the world!'

Charlotte thought how sad it would be to lose your mother as a baby. Mamma clasped Emily's hand.

'My father, Albert Waring, came from a wealthy, land-owning family in Kent,' Mamma continued. 'The Warings were descended from a Norman knight called William de Warenne, who came to England from France with William the Conqueror in 1066, and he was rewarded for his valour by becoming the first Earl of Surrey.'

'He must have been very brave,' decided James. 'I wish I could have seen him fight.' He jumped up and began swishing an imaginary battle sword over their heads.

'James, let Mamma tell the story,' Charlotte admonished.

Mamma took up her work basket and began to sew. 'My father was the sixth son, but had enough fortune to possess a large house in London, and to live in style,' she explained. 'My father amused himself drawing and rearing many pet birds and animals.'

'Just like us,' said Louisa with a gap-toothed smile.

'Exactly,' Mamma agreed. 'When my mother died, she left behind four daughters under the age of nine. Soon afterwards, my father met with an accident, and he found it too much to care for us, so I was reared by an aunt, Mrs Fisher. Eventually my father remarried, so when I was ten I was sent away to a "superior school" in Kent, where I stayed until I was fifteen. My father thought it was important that girls should also have a thorough education, which is quite an unusual notion, even now.'

Charlotte and Emily nodded. They had heard Mamma's views on the importance of education for girls many times.

'My father had another two children, a daughter and a son, Thomas Albert — and of course all my father's property and fortune were to be inherited by my half-brother.'

Mamma snipped the cotton with her silver scissors.

'The school in Kent had an excellent reputation and I received lessons from the finest masters, including the celebrated landscape artist John Glover.' Mamma gestured over to the wall, where two of her own landscape paintings were hanging. 'However, I arrived there at the age of ten, leaving behind my family. I was terribly homesick.

'The discipline, as in most schools, was harsh. Children were regularly beaten, starved and made to stand on stools for hours for the slightest infraction. My dearest friend Eliza died at the age of eleven from consumption caused by poor food and cold dormitories.

'While I believe it is absolutely vital for girls to have an outstanding education, I know what it is like to be torn away from your family and sent away to boarding school, and I would *never* allow that to happen to you.'

Mamma gazed at them all in turn. 'I will do *everything* it takes to convince the Master-in-Equity that you must stay here with me.'

Emily, James and Louisa looked up at Mamma, their faces reflecting the trust they had in her power to protect them. Charlotte wished she could have their confidence — she could only feel sick with fear.

'You tell the best stories in the world,' said Louisa.

'Especially the ones about shipwrecks and cannibals and castaways,' James added.

'You should write them down, Mamma,' said Emily. 'You could make a book of the stories you tell us. That way, other children could enjoy them too.'

'You could sell the book and make a fortune,' James said.

Charlotte felt impatient with her brother and sisters. 'When would Mamma have time to write a book, James?' Charlotte asked. 'Mamma is working day and night as it is to look after us, writing petitions to the court and visiting the lawyers. She hardly has a moment to herself except when we're asleep.'

'You are right, Charlotte,' Mamma said, smiling at their enthusiasm. 'I could write at night-time while you are sleeping. I rarely sleep well at the moment, and it would give me something to do other than rewriting petitions for the lawyers. I will write some stories and see how it progresses.'

'Be sure to put in some stories about the Aborigines near Oldbury,' Louisa said, clutching her mother's sleeve. 'And some about beetles,' she added.

'Beetles?' demanded James in disgust. 'Who would want to read a story about *beetles*?'

'I would,' said Louisa, crossing her arms and pouting.

Everyone laughed.

'Poppet, I will be sure to write a story about beetles, just for you.'

20

Unwelcome Visitor

Outside, the rain drummed down relentlessly, as it had all day. It had been too miserable to go for a walk. The sky was so dark that Charlotte had lit the lamps early, and James had started a fire in the grate. They were all sitting around the cedar breakfast table, working on various pursuits.

Mamma was writing one of her stories about the shipwreck of the *Stirling Castle* and the experiences of one of the survivors, Eliza Fraser, living with the Aborigines. There was a growing pile of paper at her left elbow, written in her precise calligraphy. Emily was testing Louisa on her French verbs, while James was building a model of the *Stirling Castle* from scraps of wood and glue. Charlotte was sketching a bouquet of white daisies and scarlet geraniums from the garden, arranged in a crystal vase.

Samson lay in front of the fire, snoring gently. Suddenly

he pricked his ears and listened. He jumped up and ran to the back door, barking loudly.

'What is it, Samson?' asked Charlotte, putting down her pencil. 'Is someone there?'

A loud clang sounded from the rear yard. Mamma frowned, peering out the window into the heavy downpour.

'Who in their right mind would be visiting in this dreadful weather?' Mamma asked.

'Perhaps it is Mrs Fisher?' suggested Emily. Their well-meaning neighbour sometimes looked after the children when Mamma had to go to town on business and was prone to dropping in to see if everything was all right.

Mamma shook her head and straightened her heavy skirts.

The back door flew open, smashing against the wall. Mamma had not locked it yet for the evening. A stooped figure swathed in a saturated greatcoat stumbled into the corridor, leaving puddles of rainwater on the floor.

Samson growled, baring his fangs, the fur on the back of his neck standing on end. The children raced to stand beside their mother. The man grabbed the dog by the collar and hauled him outside, slamming the door. Samson barked furiously, his claws scratching frantically at the back door.

'George?' asked Mamma in disbelief.

'Mr Barton?' said Charlotte in disgust.

Mr Barton leered at them. Charlotte could smell the reek of him from where she stood — raw spirits, unwashed body, stale tobacco and foul breath. Since she had last seen him, he looked older — grey skin; lank, unkempt hair; his nose rosy with broken capillaries.

'What's for tea?' demanded Mr Barton.

Mamma slipped her hand into her pocket. 'There is nothing here for you. Would you please be so good as to leave us in peace?'

Mr Barton staggered down the hall towards them. He had obviously been drinking heavily.

'Emily, take Louisa and go next door to fetch Mr Fisher and his son,' Mamma whispered. 'Hurry.'

Emily obediently grabbed Louisa by the hand and rushed towards the front door.

'Stop, brat,' called Mr Barton. 'Don't you go anywhere.' Emily paused obediently, looking back, her hazel eyes round with fear. Charlotte could feel her heart thumping and her mouth become dry.

Mamma glared at Emily. Soundlessly she mouthed an urgent command: 'Go. Now.'

Emily turned and ran, dragging Louisa by the hand. Mr Barton charged after her, shoving Mamma and Charlotte out of the way. Fortunately his reflexes were slow and his movements clumsy. Emily slammed the door shut in his face.

Mr Barton grabbed Mamma by the wrist and dragged her into the sitting room. Charlotte yelped. James backed away towards the fireplace.

'I want food and I want money,' Mr Barton demanded, spraying spittle as he slurred. 'And I want it *now*.'

'We have not had any money since you forced us out of Oldbury all those months ago,' said Mamma indignantly. 'We barely have any food either.'

Mr Barton scowled and twisted her wrist savagely, forcing Mamma down onto her knees. Mamma struggled futilely.

'Don't hurt her,' Charlotte begged, grasping Mr Barton's arm. 'Let her go. Leave us alone.'

Mr Barton shoved Charlotte away so forcefully that she fell hard against an armchair. James darted forward, brandishing the fire poker as a weapon.

'James, please put that down,' insisted Mamma. 'Mr Barton is leaving immediately.'

James paused, torn between obeying his mother and defending her. At last he dropped his hand, but not the poker.

'Don't tell me you have no money,' scoffed Mr Barton, letting her wrist go. 'Your mealy-mouthed first husband left you and the brats a fortune. Now give me some.'

Mamma stood up with difficulty, her shoulders sagging. 'Look at us, George,' she demanded, gesturing around the tiny sitting room and at her faded gown. 'Do we look like we have money? Would we be living here, dressed like this, if we had a fortune? We are virtually starving.'

'Empty your pocket,' insisted Mr Barton.

Mamma glared at him but slipped her hand through the slit in the side of her skirt to the separate pocket she wore tied around her waist over her petticoats. Mamma pulled out a linen handkerchief, a set of three keys and a small brown pebble that she held out on the flat of her palm. There were no coins.

Mr Barton whacked her hand, sending the items flying. The keys jangled to the ground and the pebble skittered across the floor, lodging under the sideboard.

Mr Barton swept his fist across the breakfast table in frustration, scattering Mamma's carefully stacked sheets of paper and smashing the vase of flowers to the floor. The water puddled on the floor, ruining Charlotte's sketch and threatening Mamma's stories.

Charlotte fell to her hands and knees, scrabbling to pick up the strewn papers and place them out of harm's way.

'Get out, George,' Mamma insisted, her voice tight with barely restrained anger. 'There is nothing for you here.'

Suddenly, Mr Barton struck Mamma across the face violently. Charlotte jumped up, her fury bubbling over, and ran straight at Mr Barton. She drove into his belly with her forehead, sending him sprawling among the broken crystal and strewn flowers.

Mamma grabbed the fire poker from James and raised it, ready to let it fly if Mr Barton moved. Charlotte rolled out of the way.

The back door flew open for the second time and a black shadow streaked down the hall, followed by Emily, Louisa and two burly fishermen. A growling Samson leapt on Mr Barton's chest, water dripping from his shaggy coat, his bared fangs pressed against Mr Barton's nose.

'I'm going,' Mr Barton whimpered, covering his face with his arms. 'Call the dog off. I'm going.'

Charlotte lay curled up against the skirting board, fear and anger churning inside her. James pulled Samson off the quivering Mr Barton, who was dragged out the back door by the two fishermen. Emily locked the door behind them. Mamma came to check on Charlotte.

'Charlotte, dearest,' whispered Mamma, lifting her up. 'Are you all right?'

Mamma had a livid red mark on her face and her eye was puffing up.

Charlotte's anger and fear were too great to contain. She shook off her mother's arms.

'Don't touch me!' Charlotte shouted. 'It's *your* fault. Why did you marry him? Why did you betray Papa's memory by marrying that disgusting drunkard? *How could you?* None of this would have happened if you hadn't married him.'

Charlotte collapsed back against the skirting board, sobbing.

'We'd still be living at Oldbury,' Charlotte murmured. 'We'd still have our home.'

'Charlotte, you mustn't talk to Mamma like that,' Emily implored. Charlotte looked up. Louisa was glaring at her. James looked disgusted. Mamma looked beaten.

Mamma hushed Emily with a wave of her hand. 'Charlotte is right,' she admitted. 'If I had not married George Barton, none of this would have happened. One day I will try to explain . . . One day I hope you will understand . . . and forgive me.'

Mamma turned away and went to her bedroom, closing the door softly behind her.

Later, when Charlotte was sweeping up the broken crystal and spilled flowers, she found the small brown pebble under the sideboard. She rolled it between her own fingers, feeling the smoothness of the polished stone. The thought crossed her mind whether to throw it away, or keep it for herself.

She hesitated, then wrapped the pebble in the handkerchief with the set of keys and left it on the breakfast table, on top of the straightened pile of slightly damp writing paper. Mamma would find it later.

21

Examinations

Winter, 1841

The children had just returned from a lovely, long ramble along the beach, chatting to the fisher-wives and searching for shellfish. Samson was wet and sandy from chasing sticks thrown into the tiny waves. Emily and James were towelling him down while Louisa and Charlotte were rinsing the mussels under the pump to make a stew for supper. Mamma was feeding kindling into the wood-fired stove, a smear of ash on her cheek.

A loud knocking sounded from the front door. Samson barked and stood guard.

'Charlotte, would you mind answering that?' asked Mamma, gesturing to her dishevelled appearance.

'I wonder who it could be?' Charlotte wiped her damp, sandy hands on her apron as she hurried down the hallway. They rarely had any formal visitors. If one of the neighbours dropped by they usually came to the back door in the kitchen.

She opened the door to find a well-dressed young man wearing grey trousers and a waistcoat, a black jacket and gold fob watch, his dark hair slicked back from his face. A shiny carriage waited in the dusty roadway, with four matched bay horses standing in their harnesses.

'May I help you?' asked Charlotte, holding Samson by the collar.

'Good morning, miss.' The young man spoke with a strong English accent. He took off his hat and smiled. 'My name is Edward Corry. Am I addressing Miss Charlotte Atkinson?'

Charlotte tucked a stray curl behind her ear and wished she'd thought to take off her apron.

'Yes, Mr Corry,' Charlotte replied.

'I'm one of the solicitors handling the court case for the executors of your father's estate,' Mr Corry explained, his chest swelling. 'I have orders from the courts, as we previously advised Mrs Barton, and have been requested to escort you this afternoon to Mrs Harvey's School for Young Ladies at Liverpool.'

Charlotte hurriedly stepped backwards into the hallway, instinctively letting go of Samson's collar. Sampson barked, darting forward onto the stone verandah.

'Perhaps you could fetch your hat and gloves?' asked Mr Corry. 'You will only need to take a few things today. Your mother can send on any further luggage.'

Charlotte stood firm against the wall. Thoughts churned through her mind. Nausea churned in her belly. She thought she might vomit.

'May I come in?' asked Mr Corry, stepping forward.

'No,' Charlotte said clearly. Samson whined.

'I beg your pardon?' the man said, the smile wiped from his face.

Charlotte pulled herself tall, searching for courage. 'No, you may not come in,' she replied. 'No, I will not fetch my hat and gloves. I will not be going to Mrs Harvey's school. I will not leave my family.'

'Now, now,' blustered Mr Corry. 'You have no choice, young lady. The court has decided that it is in your best interests to go to school. There is no point fighting it. You need to be educated as befits your position in society. Now be so good as to fetch your belongings. I do not like to leave the horses standing long.'

Samson growled menacingly, his hackles raised.

'I *am* being educated as befits my position in society,' retorted Charlotte, twisting her apron between her fingers. 'I am being educated far better than most girls in the colony — and probably better than most girls in England.'

'Charlotte, is everything all right?' Mamma hurried down the hall, frowning. She had taken off her dirty apron and tucked her hair back under her cap. She still had a grey streak of ash on her cheek.

The solicitor looked her up and down, smiling in a superior way at the small woman in her dowdy gown and the girl with her sandy apron.

'Mrs Barton, I am Edward Corry, a solicitor for James Norton. I have come to escort Miss Charlotte Elizabeth Atkinson to Mrs Harvey's School for Young Ladies, where she will be boarded, as directed by the court.'

'I told him I won't go,' said Charlotte defiantly, her cheeks flushed.

Mamma smiled at Charlotte. 'Of course not, my dearest.'

Mamma turned to the young lawyer and said sweetly, 'Thank you for your concern, Mr Corry. However, as you can see, my daughter does not wish to go away to be boarded at school. She is being educated and cared for perfectly well at home.'

'You must obey the court orders, Mrs Barton,' insisted Mr Corry, his face pale and damp. 'The court has decreed that you are not fit to care for the children. She will be much better off with Mrs Harvey.'

'I doubt that very much,' Mamma retorted, her head held high. 'Now, if you will excuse us, we have work to do.'

'But . . .' Mr Corry stammered on the verandah, his gloved hands gripping his hat tightly.

Mamma leant forward and grasped Samson firmly by the collar, hauling him backwards. 'You might want to leave before my dog becomes aggressive. He has a nasty bite, and I find I am not strong enough to hold him when he becomes vicious.' Samson obliged, growling fiercely and baring his white fangs. Mr Corry stepped back hurriedly and Mamma slammed the door shut. Mr Corry banged furiously on the other side.

Mamma held Charlotte's trembling body tightly. 'Everything will be all right, my love,' she promised, her voice wavering. 'You did well, Charlotte. I am proud of you.'

Mamma drove the buckboard outside the sandstone court-house, the bay mare skittering in the traces. A blue sky arched overhead. The sun shone warm, glittering off the shiny cobbles.

Charlotte and Emily sat beside her on the front seat, their backs ramrod straight, while James and Louisa sat in the back. Each of them had been combed, scrubbed, starched and spruced as close to perfection as their mother could get.

Their worn boots had been polished with linseed oil until they gleamed in the sunlight. Charlotte could feel the cold stone cobbles through her worn soles as she stepped down. Her white dress had been soaked, boiled and scrubbed, dried in the sun to bleach, then ironed and starched to stiff respectability. Her petticoats, stockings and gloves had been darned, and her old hat trimmed with a scrap of blue ribbon that Mamma had rescued from one of her own gowns.

All the girls had slept with rags knotted in their hair. Torn from sugar bags, these rags created perfect ringlets, although Charlotte was sure hers would go wayward before much longer.

James had his usually unruly hair slicked down into submission with oil. He was wearing his Sunday best, although Charlotte realised as he clambered down from the buckboard that a wide expanse of wrist showed below his coat sleeves, and his trousers no longer covered the tops of his boots.

Mamma was also dressed in her best gown, with a faded blue shawl around her shoulders. Even though it was tightly laced, the bodice of her gown seemed far too big for her, as though it was Mamma herself who was shrinking.

'Now remember,' warned Mamma, 'you must all have absolutely perfect manners. Charlotte, no matter what he says, do not lose your temper.'

'I don't lose my temper,' Charlotte retorted, her cheeks warming.

Mamma smiled. 'Do not worry, dearest. It will be harder for me to hold my temper than you.'

'Will he ask very hard questions, Mamma?' asked Louisa.

'Yes, he may, poppet,' Mamma replied, leaning down to look into Louisa's eyes. 'However, I have full faith that you will all answer the questions to his satisfaction.'

Charlotte felt a stab of fear in her belly. Today was the day that the Master-in-Equity had decreed that the Atkinson children should each be examined in person, without their mother, to see how well they had been educated. Charlotte was worried, particularly about her arithmetic.

There had been times when Mamma was busy writing petitions to the court or visiting the lawyers' offices, when she had hurried through her exercises so she could read a book, or sketch, or play with her siblings instead. Now she wished that she had been more diligent.

'Mamma, will you be there with us?' Emily asked, her voice quavering.

'I will be out in the vestibule,' Mamma assured her, straightening the bow on Emily's straw bonnet.

As the eldest, Charlotte was the first to be examined. She was shown into a large chamber lined with hundreds of red leather-bound books with gilt lettering. A jowly old man swathed in a black robe sat at his chair behind a huge mahogany desk, a curled powdered wig upon his head. Charlotte curtseyed nervously.

'Please, take a seat, Miss Charlotte,' invited the Master-in-Equity, indicating the chair opposite him. 'Do you understand that today I am going to ask you a great many questions about your learning to ascertain your level of education to date?'

Charlotte nodded, her mouth dry. She pressed her knees together and clasped her hands in her lap. *What if I answer incorrectly?* she thought. *My whole future depends on this examination. If I don't impress him, I'll be taken away from my family. Dear God, please don't let me fail.*

'Do not be anxious,' he said kindly. 'I understand that until now you have been educated at home by your mother? Could you tell me what you learn?'

Charlotte swallowed and took a deep breath. She licked her lips. 'We study English composition, grammar, arithmetic, English history, natural sciences, geography, drawing, music . . .' Charlotte paused, trying to think.

'Languages?' asked the Master, writing notes on a sheet of paper.

Charlotte nodded. 'French, Italian and German.'

'*Buongiorno,*' the Master greeted her in Italian. '*Come sta?*'

'*Grazie, signor, sto bene,*' replied Charlotte, thanking him and saying she was well.

The Master asked her a few more questions in Italian, then in French and German. Charlotte was able to converse in all three languages with little hesitation.

'You said you learn natural science?' asked the Master, switching back to English. 'What exactly do you learn?'

Charlotte sat up straighter. 'We study geology, anthropology, botany, zoology, palaeontology, conchology —'

'Conchology?' interrupted the Master.

'Yes, the study of shells,' replied Charlotte. 'We collect shells at Bondi Beach and the beaches around Double Bay, then we identify them and learn about the creatures who inhabit them.'

The examination continued, the Master asking Charlotte detailed questions about each branch of her knowledge. Charlotte began to relax. She was having no difficulty answering any of the questions.

She had to read aloud from a heavy law text, full of long, difficult words. She had to sketch a waratah flower in a vase on the table. She completed the drawing by identifying the various parts of the plant, including the stem, florets, stigma, style and anther, and labelling it with its common, Latin and Aboriginal names. She had to recite lists of English kings and English rivers, and write a composition on fossils.

By the time she had completed pages of mathematical exercises, her head was aching.

'Thank you, Miss Charlotte,' said the Master with a smile. 'I believe your mother has done an exceptional job with your education. You are obviously a talented young lady.'

Charlotte sighed with relief, the knot in her stomach dissolving. She thanked the Master-in-Equity then hurried outside to fetch Emily, who looked as though she was about to be taken to the guillotine.

'It was fine,' Charlotte reassured her sister. 'You'll do brilliantly, I know.'

Emily smiled back wanly.

It was a long, anxious wait in the draughty vestibule as Emily, then James and finally Louisa were examined by the Master. Finally, Mamma was summoned to the judge's chamber to collect Louisa. Charlotte, Emily and James followed behind.

The Master frowned at Mamma. Mamma bowed.

'I'd like to commend you, madam,' said the Master. 'I believe your children are diligent and talented students — a credit to your abilities as a teacher and mother.'

Mamma beamed with delight, her face losing its anxious frown. 'Thank you, your honour.'

'They certainly seem to have received a thorough education, including some branches not normally taught at schools, particularly to young ladies.'

'I believe it is just as important for young ladies to receive a thorough education as it is for young gentlemen,' replied Mamma.

The Master nodded. 'I believe you are separated from your husband, Mr Barton?'

Mamma's frown returned and she stiffened. 'Yes, I am.'

The Master steepled his hands on the desk. 'May I ask why? Surely your place is with your husband.'

Mamma crossed her arms, compressing her lips into a thin, pale line. Charlotte and Emily drew closer to her in support. 'We no longer reside with Mr Barton as his constant intoxication and violent temper make him unfit to live with.'

'Surely you exaggerate, madam?' asked the Master. 'Without a doubt it would be better for the children to be living in a stable home with a male protector.'

'Since my first husband's death, I have had to be mother, father, teacher, protector and provider for my children,' Mamma insisted, her voice rising in anger. 'Mr Barton has done *nothing* to provide for them. His behaviour has at best been negligent and, at worst, dangerous.'

The Master gazed at the four frightened children, clustered around the skirts of their mother. Mamma took a deep breath, trying to calm her temper.

'Your honour — all I wish is to be allowed to raise my children,' Mamma begged. 'I have not received a penny of our income for well over a year. I have sold everything I can and run up multiple debts.

'We are nearly destitute. I offered to rent Oldbury and run the farms, but I was refused. Instead, they leased it to a man who is now bankrupt and cannot pay the rent. Please, I implore you, allow me to receive the allowance I am entitled to so I can feed, clothe and school my children.'

The Master stood up and turned to Charlotte. 'Miss Charlotte, is it true what your mother claims about your stepfather?'

Charlotte leant forward. She gathered the full depth of her feeling for the man.

'Mr Barton is a raving lunatic,' Charlotte spat. 'I hope I never see him again.'

The Master laughed suddenly, his jowls wobbling. 'Very well — I see that you are united on your opinion of him. I wish you all a very good day.'

Mamma decided to make a feast to celebrate the children's successful examinations. She sacrificed a fowl from the coop and raided the vegetable garden. Fragrant, delicious smells of roasting meat and vegetables wafted from the kitchen.

Louisa picked scarlet geraniums from the garden and set them in a jam jar on the table. Emily set the table with a patched, embroidered tablecloth and the mismatched crockery that had survived the journeys up and down Meryla Pass.

They sat down together, still dressed in their starched Sunday best. Mamma said grace then set to work carving the crispy-skinned roast chicken. Charlotte helped herself to roasted onions and crunchy browned potatoes, her mouth watering in anticipation.

'Mmm,' said James, passing a bowl of steaming green beans. 'This smells delicious.'

'I can't remember the last time we had roast chicken,' said Louisa, pouring a lake of rich, fragrant gravy over her meal.

'I can,' said Charlotte. 'It was at Oldbury.'

Everyone was quiet, remembering the many festive meals they had enjoyed in the gracious dining room at Oldbury. Their suppers now seemed to comprise solely of fish they could forage or barter for, vegetables from the garden and home-baked bread.

'Well, I think this looks like the best meal I have ever eaten,' said Emily.

'*Bon appétit,*' said Mamma, picking up her heavy silver cutlery.

The children tucked in and there was much chattering

and joking. James was telling Mamma a practical joke he had played on one of the local fishermen. Louisa was talking over the top of him, describing an unusual wildflower she had found that morning. Emily was trying to interject, while Mamma laughed at James's prank. After the meal, Charlotte sat back, her stomach comfortably full and her heart overflowing as she looked around the table at her family.

How could anyone think she would be better off living with strangers?

22

The Verdict

A few days later, someone knocked on the front door while Charlotte was in her bedroom reading. She looked up from her book, wondering who it could be. James, Emily and Louisa had run down to the beach to throw a ball around with Samson.

'Good afternoon, Mr Broadhurst,' came Mamma's voice from the hallway. 'I did not expect to see you here — come in. What can I do for you?'

Charlotte remembered that Mr Broadhurst was Mamma's lawyer.

'I wanted to bring you the news myself,' replied Mr Broadhurst. 'Is there somewhere we can sit down?'

Charlotte could hear their footsteps entering the sitting room.

'Would you like some tea?' asked Mamma, her voice strained.

'No, thank you, madam,' replied Mr Broadhurst. 'I'm afraid we have bad news for you. The Master-in-Equity has made his interim report.'

'Oh?' asked Mamma. 'I see.'

'He has found that you are not fit to be guardian of the children.'

Charlotte drew in her breath sharply and held it.

'Not fit to be their guardian?' Mamma repeated, her voice raised.

'He has appointed Mr Edward Corry as the children's guardian.'

'Mr Corry!' Mamma exclaimed. 'You mean that idiotic young clerk who works for the executors' lawyers? That is *outrageous*. The man has barely been in the colony a few months — he is almost a child himself. What on earth would he know about raising children?'

Charlotte crept down the hallway.

'I am so sorry, madam,' soothed the lawyer. 'Mr Corry is now the children's legal guardian and will make decisions about the children's future. He has determined that Miss Charlotte and Miss Emily should be sent immediately to boarding school. Master James is also to be sent away to board with a suitable clergyman. Miss Louisa, however, will be allowed to stay with you for a little while longer.'

'How can this be?' asked Mamma, her voice trembling. 'How can they take away my children? We went to court to ensure that we would receive the allowance that I was owed, and now they have decided to take away my *children*?'

'The report does say that you have instructed them exceptionally well, but, due to your peculiar circumstances, he can't approve of you continuing to care for the children.'

Charlotte crept closer.

'My "peculiar circumstances"!' Mamma shouted. 'What does that mean? That I can't feed and clothe my children properly because the lawyers won't let me have the money left to us by their father? That we are virtually starving because a gaggle of old men do not think I can be trusted to organise my own affairs?'

'The crux of the problem is Mr Barton,' Mr Broadhurst explained. 'The Master-in-Equity does not think it is proper that you have left your husband. In addition, Mr Barton has made several slanderous claims about you. Even though he has subsequently retracted them, I'm afraid the damage has been done. I am so sorry.'

There was silence for a moment as Mamma gathered herself.

'I will fight them,' said Mamma, her voice dangerously calm. 'I will not let them take my children. It is not right that a twenty-eight-year-old stranger should be able to make decisions about my children's upbringing just because he is a man.'

Charlotte crept into the sitting room and to her mother's side. 'Mamma?'

Mamma hugged her fiercely. 'You heard, dearest?'

Charlotte nodded.

'I will not let them take you,' Mamma insisted. She slipped her hand into her pocket, unconsciously pulled out the little brown pebble and rolled it between her fingers.

Charlotte put her hand over her mother's hand, squeezing it tightly over the pebble.

'We will not go,' said Charlotte.

In July, Mamma was summoned to the Equity Court for a hearing in front of Chief Justice Sir James Dowling. Mamma spent many hours writing and rewriting her petition, begging that she be allowed to keep her children. Charlotte could hear her in her bedroom, reading and re-reading the petition, calling out with exasperation, striking out sentences then writing them again.

On the day of the court hearing, their neighbour Mrs Fisher came in to watch the children, as she always did when Mamma went to town. Mamma looked pale and thin, as though a strong southerly wind would blow her away.

The children stood in the street and watched her drive the buckboard to town. It was one of the longest days that Charlotte had ever known. She could not settle to anything. They went for a walk, tried to read and draw, played knuckles with Louisa, but all day Charlotte had a pit of dread in her stomach.

It was nearly dark when James, who had been keeping watch on the front verandah with Samson, yelled, 'She's coming! She's coming!'

Charlotte, Louisa and Emily ran to the front door. Mamma turned the buckboard down the side street to drive it around the back to the stables. All four children ran through the house to meet her at the carriage house, Samson barking with excitement.

'Mamma?' called Charlotte. 'Are you all right?'

Mamma slid down off the buckboard, her knees buckling with weariness. James took her driving whip and hung it up on its hook. The horse stamped its hooves in the chilly air and whinnied for its stall.

'Mamma, why were you so long?' demanded Louisa, clasping at Mamma's crumpled skirts.

Mamma laughed hysterically, her hair cascading from its bonnet and her shawl askew.

'They fined me for *impertinence*,' Mamma cried. 'They said my petition was too long and its content scandalous. I asked them what was scandalous about a mother begging to be allowed to keep her dear children?'

'Mamma, what happened?' asked Charlotte, panic rising.

Mamma sank to her knees in the straw, her shawl falling to the ground. She was trembling violently. Louisa and Emily gathered around to comfort her. Charlotte clung on to the horse's head.

'The Chief Justice, Sir James Dowling, disregarded the conclusions of the Master-in-Equity,' said Mamma. 'He has appointed me as your guardian and ordered that I be paid three hundred and fifty pounds a year to cover our expenses.'

Charlotte and Emily looked at each other.

'You mean —' Emily began.

'I mean we won the case!' Mamma cried, tears falling down her face. 'They will not take you away from me. We will have money to live on.'

'We won!' James shouted, dancing around the stable yard. 'We won!'

Louisa buried her head in Mamma's skirts and cried because Mamma was crying. Emily hugged Mamma, then Charlotte.

Charlotte dropped the reins, her mind numb. *We won*, she thought. A feeling of euphoria flooded her. She smiled, then a loud 'whoop' escaped her throat. 'We won!'

Mrs Fisher bustled out the back door, alerted by all the noise.

'Oh, goodness gracious! What's going on?' she asked. 'Come in out of the cold, all of you. I've made a hot fish pie for your supper. Miss Charlotte, help your mother inside. She's all done in and will catch her death out there. Master James, you put that horse and carriage away. Miss Louisa, will you come and set the table for me?'

Charlotte and Emily helped Mamma to her feet and soon she was wrapped in a blanket in front of the roaring fire, sipping hot tea. Mrs Fisher served the steaming hot pie, which was filled with chunks of fish, seafood and leek in a creamy sauce topped with flaky pastry.

'Will you be all right?' Mrs Fisher whispered to Charlotte.

'Yes, thank you, Mrs Fisher,' Charlotte reassured her. 'Everything will be fine now. Mamma just needs a rest and some good, hot food — she's completely exhausted.'

'I take it there was good news today?' asked Mrs Fisher.

'Very good news.' Charlotte beamed, her cheeks aching.

'I'm glad to hear it, pet,' said Mrs Fisher. 'You and your mother deserve some good news. There's some around here who say she's haughty, but I think she is just stretched to breaking point.'

Soon afterwards there was even more good news. A letter finally arrived from Mr Evans, a publisher, to say that he had read Mamma's collection of stories and planned to print it in time for Christmas. It would be the first children's book published in Australia, and he trusted that its mix of amusing anecdotes and educational content would have wide appeal to the younger generation of the colony.

In early December a messenger arrived with a parcel for Mamma wrapped in brown paper and string. The children crowded around, curious to know the contents. Mamma opened it at the kitchen table with trembling fingers. Inside was a small hardback book.

Mamma stroked the cover with her fingertips, then held it up. 'Merry Christmas, my dears. This is for you.'

'*A Mother's Offering to Her Children*,' read Emily. '*By A Lady Long Resident in New South Wales.*'

Charlotte touched the paper. It seemed strange to see Mamma's familiar stories of Australian animals, plants, landscapes and characters printed inside a real book.

'It's Mamma's book,' said Louisa.

'Look, it has us in it,' said Charlotte. 'Julius is James, Clara is me, Emma is Emily and Lucy is Louisa.'

'And Mrs Saville is Mamma,' added James.

The children crowded around, reading excerpts aloud.

'It has my favourite stories of shipwrecks,' said James.

'And a story about a purple beetle,' added Louisa with glee. 'That was my idea.'

Mamma picked up the book. 'Let us pray it sells well,' she said. 'The first thing I am going to buy with the royalties is a spinet so we can have music in the house again.'

'Oh, yes,' Emily said wistfully. 'I have sorely missed our piano.'

'Perhaps a new dress?' asked Charlotte, examining her oft-mended skirt.

'I really, really need a new doll,' added Louisa.

Mamma scooped up her youngest and kissed the top of her head. 'Well, poppet, let us hope that everyone in New South Wales buys a copy.'

Mamma's book was a bestseller and the newspapers reviewed it favourably. With the money from the book and the allowance from the estate, life improved dramatically. There were new clothes and boots, books and drawing materials. There was meat on the dinner table, and Emily was overjoyed when a new spinet was delivered for her to play. Mamma was able to engage a maidservant to help with the heavy work, and she enrolled the three eldest children in College High School in Elizabeth Street, run by Professor Rennie. She also began to look around for another house at Woolloomooloo, closer to the school.

In the New Year, Charlotte, Emily and James began attending the day school. The girls were taught by the professor's daughter, Miss Rennie, in a separate part of the building. Mamma approved of the school because it was run on very advanced educational principles – strong academic teaching for both boys and girls, a particular focus on art and music, and an unusual policy of not flogging students for punishment. It was a novel experience for the children. For the first time in their lives, they were regularly socialising with other children outside their immediate family.

A few weeks after they started school, Charlotte and Emily were walking in the school gardens at lunchtime with their new friend Kitty when they were greeted with unusual warmth by a popular red-headed girl called Ettie. She was followed by her crowd of hangers-on, who seemed to spend most of their free time discussing the latest fashions and hairstyles from London.

'Did you hear about the Berrima murders?' whispered Ettie, with delight. 'It's in all the newspapers.'

'No,' replied Emily. 'What murders?'

The other girls gathered around like bright butterflies around a honey flower. Ettie always had amusing stories to share, and she *loved* an audience. Charlotte glanced over to see if Miss Rennie was watching.

'A convict named John Lynch has been arrested, charged with murdering at least nine people in the Berrima district, and probably more,' Ettie continued. 'He murdered an entire family, including the sixteen-year-old son and the fourteen-year-old daughter, and moved into their house, passing himself off as the new owner.'

Charlotte and Emily exchanged frightened glances. *Wasn't John Lynch the convict that Mr Barton was so terrified of?*

'Apparently he was an assigned convict on a property

231

down there called Oldbury.' Ettie paused and looked at Charlotte with wide, innocent eyes. She frowned, twirling one of her red curls around her finger. 'I thought you and your sister used to live somewhere down near Berrima, didn't you?'

Emily went pale.

Charlotte swallowed. 'A few miles south of Berrima,' she admitted.

'Well, apparently a few years ago this John Lynch murdered one of the other Oldbury convicts by bludgeoning him to death with a cudgel.' Ettie paused for effect as the other girls exclaimed in horror. 'He was arrested, along with his accomplices, but when the convicts were brought to trial, their master, George Barton, turned up to court so drunk that he was unable to give evidence, so they were acquitted.'

'Oh, that's terrible,' said Kitty. 'Surely murderers could not be acquitted so easily.'

Ettie flashed a glance at Charlotte. 'My father says all those poor, unfortunate people would never have been slaughtered if Mr Barton had not been such an irresponsible drunkard. The murderer Lynch claims that it was getting away with the first killing at Oldbury so easily that gave him the courage to continue his murderous rampage.'

Emily began to shake, her eyes filling with tears.

'I dare say it is all exaggerated,' said Charlotte, tossing her head. 'I doubt that convict could possibly have murdered so many people without being discovered earlier.'

Ettie smiled at Charlotte. 'I wondered if he was perhaps any relation to *you*, this Mr Barton?' asked Ettie, a sly expression on her face. 'Your mother is Mrs Barton, is she not — the celebrated author?'

'Don't be foolish, Ettie,' scoffed Kitty. 'As if Charlotte and Emily's mother would be related to anyone like that.'

Ettie smiled enigmatically. 'I didn't think it could be her. Apparently the wife of Mr George Barton is not at all respectable.'

Charlotte flushed and grabbed Emily by the hand. 'Come on, Emily,' she said sternly, her black eyes flashing with temper. 'This all sounds like a lot of scurrilous gossip to me.'

Ettie simpered. 'I am sorry, Charlotte — did I say something to offend you?'

Later in class, when Miss Rennie turned her back, Charlotte was sure there were girls up the back staring at her and Emily and whispering behind their hands.

'What did she mean?' asked Emily as they were walking home. 'Why did Ettie say Mamma is not respectable?'

'Do not listen to her,' Charlotte insisted, swinging her bag to knock off the head of a weed. 'She is just jealous and means to cut us down. Our best revenge is to rise above it.'

23

Kitty's Ball

November, 1843

'Mamma, Mamma,' Charlotte called, running into the sitting room after school. 'Kitty's papa says he is going to hold a ball, and Kitty has asked if I can come along.'

Mamma frowned. 'Charlotte, you are only fifteen — you are too young for balls.'

'But, Mamma, lots of girls from school have been invited. It will be held at Kitty's house over on the North Shore. She has a huge house, and Kitty has asked me to stay for the weekend. There'll be music and dancing and lemonade and supper.'

Charlotte twirled and dipped in a curtsy. Mamma smiled at her enthusiasm.

'What about me?' Emily begged. 'Can't I go too?'

'Emily, no,' insisted Mamma with a laugh. 'Thirteen is definitely too young for a ball.'

'Don't worry, Emily, I promise I'll tell you all about it. Please, Mamma, please say I may go.'

Mamma looked at her eldest daughter lovingly. 'I remember when I was fifteen,' she admitted. 'I had my first job as a governess, and there was no opportunity for balls then. All right then. I will write to Kitty's mother and say you may go.'

'Thank you, Mamma,' she cried. 'Oh, thank goodness we've been having dancing lessons at Miss Rennie's.' Charlotte grasped Emily by the wrist and twirled her into a waltz, their skirts flying around them. Emily laughed, her disappointment forgotten.

Charlotte stopped dancing and looked at her mother beseechingly. 'Do you think . . .?' she began. 'Do you think I could possibly have a new dress, Mamma? We could sew it ourselves?'

Mamma pursed her lips, as though disapproving, but her twinkling eyes belied her stern expression. 'I suppose I could sew you a new dress,' she admitted finally. 'It has been a long while since you had any special new clothes.'

Charlotte twirled again, then ran to kiss her mother. 'Thank you, thank you. Now, what colour — blue or green? Tarlatan or muslin?'

'I think white muslin,' Mamma decided. 'You will look beautiful in white, with your dark hair and black eyes.'

Mamma was as good as her word and stayed up late, night after night, her eyes straining by candlelight as she sewed Charlotte's new dress. The night before the ball, Mamma gave it to her eldest daughter wrapped in tissue paper.

'Try it on, my love,' she said, 'but let me do your hair first.'

In Mamma's room, Charlotte sat in front of the dressing table on a stool. Mamma loosed her hair from its braids and pins so that it tumbled around her shoulders, and she ran her fingers through it. Carefully, Mamma twisted it up into an ornate bun at the back of Charlotte's head and fixed it with hairpins. She left a long segment on either side of her face, and these she coaxed into soft curls. Mamma then helped Charlotte tie on extra layers of petticoats and lifted the dress over her head.

Charlotte was enveloped in soft swathes of white, filmy muslin. She tugged on the tightly fitted bodice, which Mamma buttoned up at the back.

'It fits perfectly,' said Mamma, smoothing out the fabric so that it belled out over the flounced petticoats. Charlotte twirled, watching the fabric spin out about her.

'I have another present for you,' said Mamma, presenting Charlotte with a pair of white satin low-heeled dancing slippers, matching long gloves and a pale-pink reticule. Charlotte pulled the slippers on, turning her foot to admire them, and 'oohed' over the small bag that Mamma had decorated with tiny crystal beads and embroidered flowers.

Lastly, Mamma pinned a soft, pink silk rose to the nipped-in waist.

'This reminded me of the gorgeous pale-pink cabbage roses we used to grow at Oldbury,' said Mamma. 'Now look.'

Charlotte gazed into the mirror and was met with a reflection she barely recognised. Her hair was soft and elegant, curling around her face, a startling contrast to the billowing white gown and pink accessories.

'Oh, Mamma.' Charlotte stroked the short, puffed sleeves with her gloved fingertips. 'It is so beautiful. In fact, it is the most beautiful gown I have ever seen. Thank you so much.'

Mamma kissed her gently on the forehead. '*You* are what is beautiful, Charlotte,' her mother contradicted. 'I do not think I have ever seen you look more lovely. You are truly growing up into an elegant young lady.'

Kitty's father sent a servant to meet Charlotte at Dawes Point wharf and row her across the harbour to the North Shore, her carpetbag at her feet and the new dress safely stowed in a calico gown bag on the seat beside her. Kitty met her in a carriage to escort her to Rosedale on the fore-shore of Lavender Bay.

Kitty's father was a wealthy Sydney merchant who owned a number of ships that plied up and down the New South Wales coast and carried people and goods to and from England. He had built a large mansion overlooking the harbour, surrounded by lush, manicured gardens.

'Charlotte, you're here at last,' squealed Kitty, flinging her arms around Charlotte in a tight embrace. 'I thought you would *never* arrive. We are going to have so much fun this weekend. Mamma has invited a number of eligible young gentlemen, so we will have lots of dancing partners, and the orchestra is simply divine. They are the same musicians who played at Ettie's ball last week.'

Charlotte and Kitty chatted and giggled about dresses, dancing slippers and filling their dancing cards.

At Rosedale, there was an army of servants bustling about the house and grounds, preparing for the party, hanging lanterns, arranging flowers, polishing silver and setting up crystal glasses — all under the eagle eye of the housekeeper. Charlotte was whisked upstairs, where there were two maidservants to help them dress.

Charlotte had to remind herself that she, too, used to live in a gracious house with elegant furniture, servants, and the finest silver and crystal. She felt a wave of longing for the old life at Oldbury. The nostalgia was soon banished by Kitty's enthusiasm as she gushed over Charlotte's new gown.

It took the girls a long time to dress as the two maids, Mary and Bridie, fussed over their hair, curling it with hot tongs and pinning the back up into elaborate coils and braids. Bridie laced up Charlotte's corset stays far tighter than Mamma would ever have done. Kitty's mother had sent a bunch of creamy, fragrant gardenias from the garden to be pinned in their hair.

At last they were ready. Charlotte felt a flutter of excitement as she and Kitty stood side by side in the mirror. Kitty also looked gorgeous in her pale-green gown with a ruffled undergown of cream lace. A cluster of chestnut ringlets hung down on either side of her face, garlanded with gardenia blossoms, their rich scent wafting through the air each time she moved.

'It's a shame you don't have any jewellery,' observed Kitty. 'You should have borrowed some from your mother.'

Charlotte thought of all Mamma's beautiful gold

jewellery — the locket, pendants, bangles and rings — that she had sold to keep the family afloat.

'Mamma says a young girl doesn't need jewellery,' replied Charlotte. 'Her youth is adornment enough.'

Kitty rummaged through her jewellery case on the dressing table and brought out a gold bangle studded with tiny green peridot gems and seed pearls.

'Here — this will look gorgeous on you,' Kitty offered.

'Kitty, I can't,' said Charlotte. 'It's too precious — it might get lost or broken.'

'Nonsense,' Kitty retorted, pushing the bangle onto Charlotte's wrist. 'See how glamorous it looks?'

Charlotte felt torn. She had never worn anything so fine before.

'It is gorgeous,' Charlotte agreed. 'Well, thank you, Kitty. I'll look after it.'

The girls swept down the grand staircase, their frothy skirts trailing behind.

Kitty's mother, Mrs Curlewis, was waiting in the entrance hall, directing the final preparations. Through the windows Charlotte could see paper lanterns strung from the tree branches and along the verandah. Candles blazed in the candelabrum overhead. The orchestra was already playing in the drawing room, filling the house with lilting melodies. The air smelt sweet with gardenia blossoms and melting candles.

'Brown, move that vase a little to the left,' Mrs Curlewis ordered. 'Girls, come and let me take a look at you.'

Charlotte fingered the peridot bangle nervously, as though Mrs Curlewis might command her to take it off at once.

'Lovely.' She nodded her approval. 'You both look most becoming. The guests should be arriving any moment, so come and stand beside me to welcome them.'

On cue, a carriage trundled into the driveway and delivered the first visitors at the front steps, the gentleman descending first to help the ladies out.

'Pour the champagne, Brown,' Mrs Curlewis ordered, then turned to gush over the first arrivals. In minutes the reception rooms were filled with ladies in their rich, full ball gowns and gentlemen in their white cravats and tails. Servants in uniform offered sparkling glasses of champagne and lemonade.

Charlotte was introduced to dozens of people in a confusing whirl of names and bows.

Mr Curlewis stood nearby, chatting about the devastating effects of the drought and depression, his silvery whiskers quivering with indignation. 'I have three ships moored out in the harbour filled with goods from England that no one can afford to buy,' he boomed, one hand behind his back. 'The economy must improve soon or we will all be bankrupted.'

'It was only three years ago when my ships would sail to England filled with the finest wool in the colony,' replied his colleague. 'Now the sheep are worth barely thrippence a head, and thousands of them are being boiled down to make tallow. It's appalling.'

Kitty raised her eyebrows at Charlotte. 'Boring business,' she whispered, shrugging her bare, white shoulders. 'Come on – let's find some fun.'

They wandered through the shifting crowds. Kitty spied a couple of young gentlemen, about eighteen years old, chatting across the room. Both wore the correct evening dress of black trousers and tailcoats with white shirts, cravats, waistcoats and shiny patent-leather boots.

'Alexander,' she called, pulling Charlotte forward. The men smiled at the girls and bowed. 'This is my friend from school, Charlotte Atkinson. Charlotte, this is my cousin, Alexander Curlewis.'

Charlotte could see that there was a strong family resemblance between Alexander and Kitty — the same chestnut hair and hazel eyes.

'Delighted to make your acquaintance, Miss Atkinson,' said Alexander, turning to his friend. 'Will, this is my irrepressible cousin Kitty Curlewis. Kitty, Miss Atkinson, may I introduce my friend William Cummings.'

Charlotte turned to William and smiled shyly. Will was tall with dark-blond hair slicked back, brown eyes and a gentle face.

'Mr Curlewis, Mr Cummings, delighted to meet you,' Charlotte replied, curtseying. At first Charlotte felt shy in the company of the two young gentlemen. She had not had much opportunity to socialise with young men of her own class. She was quite used to the convicts and stockmen of Oldbury and Budgong, but Will and Alexander were completely different, treating each other and Kitty with a teasing familiarity.

She was soon laughing and joking along with Kitty.

'I suppose I must do my duty and dance with my tiresome cousin,' Alexander said in a loud aside to Will. 'Miss Curlewis, will you do me the honour?'

Kitty giggled and swiped his shoulder with her gloved hand. 'Dreadful Alex — you are abominably rude.'

'And you, Miss Atkinson, may I have the pleasure of a dance? asked Will, bowing and offering her his right arm.

'Thank you, sir,' Charlotte replied, placing her hand on his proffered arm. 'I would be delighted.'

'Of course she would,' said Kitty. 'Come on, Charlotte – I hope we have partners for every dance this evening.'

A trumpet sounded to signal the beginning of the dancing. The ballroom filled with dozens of girls in their filmy dresses of palest pinks, blues, greens, creams and white, all festooned with ribbons, lace and flowers. Each girl had a dance program in their reticule where the gentlemen could reserve a dance or two – daring waltzes, stately quadrilles, lively Scotch reels, jaunty mazurkas and old-fashioned cotillions.

Kitty was right – the girls soon had their dance cards filled by dozens of eager young men and spent the evening dancing, chatting and laughing. Charlotte danced until her feet ached and her cheeks were sore from smiling. She waltzed with William Cummings four times, exhilarated by the novel sensation of dancing in the arms of a charming young man.

When she tired, Will fetched her glasses of lemonade or delicacies from the supper table – cold chicken and ham sandwiches, followed by chocolate cake and strawberry meringue, which he delivered with cheerful gallantry.

Charlotte thought it was probably the best night of her life.

The party lasted until well past midnight. Charlotte had never been up so late. Her eyes were grainy and heavy when the last guests finally left. The servants bustled around, collecting dirty glasses and dishes and blowing out candles.

Will Cummings took Charlotte's hand. 'Good night, Miss Atkinson. I hope we meet again soon. Alex and I are planning a boating party next week. Perhaps you and Miss Curlewis would be able to join us?'

Charlotte felt her heart flutter. 'Thank you, Mr Cummings,' she replied. 'That would be most pleasant.'

Will pressed her hand. Charlotte realised he was still holding it and retracted it swiftly.

'Do you like to ride, Miss Atkinson?' asked Will.

'Oh, above all things,' replied Charlotte. It had been so long since she had ridden a horse. A wave of longing washed over her for Ophelia and all the long, adventurous rides she had enjoyed at Oldbury and Budgong. 'I don't keep a horse in Sydney, but I always rode when we lived in the country.'

'Wonderful,' he replied. 'My father keeps a stable of fine horses at his property in Liverpool, and one of the mares is broken to the side-saddle. Perhaps you would like to ride with me sometime?'

Charlotte's eyes shone. 'Yes, please.'

'We are wine merchants,' explained Will, 'so I am often up in Sydney and would be delighted to have a riding companion.'

Will raised his hand and pulled a gardenia from behind her right ear.

'Your hair has come undone,' he explained. 'It must be all the dancing. May I?'

Charlotte realised he was asking her if he could keep the wilted blossom.

'Yes, of course,' she murmured in some embarrassment.

Will carefully tucked the flower away in his breast pocket. 'Until next week then?'

'Goodnight, Mr Cummings,' Charlotte replied.

Kitty was all agog when they went upstairs to sleep.

'It's nearly dawn,' Charlotte exclaimed in astonishment, seeing a streak of pink on the eastern horizon through the bedroom window.

'Did you give Mr Cummings a flower from your hair?' demanded Kitty as she kicked off her dancing pumps and massaged her aching feet.

'It was falling out,' Charlotte explained, examining her tousled hair in the mirror.

'The Cummings family is very wealthy,' said Kitty. 'His father has run a number of very successful coffee houses and inns catering to the gentry. Alex told me that Will Cummings is taking the business over from his father.'

Charlotte shrugged as she began to pull the pins from her hair. 'Mr Cummings seems most pleasant.'

'I think he likes you,' said Kitty. 'Greatly.'

'Nonsense,' retorted Charlotte, her face feeling warm. 'Don't be foolish, Kitty. He was merely being polite.'

'He didn't ask me for *my* gardenias,' Kitty observed with a roguish smile. 'What were you talking about?'

Charlotte began to unbutton her dress with difficulty. 'He asked if we might both like to join a boating party he is organising,' she replied nonchalantly. 'And he asked me if I like to ride.'

Kitty laughed, pretending to swoon on the bed. 'I told you he liked you . . .'

24

William Cummings

The boating trip was followed by a riding expedition to Bondi Beach. Alex Curlewis drove an open carriage with three young ladies from school — Kitty, Ettie and Blanche, who were all dressed in wide-skirted summer dresses. The accompanying gentlemen rode on horseback, with Will Cummings leading a pretty chestnut mare by the reins. Will knocked on the front door to collect Charlotte.

Charlotte greeted him wearing a dark-blue riding habit with a fitted jacket, full skirts and a white lace cravat. A black straw hat sat perched on top of her piled hair.

'Good morning, Mr Cummings,' said Charlotte, shaking his hand.

Samson sniffed at the visitor then wagged his tail. Will ruffled Samson's ears.

'Good morning, Miss Atkinson,' he replied with a bow. 'Are you sure you would like to ride with me? If not, the ladies can make room for you in the carriage.'

Charlotte examined the chestnut mare with longing. 'Nothing on earth would induce me to ride in the staid old carriage,' she assured him. 'I have been longing for a good gallop.'

Will laughed. 'Her name is Amber and my father bought her for my sister, but alas Harriet is more interested in shopping and balls than riding these days. I brought her with me up from Liverpool.'

Mamma came to the door to meet Will and greet the rest of the party. She carried a large wicker basket. The smell of hot pastry wafted from inside, mixed with the sweet scents of cinnamon, nutmeg and caramelised brown sugar.

'Is there room in the carriage for this?' Mamma asked. 'Charlotte and I have baked some apple tarts for your picnic.'

'My favourite,' said Will, taking the basket and stowing it on the floor of the carriage. 'Now, Miss Atkinson, may I help you up?' Will offered her his hand and led her to the mare.

Charlotte was more than capable of mounting the chestnut mare herself, but Will treated her like a precious porcelain doll, holding the horse's reins and fussing over her as she stepped up on the mounting block. Charlotte delighted in the thrill of being on horseback again. The mare cavorted under her weight, arching her neck and tossing her head.

The carriage pulled out with the girls giggling and waving goodbye to Mamma and Emily on the verandah. The men trotted along behind, conversing cheerfully.

'Shall we go for a little trot?' asked Will, gesturing to the group of riders on the dusty road ahead.

'A trot?' asked Charlotte. 'How about a good gallop?'

'I don't think that would be wise,' began Will. 'You haven't ridden for a while and the mare has not been mounted with a side-saddle lately —'

Charlotte was impatient. She longed to feel the wind whipping through her hair and the ground thrumming beneath her horse's hooves. She longed to feel like she could fly. Charlotte used her crop to urge the chestnut mare into a trot and then a rolling canter.

The mare responded beautifully. Charlotte overtook the gallant riders and the carriage of fluttering butterflies. The dirt track stretched before her, winding its way out of the village and into the bushland. To her left, labourers were working on building a huge mansion on the foreshore overlooking the dazzling blue harbour. Charlotte clicked her tongue and leant forward, kicking her heels into Amber's side.

Amber responded by breaking into a flying gallop. The green-grey trees blurred by. A kookaburra laughed raucously on a nearby branch. The blue sky soared overhead. Charlotte could hear the sound of Will charging behind her. She remembered the heart-pounding adventures on Ophelia at Oldbury, with Emily on her gentler horse, Clarie.

The two riders galloped on for a few miles, leaving the carriage and its escort far behind. A fallen tree lay to the side of the road in a clearing. Charlotte veered right so Amber could sail over the jump.

Amber was slowing, her sides heaving and her neck slick with sweat, so Charlotte eventually pulled her up into a walk, with Will beside her.

Charlotte laughed out loud. 'That was wonderful.'

Will laughed too. He looked at Charlotte. Her cheeks glowed and her hair had escaped its pins to tumble down her back.

'I was expecting a sedate ride, like the ones I take in the park with my sister, Harriet,' said Will. 'She never goes above a walk because it might ruin the fall of her perfectly tailored riding habit. I am there as an escort to beat off the crowds of admiring young gentlemen.'

Charlotte tossed her head. 'That sounds terribly tedious,' she confessed. 'There is nothing better than a gallop through the bush. When we lived at Budgong we would go for the most wonderful rides over the mountain and down to the sea.'

'Was that far?' asked Will in surprise.

'It was about thirty miles, but it was through thick wilderness, over the high ridges and across several rivers. It would take two days each way, so we'd camp out in the bush.'

'That sounds like rather more of an adventure than our ride to the beach today,' Will replied.

'Yes, but I haven't ridden for so long that this is heavenly.' Charlotte leant her head back and closed her eyes so the sun could shine on her face.

'Do you like riding Amber?' asked Will.

'I still miss my own mare, Ophelia,' admitted Charlotte. 'But Amber is a lovely horse. Thank you for letting me ride her.'

'It is absolutely my pleasure,' replied Will with a warm grin, doffing his hat in salute. They chatted on about Will's involvement in his father's business and discussed plans for another riding expedition over to the North Shore.

They paused at the top of the hill. As far as the eye could see, the wide blue ocean rippled like silk. Down below was a deserted crescent of white sand fringed with thick green bush and white breakers foaming on the shore. The air smelt of salt and seaweed and the tang of eucalyptus oil.

'Bondi Beach,' announced Will.

'Mamma used to bring us here often when we lived at Double Bay,' said Charlotte. 'I remember finding an enormous squid washed up on the shore, just over there. It was still alive and thrashed about violently.'

The remainder of the party was far behind them, so Charlotte and Will rode along the beach, splashing through the waves and cantering along the hard, wet sand. When they returned, the other horses were tethered under the shade of a tree while Alex and Kitty were unpacking the picnic baskets from the carriage.

'Where are the others?' Will asked as he dismounted.

Kitty gestured to a track that wound up through the bush towards the headland. 'Walking out to admire the view. However, I think the view is perfectly fine from here.'

'It is a charming walk to the headland,' said Charlotte, shading her eyes with her gloved hand.

'I'll tend to the horses,' suggested Will. 'Why don't you set off and I'll catch up with you in a minute.'

Charlotte nodded and Will lifted her down from the saddle. She flushed at the closeness of his touch. Picking up her skirts, she set off, her boots sinking in the thick sand. It was easier going on the harder track through the bush. Charlotte heard voices ahead and paused to listen.

'Did you see how Charlotte was flirting with Mr Cummings?' Charlotte recognised Ettie's voice and froze. 'Galloping off like that, forcing poor Mr Cummings to chase her. He must think her a complete hoyden.'

'It wasn't very ladylike,' agreed Blanche. Charlotte felt a lump swell in her throat. She felt sick. She had thought Blanche was one of her friends.

'Gentlemen don't like girls who behave in that fashion,' continued Ettie, her tone increasingly spiteful. 'He may flirt with her, but Mr Cummings would never marry her. Mother always says gentlemen prefer their ladies to be demure and well bred.'

'Charlotte's very clever, though,' added Blanche. 'She was dux of the school and her drawing is just marvellous.'

'Clever?' sneered Ettie. 'She's just a show-off. She was always trying to be top of everything. Her mother has some odd notions about educating girls. Gentlemen don't like ladies to be more clever than they are.

'You mark my words: Mr Cummings will toy with her for a few weeks then abandon her for a more appealing prospect. Mr Cummings comes from a wealthy family who won't want him to throw himself away on an impoverished girl.'

Charlotte turned and hurried away silently, her eyes blinded with angry tears. She had not gone far when she met Will, who was striding towards her.

'Miss Atkinson, are you all right?' he asked. 'You look distressed.'

Charlotte groped in her pocket for a handkerchief. 'Thank you, I'm fine,' she said, smiling tightly. 'Just some pollen making me sneeze.'

Will rummaged in his coat pocket and pulled out a fine linen handkerchief embroidered with his initials, which he presented to her with a flourishing bow.

Charlotte took it and dabbed her nose.

'Shall we go back to the beach?' asked Will, gesturing back up the track. 'It looks like the ladies have had enough of admiring the view.'

Charlotte glanced over her shoulder at Ettie and Blanche strolling towards them. Ettie began waving madly and urging Blanche to walk faster. Charlotte walked away hurriedly. Will followed, teasing and chatting and cajoling, trying to cheer Charlotte up as they strode along.

It was impossible to avoid Ettie and Blanche back at the camp site. Kitty and Alex had spread out blankets on the sand, set out the picnic baskets and lit a campfire. The other two gentlemen followed a few minutes later. Charlotte made tea in the quart pot, keen to busy herself so she needn't talk, pouring it into tin mugs.

'Why, Charlotte, your hair has come all undone,' cooed Ettie, twisting one gloved finger through her own perfectly curled red ringlets. 'Do you not think, Mr Cummings, that Miss Atkinson looks like a gypsy with her flashing black eyes and black hair? I quite expect her to start telling our fortunes from the tea leaves.'

Everyone looked at Charlotte as she fumbled with her pins, trying to tuck up the flyaway curls.

'Let me help you,' offered Kitty, taking the pins and moving behind Charlotte.

'I think Miss Atkinson looks most becoming,' said Will with a smile. 'I hope she does tell my fortune.' Will peered into the bottom of his tin mug, frowning with concentration.

'Ah, you vill meet de gorgeous young lady,' predicted Will, putting on a thick Slavic accent. 'She vill fall deeply in love vith you — because you are so handsome and vitty. She will have de thick black hair and de beautiful black eyes —'

Charlotte took the mug from Will. 'No,' she disagreed, peering into the tea leaves. 'It quite clearly says that you will meet a prim young lady from a wealthy family. Her mother will be a tyrant and her father a business tycoon. She will seem sweet and demure but will really be a spiteful cat. You will have eight children and be miserable, but at least you will be respectable.'

Charlotte smiled sweetly and handed back the mug.

'Good God, I hope not,' exclaimed Will. 'Please don't sentence me to such a dreadful existence.'

Ettie pouted then quickly changed her expression into an arch smile. 'Why, Charlotte — do you think respectability is such a curse?'

'Not at all, but perhaps it would be better to be an impoverished gypsy than a spiteful cat?'

Kitty and Blanche giggled and Ettie had the grace to look ashamed.

The summer was a whirlwind of social engagements — picnics, balls, tea parties, boating expeditions and weekly rides on Amber, accompanied by Will. For Charlotte, it was a complete change from her usual family life of study and chores.

In February, Will's mother and sister, Harriet, invited her to tea at their spacious villa in Liverpool. Will came to collect her for the two-hour drive in his father's carriage, drawn by four matched horses. He was escorted by a coachman and attendant groom in their smart livery.

Charlotte was wearing her best afternoon dress — a sprigged muslin with short, puffed sleeves over full petti-coats. Will sat opposite Charlotte, his back to the horses, and chatted to her on the long, dusty drive.

The Cummings' villa was graceful and large, sur-rounded by landscaped gardens and orchards. Will went to discuss business with his father, while Charlotte was shown into the drawing room, with its spindly furni-ture, lace doilies and china knick-knacks. A large, gilded cage held a crimson parrot with blue-and-black speckled wings.

Mrs Cummings and Harriet Cummings were seated in delicate armchairs covered in gold brocade. Harriet was much as Charlotte had imagined her — pretty, perfectly groomed and vacuous. Her mother was an older, stouter version of her daughter.

'Miss Atkinson, how do you do?' asked Harriet, shaking hands.

'Quite well, thank you, Miss Cummings. And you?'

The conversation covered the weather, the price of silk and the latest news from London on Queen Victoria and her two young children, Princess Victoria and Prince Albert Edward.

'Tell me,' began Mrs Cummings, pouring tea from a silver teapot into a delicate cup. 'Now that you have finished at Miss Rennie's school, what do you plan to do with yourself?'

Charlotte paused, taking the tiny cup in her gloved hand. 'I am thinking of gaining employment as a teacher. My mother was a governess before her marriage, and Miss Rennie has asked me to help with some of the younger students.'

Mrs Cummings and her daughter exchanged quick glances.

'Surely not, my dear,' said Mrs Cummings, smiling kindly at Charlotte. 'I have heard that your mother has some . . . unusual notions, but surely a young lady in your position will not seek *paid* employment. Harriet, for example, is on a committee of young ladies who organise regular balls, and she does seem to spend a lot of time shopping, much to her father's chagrin when he receives the bills.'

Mrs Cummings smiled fondly at her daughter.

'I am not totally self-indulgent, Mother,' complained Harriet, raising her eyebrows at Charlotte. 'I do help with the church charities and have French and piano lessons. Although I must confess it is quite difficult to practise. I always seem to be so busy.

'Actually, Miss Atkinson, I must introduce you to my darling dressmaker. She is an absolute treasure. She is quite up-to-the-minute with London fashions and has a gorgeous array of fabrics.'

Harriet checked over Charlotte's dress, which Mamma and Charlotte had worked together to sew. Charlotte felt a flush of embarrassment mingled with annoyance rush through her. Suddenly the dress felt dowdy and plain, instead of fresh and pretty. She doubted very much that Mamma's allowance could stretch to cover bills from Harriet's dressmaker.

Charlotte was relieved when Will joined them. He kissed his mother and sister on the cheek, and bowed over Charlotte's proffered hand.

'I hope my sister has not been boring you with details of her latest shopping adventure?' joked Will, shooting a grin at Charlotte. 'Apparently she was able to snap up a pair of darling kid gloves at half price yesterday.'

Harriet pouted. 'Don't be ridiculous, Will. Don't pretend that you know what ladies such as Miss Atkinson like to do.'

Will smiled at Charlotte. 'Of course I do,' he retorted. 'Miss Atkinson's idea of an adventure is riding through the wilderness for days on end, sleeping on the ground with a saddle for a pillow and drinking tea out of a pannikin.'

Mrs Cummings and Harriet glanced at Charlotte in dismay.

'Good heavens,' exclaimed Mrs Cummings. 'I should sincerely hope *not*.'

'Mamma, of course Will is only funning,' replied Harriet. 'As if Miss Atkinson would really do anything so . . . indecorous.'

Charlotte smiled brightly. 'By the way, Miss Cummings,' she said, changing the subject. 'I have been meaning to thank you very much for allowing me to ride your mare, Amber. She is a lovely horse, and I have enjoyed the opportunity to ride again. I hope you don't mind that I have taken her out so often?'

Harriet waved her hand languidly. 'My pleasure. As Papa says, it is better someone rides her than she eats her head off in the stable all day. Although I do hope you don't ride her above a slow trot — I would hate her to become too spirited.'

'Indeed,' Charlotte replied, sipping her tea and wishing she could escape home to her sketchbook.

It was with great relief that the visit finally came to an end and Will offered to escort her home.

25

The Question

On the return drive, Will seemed nervous, ordering the coachman to drive along at a clipping rate. He was unusually silent, and Charlotte worried that she may have said or done something to upset him or his mother at teatime. As they approached Sydney, Will ordered the coachman to pull the horses up on a grassy knoll over-looking the harbour, under the shade of a huge gum tree. The groom jumped down to hold the horses.

'Shall we stretch our legs for a moment?' suggested Will. He handed her down from the carriage and they strolled towards the rocky foreshore.

Charlotte gazed out at the view, admiring the sight of white sails skimming over the water.

'Miss Atkinson,' Will began nervously, gripping his hat in his hands. 'There is a question which I would like to ask you. That is to say, I wondered whether you would do me the honour of . . .'

Charlotte looked at Will sharply, her heart pounding. Will fumbled in his jacket pocket and pulled out a ring. It was a lustrous pearl, surrounded by a circle of smaller diamonds on a rose gold band.

'Miss Atkinson . . . Charlotte . . . will you marry me?'

Charlotte paused, searching for an answer.

'Mr Cummings — I don't know what to say,' Charlotte stuttered. 'I'd not thought of marriage for years yet. I thought we were . . . friends. What will your parents think?'

Will took her gloved hands in his.

'I know I should have knelt down, but it's hard to do that on these rocks. My parents will adore you, just as I adore you.'

'But, Will, I have no money . . .'

Will pulled her leather glove from her left hand and kissed her skin. Charlotte shivered.

'Please say yes, Charlotte,' begged Will. 'Please say you'll marry me. You are the most bewitching girl I have ever met.'

Charlotte felt a rush of happiness — she was adored; she was bewitching — but marriage was such a big step. Marriage was forever, and she was only fifteen.

She looked at Will and the ring he held out. *How can I say no?*

'Yes, I mean, I think so . . .' murmured Charlotte, looking down at her slippers.

Slowly, reverently, Will slipped the gold band onto her ring finger. The diamonds glittered in the sunlight around the creamy pearl. Then he kissed her.

'You have made me the happiest of men,' Will whispered. 'Please say we can be married straightaway — today!'

'Don't be silly, Will,' said Charlotte. 'I'm only fifteen. We couldn't possibly be married until I turn sixteen in July. Besides, I have to talk to Mamma.'

It was dusk when Will dropped Charlotte home. He whispered nonsensical endearments to her, which made her giggle. She was still giggling when she ran up the steps and through the front door.

'Mamma,' Charlotte called. 'May I speak with you?'

Mamma was in the sitting room at the breakfast table, working on the accounts. She looked tired.

'Yes, dearest, of course,' Mamma said, pushing away the ledger. 'These accounts are giving me a headache. I do not know how James manages to go through so many pairs of boots, and the executors have just written to say that our allowance is to be cut back again. I do not know how we are to manage.'

Charlotte took a seat beside her mother, her ring hand hidden by her side.

'It would be easier if I did not live at home,' Charlotte said. Mamma waved her hand to dismiss such a suggestion.

'We will manage somehow. How was tea with Mrs Cummings?'

Charlotte paused, wondering how she would get the words out. 'Mamma . . . William Cummings has asked me to marry him.'

Mamma took a sharp breath and hugged her daughter. 'Charlotte, dearest, I knew you were seeing a lot of Kitty's cousin, Mr Curlewis, and his friend Mr Cummings, but

I did not realise that things had progressed so far. Emily said you seemed struck with him.'

Charlotte showed Mamma her ring finger with its sparkling jewels.

'Mr Cummings says he loves me and would like to be married as soon as possible,' Charlotte explained. 'He asked me on the way home today.'

'It is a beautiful ring and very expensive,' said Mamma, frowning. 'Do you reciprocate his feelings?'

'He is charming and funny, and we have lots of laughs together,' Charlotte explained. 'He treats me like a princess.'

Mamma sighed and took Charlotte's hand, stroking the ring finger. 'You have not known him very long. I would not wish you to wed in haste.'

'I have known him for three months,' Charlotte replied. 'You had known Papa only three weeks when you became engaged.'

'Yes, but you are only fifteen, Charlotte,' Mamma pointed out. 'I was nearly thirty.'

Charlotte bit her lip with uncertainty.

'I will be sixteen later this year, and many girls are married at sixteen,' Charlotte said. 'It would make it easier for you all if I were married. Then you wouldn't need to worry about my expenses.'

Mamma took Charlotte's hand. 'My dearest, above anything else I wish you to be happy,' she began. 'I pray you would never marry for the wrong reasons. I know Mr Cummings is from a well-to-do family, and you have been enjoying the richer things in life — riding a fine horse, dancing at balls, wearing pretty clothes . . .'

Charlotte nodded, smiling. It had been fun to be treated like a princess after years of struggling.

Mamma paused for a moment. 'I do not want you to make a bad decision that will affect your life for years,' Mamma warned. 'I of all people know that one poor decision can ruin your life.'

Charlotte held her breath. *What does she mean?*

'Charlotte, you know that I loved your Papa dearly. We had only known each other for three weeks, but I knew without a doubt that I loved him. When he died, I thought I would die too. But never underestimate the power of human endurance.'

Charlotte nodded, encouraging her mother to continue.

'I had four children under six and a huge estate to run with the outstations at Budgong, Belanglo and Wollondilly River,' Mamma explained. 'Louisa was a sickly baby and I thought she, too, would be taken from us. The convicts were difficult to manage — neglecting their tasks and stealing from me at every turn. The estate was the target of bushrangers and moonlighters, who picked off our cattle and horses, and raided our stores. Our properties were robbed at least ten times by bushrangers in the two years after your father died.'

Charlotte could remember glimpses of that terrible time, when Mamma had been so distracted and Papa was gone, and the delicate new baby was endlessly fussing and squalling. She squeezed her mother's hand in sympathy.

'It must have been unbearable,' Charlotte whispered.

'Your papa and I had many friends in the district who were kind and offered help. There was one — a local miller with a property near our outstation at Belanglo called

George Barton. He had known James back in England in Kent, and had been persuaded to come to Australia by James's stories of the boundless opportunities here. When James built the flour mill at Oldbury, he employed George Barton to operate it for him.'

Papa must have liked Mr Barton, thought Charlotte, confused. *It was Papa who brought him into our lives.*

'After your father died, Mr Barton helped me to make an inventory of all our stock and possessions. I employed him to become overseer, to help me run the estate. Your father had always believed in being lenient with our convict labourers. Unlike many masters, we made sure they had plenty to eat and were not punished unduly. Your father even arranged to bring out the wives and children of two of our convicts from England, so their families could be reunited at Oldbury.

'Mr Barton, however, thought we had been too soft with the convicts and that if anything "disappeared", the convict responsible should be sent to the Berrima lockup.'

'I remember him sending our groom, Thomas Smith, to the lockup when one of the saddles disappeared,' said Charlotte. 'That was just a few days before Thomas was killed by John Lynch.'

'That's right,' Mamma said. 'Well, about two years after your father died, Mr Barton escorted me on a visit to check on the sheep stations at Belanglo. You know we had to visit the outstations several times a year to check on the sheep and cattle?'

Charlotte nodded, although she could never remember Mr Barton going on these journeys. It was usually Mamma accompanied by a couple of the men.

'We left on the morning of January 30th, 1836, and had ridden about ten miles when we came to a steep mountain descent, similar to the one we had to descend at the Meryla Pass on our way to Budgong. We were walking down, leading the horses, when two bushrangers jumped from behind a rock armed with large pistols.'

Charlotte's stomach clenched. She had heard many stories of the violence of the Southern Highland bushrangers, but she had never heard that her own Mamma had been held up.

'In the most dreadful language imaginable, they ordered us to stop and turn the horses loose, demanding our money and valuables. When they had taken all that we had, they tied Mr Barton to a tree, tore the back out of his shirt and began to flog him with a heavy stockwhip over and over again.'

Mamma paused and covered her eyes, the memories pressing in.

'They whipped him until the blood ran down his back and his skin was hanging in shreds. I begged them to have mercy, yelling that they would surely kill him. At last they allowed me to untie Mr Barton, who was screaming in agony.

'I lost my temper, which perhaps was not wise, and chastised the villains for their unchristian behaviour. One of the bushrangers pointed his pistol in my face and threatened me with his stockwhip. He declared that he thought he should flog me as well, as I allowed Mr Barton to mistreat the men.'

Charlotte clutched Mamma's arm, her heart pounding with fear. 'Mamma, no — they wouldn't!'

'I vehemently denied this charge and defied him to name any man who could complain of being mistreated on my property.' Mamma's voice rose with indignation. 'He retreated somewhat after that and said he made a habit of flogging any gentleman he could so they would know what it was like to be punished.

'At last, they let us go, telling us they would shoot us if we didn't turn back. I had to drag Mr Barton up on his horse and lead him back up that steep mountain path. It took us three hours to return to Oldbury. By that stage, Mr Barton was unconscious and I thought he might die. It was terrifying. I had to nurse him back to health over the following weeks. The doctor recommended that I give him rum to kill the pain.'

Mamma shook her head in disbelief.

'News of the attack spread like a bushfire around the district. Mr Barton had to give a sworn statement, which was subsequently published in the *Sydney Herald*. Everyone in the colony knew that we had been attacked and Mr Barton flogged.

'It also came out from our groom, Thomas Smith, that it was actually convict men from Oldbury who were behind the attack, as well as the robberies at our sheep stations and highway hold-ups on the drays travelling from Sydney. It seems that many of the local bushrangers were not hiding in the caves but living openly on Oldbury — they'd work for us by day and steal by night.'

Charlotte felt a shiver run up her spine.

'Gossip is a terrible thing, Charlotte,' Mamma continued. 'Rumours abounded that I had been travelling alone with my overseer, without a female companion. I was snubbed at church.'

Charlotte remembered the many hints she had heard over the years, that Mamma wasn't respectable. She hated the idea that people had been gossiping about her mother and criticising her behaviour.

'I felt desperate, frightened and so alone,' Mamma confessed. 'Mr Barton suggested that we should marry to stop the rumours; he could protect me. That was what I wanted more than anything — someone to protect us and keep us safe, just like your papa had done.

'Four weeks after the attack, George Barton and I were married by special licence in the very same church where I married your papa. The two weddings could not have been more different. It was a terrible mistake. The next day, Thomas Smith was bludgeoned to death outside his hut by two of our convicts — John Lynch and John Williamson — apparently for informing on them.

'As John Lynch was being taken away by the constables, he whispered to Mr Barton to watch his back — he would be next. He said the forests around Oldbury would always be filled with spying eyes and assailants, ready to strike. Mr Barton would drink himself into stupors that would last for weeks at a time. From the first day of our marriage he revealed himself to be a violent drunkard, deranged with fear.'

He certainly was, Charlotte thought, remembering her own aches and bruises.

'You asked me once why I married George Barton and why I had ruined our lives,' Mamma reminded her. 'It simply came down to making a poor decision under difficult circumstances. Yet, it was a decision that I have lived to regret every waking moment of my life.'

Mamma took Charlotte's hand and smiled.

'Now I am not for one moment suggesting that your dashing William Cummings will turn out to be a scoundrel like Mr Barton — but I do wish you would think very carefully upon your reasons for marrying him. I would not want you to marry for money or position in society or to escape a difficult situation — you must only marry if you truly, deeply love him.'

Charlotte glanced down at the pearl-and-diamond ring on her finger. *Do I love Will? Am I tempted by his family's wealth? Am I blinded by the attention he gives me? Am I determined to prove Ettie wrong?*

'Mamma, of course I love him,' Charlotte reassured her. 'Of course I wish to marry him.'

Mamma sighed and kissed Charlotte on the forehead. 'Good, my dearest. Then marry him you shall.'

26

The She-Dragon

'Is there something wrong, Will?' asked Charlotte as they strolled along a footpath in the Botanic Gardens on their way home from church. Workers and their families were enjoying the Sabbath, sitting on blankets on the grass, sharing picnics and playing with balls. Mamma and the children were walking ahead, giving Charlotte and Will a chance to talk.

'Sorry?' he asked, patting her hand absent-mindedly.

Since summer had finished, Will had been much busier with his father's business and had spent most of his time at Liverpool. Charlotte had not seen him for weeks. Now his mind was definitely elsewhere.

'You seem very distracted today,' Charlotte said, twirling the parasol that shaded her from the brilliant autumn sun.

'I beg your pardon,' said Will with a forced smile. 'I was just thinking through a few business issues, which was unbearably rude of me.'

'Tell me,' Charlotte invited with a smile.

'What do you mean?' asked Will.

A boy with a kite ran across the path, nearly bumping into them.

'Tell me about the business issues that you are concerned about,' Charlotte repeated.

Will shook his head and laughed. 'No, I wouldn't be so boring. It is nothing to worry your sweet little head with.'

A flash of annoyance surged through Charlotte. There was obviously something worrying Will and his response irked her, as though he thought her too young or too foolish to confide in.

'We are to be married, Will,' Charlotte reminded him. 'I would like to share any problems you might have and learn about your company. Perhaps there is something I can do to help?'

Will laughed again. 'In twenty years of marriage, I don't think my father has ever discussed his business affairs with my mother. She doesn't even know —' Will stopped abruptly then changed the subject. 'Well, never mind. I won't be up in Sydney for another four weeks; perhaps we can go for a ride then? Amber has been missing you.'

'Four weeks is such a long time,' Charlotte complained. 'And I haven't seen you for several weeks already. Can't you come up next week? We could go for a picnic at the beach.'

Will shook his head, a furrow between his brows.

'I cannot, Charlotte,' Will explained. 'I have other things I need to do.'

Will seems so reserved, thought Charlotte. *Where is my fun-loving, teasing companion?*

'Are you worried about the petition?' asked Charlotte, suddenly sympathetic. As Charlotte was still officially underage and a ward of the court, they had to apply to the Equity Court for permission to marry, even though Mamma had given her consent.

'No, Charlotte,' snapped Will. 'When we are married will you be constantly asking me questions about my business? It is not your concern.'

Charlotte fumed. This was a side of Will she hadn't seen during the relaxed, holiday atmosphere of summer.

'I would think it is very much my concern,' Charlotte said, raising her voice. 'I don't want to be an empty-headed wife who spends my days shopping and gossiping — I would be bored to tears. My mother always helped and supported my father.'

'My mother is not an empty-headed wife,' Will insisted. 'At least my mother is not a "notable she-dragon", as they call your mother. You will be busy enough looking after the house and our children without worrying about business affairs.'

Charlotte gazed ahead up the path. There was Mamma, walking along straight-backed, holding Louisa's hand, chatting to Emily while James was running in front, chasing Samson.

A notable she-dragon, thought Charlotte. *Is that what people think of my mother? Is that what Will thinks of her?*

'A she-dragon?' Charlotte asked stiffly. 'Who calls my mother that?'

Will paused and flushed. 'I apologise. I should not have said that.'

Charlotte stopped walking and glared at him. 'Who calls

my mother a she-dragon?' she repeated, her voice rising. A group of women sitting on a picnic rug turned to stare. Will hurriedly took her arm and led her on.

'One of the executors of your father's estate told my father that your mother had been difficult to deal with,' Will murmured reluctantly. 'That she was . . . well, you know.'

Charlotte shook off Will's hand. 'My mother has always fought for what she thinks is right. The executors drove us from our home, refused to pay us our allowance and tried to take us away from our mother. Is it any wonder she was difficult?'

Will looked shamefaced. 'I'm sorry, Charlotte,' he said, his shoulders sagging. 'I have been a little preoccupied.'

He paused, then continued with a rush, 'You see, my father has been in poor health for the last few years, and I have taken over running the family business concerns. However, with the ongoing economic depression, so many people are unemployed or spending less money, so the business has not been thriving.'

Charlotte nodded, feeling mollified. 'Mamma says that the income from our estates has dwindled drastically over the last four years because of the depression. The tenant who was leasing Oldbury went bankrupt and was unable to pay the rent. The house has been lying empty and neglected.'

Will sighed, shaking his head in agreement. 'It is happening all over the colony. Many of the leading businessmen have gone bankrupt . . .' He eyed the path ahead. 'I am applying for a licence to run an inn at Macquarie Street in Liverpool – The Liverpool Arms. I must make it a success. If I cannot turn the business around, Father will be declared insolvent. The shame would kill him.'

Charlotte looked at Will. He suddenly seemed so young and vulnerable with the weight of his family's expectations on his shoulders. She was only fifteen. He was only eighteen. She felt like they were children playing at being adults in a complex, harsh world.

'My whole family is depending on me,' Will said. 'If I fail we will lose everything — our house, our land, our reputation.'

She took his hand and squeezed it. 'You will make a success of the business, Will. The depression must end soon.'

Will smiled at her, his face still strained. 'It will be difficult for me to get up to Sydney once I am running The Liverpool Arms,' he explained. 'As father keeps reminding me, it is more than a full-time occupation running a hotel. There is no time for anything else.'

'I understand,' replied Charlotte, her heart sinking.

Mamma and Emily were waiting at the end of the gardens, near the gate that led towards Woolloomooloo. James was throwing sticks into a nearby pond, while Louisa was trying to catch a dragonfly in her hands. Mamma looked enquiringly at Charlotte's pale face and Will's stiff posture, but she did not comment.

'Would you like to join us for a family lunch, Mr Cummings?' asked Mamma. 'We are just having a simple roast, but you have a long drive ahead of you back to Liverpool.'

'Thank you, ma'am,' Will replied. 'That would be delightful.'

There was an awkward pause, as Charlotte couldn't think of anything to say.

'The children and I were just talking,' Mamma began. 'We were thinking that once you are married, Charlotte, perhaps we should move back to Oldbury?'

Charlotte's heart beat faster. She twisted the pearl ring on her finger.

'Move back to Oldbury?' Charlotte's voice croaked.

'Well, you will be living at Liverpool, busy with your new life,' Mamma explained, smiling. 'The house at Oldbury is empty, and it is nearly time that James began to learn how to be a farmer. It will certainly be a lot more affordable for us to live in the country than here in Sydney.'

'It will be wonderful to go home at last,' Emily sighed, clasping her hands together under her chin. 'Although we will miss you so much, Charlotte.'

James ran up to Charlotte. 'Did Mamma tell you we will be going home soon?'

'That is good news,' Charlotte agreed. Even to herself, her voice sounded hollow.

It was late afternoon, several weeks later, and Mamma was cooking in the kitchen. It was the new servant girl's day off, so Mamma and Emily were preparing the meal. Emily was peeling potatoes while Mamma was dressing a leg of lamb with butter, lemon and rosemary. In the corner, James was reading a book on Greek mythology. Louisa was sitting in a chair, topping and tailing the beans with a sharp knife.

Samson lay across the doorway. He wasn't supposed to be in the kitchen, but he believed that lying in the doorway didn't count. Charlotte stepped over him and dropped her new bonnet and gloves on the dresser.

'Mmm — that smells delicious,' Charlotte said. 'I haven't had Mamma's roast leg of lamb for an age.'

'That's because you are never home,' Emily said, sounding aggrieved. 'You are forever gallivanting about Sydney Town with your friends or your fiancé.'

'It is an exciting time in a girl's life being engaged,' Mamma explained. 'It is nice that the Cummings are up in Sydney for a few days. How did you go shopping for your trousseau with Miss Cummings today?'

'I didn't go after all,' Charlotte said, looking embarrassed. 'I had a headache.'

'Too many late nights, I suspect, my dearest. You have been on a whirligig of social engagements this past week. Please try not to overdo it.'

'I cannot wait until the ball at the Cummings villa to celebrate your engagement,' Emily said. 'Mamma and I have started making a new gown for me to wear. It is pink with pale-green ribbons.'

Charlotte paused, took up a knife and began to peel a potato in a single, sweeping cut.

'Actually, Mamma, there was something I wished to speak to you about,' Charlotte confessed, her eyes on the long curl of potato peel.

'You have not quarrelled with Mr Cummings, have you?' Louisa teased, pointing a bean at Charlotte. 'Not after he gave you all those lovely presents?'

Charlotte glanced at Louisa and frowned. 'I told

Will today that I could not marry him,' she explained, her voice thick.

'Oh, Charlotte!' Mamma exclaimed, wiping her hands on a linen towel. She came and hugged her daughter against her. Charlotte breathed in the soft, familiar scent of her mother mixed with lemon and rosemary. 'I am so sorry. What made you change your mind?'

Charlotte glanced around the warm kitchen, with its blazing wood fire and her beloved family grouped around their household tasks.

'I have been thinking about things,' Charlotte explained slowly. 'I'm not sure I really understand why, but it just didn't feel right.'

'You were not put off by his family, were you?' asked Mamma. 'I know you said Will's mother did not seem terribly pleased with the prospect of you being engaged?'

Charlotte laughed. 'I am sure she and Harriet are most relieved. Mrs Cummings would adore me if I were a wealthy heiress — especially now Mr Cummings has lost his fortune.'

A look of pain crossed Mamma's face. Charlotte took her hand and squeezed it.

'So why have you broken your engagement?' asked Emily.

'Will has been so tense about the new inn and working so hard,' Charlotte explained. 'He says it is almost certain now that his father will be declared bankrupt after all these years of hard work. The whole family must depend on what he can earn.'

'Oh, that is a dreadful shame,' Mamma sympathised. 'But I would not let that deter you. You are both young and can work hard to get established.'

'No, it's not that,' Charlotte replied, shaking her head. 'I'm not afraid of hard work. Actually, it was when you said that you would move back to Oldbury after the wedding. I imagined you all living at Oldbury without me, and I realised that I wanted to go home too.' Charlotte started peeling another potato. 'I suddenly felt that both of us are too young to get married just yet. I remembered what you said about making a bad choice that I might regret my whole life.'

Mamma brushed a wisp of loose hair from Charlotte's forehead. 'That was a hard decision, dearest.'

'But I am to be your bridesmaid,' Louisa wailed. 'And wear a long dress with pink roses in my hair.'

'I'm sorry, poppet,' Charlotte apologised. 'I'm sure I will get married one day when I'm a little older, and you and Emily can be my bridesmaids then.'

Emily exchanged glances with Charlotte and smiled.

'I have missed you,' Emily confessed.

'I've missed you all too.'

27

Return to Oldbury

April, 1846

The carriage drawn by two bay horses swept up the driveway, between the avenue of elm trees with their blazing golden foliage.

Mamma leant out of the carriage window, her black eyes dancing with excitement. 'Thomas, would you mind stopping for a moment, please?' she asked.

The new coachman, Thomas McNeilly, obligingly pulled the horses up beside the overgrown hawthorn hedge.

Mamma climbed down out of the carriage, followed by Charlotte, Emily and Louisa. They were all rugged up against the autumn chill, with dark woollen travelling dresses, thick cloaks and straw bonnets. James jumped down last, followed by Samson.

'There it is,' Mamma whispered.

Through a gap in the hedge they could see the honey-warm stone of Oldbury in the distance, nestled among the green-and-gold foliage.

'We're home,' Emily murmured. James leant down and picked up a handful of dirt and pebbles from the roadway and squeezed it in his fist.

A sense of excitement bubbled up inside Charlotte. At last, they were finally here.

Charlotte glanced back at Thomas McNeilly. He was a handsome, dark-haired Irishman with a thick brogue. Mamma had employed him to help with the farm, drive the carriage and tend to the horses.

'Must be grand to be home, miss?' Thomas asked with a grin.

'Marvellous,' Charlotte agreed. 'It has been a long, long time.'

'Come on,' Louisa called, pulling at Charlotte's arm. 'Stop talking. Let's get there.'

'Good idea, poppet,' Mamma agreed.

They all clambered back into the carriage, which rumbled over the creek crossing, through the garden gateway and into the front carriage loop. Charlotte felt tears of exhilaration well up. She blinked rapidly and surreptitiously smudged them away with a gloved finger. Mamma blew her nose on her handkerchief and took a deep breath.

The grounds were overgrown and a cow was grazing in what had once been the rose garden. Up close, the house looked forlorn — the paint peeling and the front windows cracked. Thomas pulled the horses up and opened the carriage door.

Mamma led the way up the front steps and opened the double French doors with a large key. Silently, they wandered into the vestibule. The house had lain empty for years. All their remaining furniture was coming down slowly from Sydney by bullock dray. Inside, the wallpaper was peeling and stained by the damp. Large cracks ran through the plaster.

They wandered from room to room, checking the upstairs bedrooms, the empty cellars, the derelict dairy and kitchen. Charlotte felt a mixture of jubilation to finally be home, tinged with sadness that their once-graceful estate was in such disrepair.

Thomas carried in the carpetbags from the carriage. 'Where would ye like me to put these, ma'am?' he asked.

'Just here in the drawing room is fine,' Mamma replied. 'I think we will camp in here together around the fire until the furniture arrives.'

'Aye, ma'am,' replied Thomas. 'To be sure.'

It had been a long, uncomfortable two-day drive from Sydney, with the anticipation mounting as they neared Berrima and then Oldbury itself.

James and Thomas collected wood and made a fire in the sitting room grate. Charlotte began preparations for a damper to bake over the coals, while Emily made tea in a quart pot.

Mamma sat down on the floor at her battered writing desk, pulled out a sheet of paper, a bottle of ink and a metal-nibbed pen, and she began to write.

'What are you writing, Mamma?' Charlotte asked, mixing the flour and water in a tin pannikin.

Mamma smiled, her face softened and transformed, her

eyes sparkling with energy. 'I am writing a list. Tomorrow we will clean all the rooms on this level, then we can work on the upstairs bedrooms. There is no money to repair the building just yet, but we can make it quite comfortable.'

Charlotte and Emily exchanged a smile.

'When the furniture is delivered, we can start on the garden.' Mamma slipped her hand in her pocket and unconsciously rolled the smooth, brown pebble between her fingers. 'James, we will make a fine farmer out of you yet.'

Charlotte stood up and wiped a smear of dust from her dark-blue travelling skirt. 'I'll go out into the garden and see how it looks,' she announced. 'Come on, Samson — walk time.'

Samson jumped to his paws, his whole body wriggling with excitement. Charlotte ruffled his silky ears and grabbed her cloak. They wandered out through the back door into the courtyard, then further back towards the stables and outbuildings. The vegetable garden was overgrown with weeds. In the stable yard, Thomas was grooming the two bay horses, brushing them until their coats gleamed.

Charlotte came and leant against the stable wall, breathing in the comforting smell of horse sweat and old hay. Samson pushed his nose against Thomas's leg, begging for a pat.

'He's not a shy creature,' said Thomas with a grin, rubbing Samson between the eyes.

'Only to people he likes,' Charlotte agreed. 'He usually takes longer to get to know people. He's decided you can be trusted.'

'Well, tha' is a relief, at any rate,' Thomas replied. He jerked his thumb back towards the house. 'It must ha' been a splendid place once.'

'Yes,' Charlotte agreed. 'And it will be again if my mother has her way.'

Thomas untied the horses and began to lead them away.

'Oi'll let them loose in the ol' orchard,' he said. ''Tis full of grass.'

Charlotte wandered along beside Thomas, her eyes soaking up the sights — the tumbledown fences, the long grass choking the garden beds, the familiar paddocks and the abandoned outhouses. To the east, past Gingenbullen a single spiral of smoke curled lazily in the air. Charlotte wondered if Charley and the Gandangara clan might be camping there.

Thomas clicked his tongue softly as he let the horses go. The orchard was indeed lush with grass, and the gnarled apple trees were laden with rich, red fruit.

'The apples are ripe,' Charlotte cried in delight. She stretched up to a branch and picked one. 'It will be apple tart for supper tonight.'

Suddenly, Charlotte scrambled up the tree and onto a low-lying branch, just as she had done when she was a child, to pick some of the higher fruit. From her vantage point she could see back towards the golden house, the distant waterhole choked with white waterlilies and then behind her towards the forest-covered mountain of Gingenbullen. Her eyes filled with tears.

'It is part of me,' whispered Charlotte to the tree trunk. 'And I am part of Oldbury.'

She was overflowing with hope, joy and relief. No matter what happened now, no matter how much hard work it would take to restore Oldbury, this was the start of a wonderful new stage in her life.

'Are ye all roight up there, miss?' Thomas asked, sounding concerned. 'Can I help ye down?'

'Catch,' Charlotte cried, raining a shower of fruit upon Thomas. He laughed and caught the apples deftly, one by one, stowing them in his hat. Samson barked with excitement, chasing an apple that Thomas missed.

Charlotte jumped to the ground, her skirts and petticoats flying. 'We're home!' she shouted, throwing her dark head back against the sky. 'We're home at Oldbury, together.'

28

Afterwards

Present Day

Aunt Jessamine paused. 'So the Atkinsons returned to Oldbury just before James's fourteenth birthday, when Charlotte was seventeen,' she explained.

Millie sighed, the spell broken. She pushed her hair back behind her ear, the gold charm bracelet jingling. 'That was a wonderful story, Aunt Jessamine.'

'I had heard parts of their history over the years,' Mum added. 'But I had never heard the full tale.'

'Well, lots of the history is documented, and lots of it has been passed down as family folklore, so who knows what the real story was?' Aunt Jessamine confessed.

'But the story doesn't end there,' Millie reminded them. 'What happened when they all grew up?'

Aunt Jessamine rubbed her hands together. 'Well, Charlotte fell in love with the charming Irish coachman,

Thomas McNeilly, and they eloped. She was married on her nineteenth birthday. They lived at Oldbury, then on their own farm near Berrima for many years. Charlotte and Thomas had six surviving children, but eventually they moved away to Orange, where Charlotte established a school. She lived to a ripe old age, a true matriarch, continuing to paint and write to newspapers and in journals until she was in her eighties.'

'I hope she was happy,' Millie whispered.

'I'm sure she had her fair share of happy and sad times,' Mum said, ruffling Millie's hair.

'What about Emily?' Bella asked. 'Did she marry too?'

Aunt Jessamine sighed. 'Emily married a farmer called James Johnson when she was twenty-three. She died ten months later, after the birth of her first child. The baby survived only a few months.'

'Oh, no!' Millie felt tears welling in her eyes and she tried to blink them away.

'Louisa lived with her mother up in Kurrajong and at the cottage at Swanton,' Aunt Jessamine explained. 'Louisa scandalised Kurrajong society by riding out through the mountains on her botany excursions wearing men's trousers! Absolutely shocking behaviour for the times!'

Millie giggled and rolled her eyes.

'When her mother died, she finally married James Calvert,' Aunt Jessamine continued. 'Her mother was always against Louisa marrying because she had such delicate health. Her mother was proved right. Louisa only had three short years of marriage. She died at Oldbury eighteen days after the birth of her daughter from a heart attack caused by seeing her husband's horse returning without a rider.'

'Tell me James didn't die young as well!' Mum begged.

Aunt Jessamine laughed. 'No, James inherited Oldbury when he was twenty-one and later married and had lots of children. It was after his death that his widow auctioned off Oldbury and had a huge bonfire, burning most of the family's paintings, sketchbooks, drawings and scientific specimens. Louisa's daughter, as a teenager, could only take what she could carry away on foot.'

'Those poor girls,' Bella said. 'Can you imagine how different their lives would have been if Charlotte Atkinson hadn't married George Barton?'

'It seems to me, Bella,' said Mum, 'that lots of good things came from that misfortune too.'

'Really?' asked Bella, screwing up her nose.

'Well, for one, Charlotte Waring Atkinson would never have written her children's book if she had not been destitute. Louisa would never have become a journalist or author if she had not had to earn her own living, and she may not have become such an outstanding botanist.'

'The girls would probably not have been brought up to be so independent if they had grown up with a father,' added Aunt Jessamine. 'By the way, did I tell you that George Barton was eventually charged with murder? During a drunken argument, he shot one of his workers in the stomach. He was convicted of manslaughter and sentenced to two years hard labour at Parramatta Gaol. He survived that and outlived most of the Atkinson family.'

Aunt Jessamine shook her head then stood up, turning

to Millie. 'Millie, don't be frightened of life. Be brave. Be adventurous. And be true to yourself.'

Millie thought for a moment, then smiled. 'Just like Charlotte?' she asked.

'Just like Charlotte,' Aunt Jessamine agreed. 'Let's go back home.'

Images from Aunt Jessamine's stories played through Millie's mind like scenes from a movie. She stood by the water's edge and stared out over the waterhole, then at the ancient elms towering overhead.

Aunt Jessamine and Mum started walking back to the house, with Bella skipping along between them.

Millie picked up a pebble and threw it at the waterhole. It skimmed perfectly across the surface —*skip, skip, skip*. She picked up another pebble and it, too, skimmed perfectly across the water.

'Did you see that?' called Millie. The others had already gone.

Millie laughed with exhilaration. She turned to follow them back to the house, the bracelet she wore jingling against her wrist. At the rose garden, a slight noise made her pause. It was the sound of laughter.

She turned and looked back to the creek.

Under the elm tree were four children dressed in old-fashioned clothes. The boy, James, was fishing in the waterhole, the cap on his head covering his shock of unruly hair. He gave a shout as he reeled in a wriggling eel.

Two girls sat on the bench under the tree, playing a game of chess, both with curly brown ringlets and long, pale gowns. A third girl in a white dress stood up, her dark hair waving about her face. She knelt down under the tree and picked a bunch of creamy, star-shaped flowers. The girl was humming to herself.

She turned and walked towards Millie, a dreamy smile on her face. She stopped and handed Millie the bunch of flowers.

'Thank you, Charlotte,' Millie whispered, reaching out to take the gift.

Millie blinked. The girl and her siblings disappeared. She glanced at her hand. It was empty, but Millie felt a sensation of warmth spread through her body. Was it love? Was it courage?

She turned and ran towards the house, following her family.

Two weeks later, back in Sydney, it was the night of the Young Artist Awards at the Art Gallery of New South Wales in the city. Mum had surprised Millie with a brand-new floral sundress and a pair of rose-pink ballet flats. For once she wore her hair out of its tight plait, and it flowed down her neck, wavy and brown. Mum, Dad, Bella and Millie arrived and took their name tags. Next, they saw Mrs Boardman and two of the young teachers from the art department. Mrs Boardman waved madly.

Millie nibbled her nails then stopped — she had promised herself she wouldn't bite her nails anymore.

The room was packed with people all dressed in suits and cocktail dresses, sipping on champagne and discussing the artwork. Waiters dipped and flitted among the crowd. A television crew set up their equipment; the camera scanned the crowd. An impeccably dressed woman interviewed a handsome boy about Millie's age, a student from another local school.

'Can you tell us about your artwork, Zach?' the television host asked, flicking back a tress of platinum blonde hair and unleashing a dazzling smile.

'I was inspired by the themes of grief, love and loss,' said Zach. 'I wanted to paint the alienation that immigrants feel when they have left their homelands and settled here, in a strange land.'

A photographer flashed a picture.

Millie took a second look at Zach's painting. To be honest, she hadn't felt any of those emotions when she observed his painting. However, it was very good.

All the finalists' paintings were displayed on easels on the stage — each one uniquely different, but all outstanding. To the side was her own painting, *The Dream Girl*.

The television presenter checked the tag. 'Has anyone seen Millie Mitchell? We haven't interviewed her yet.'

Millie ducked out of sight.

The mayor in her gown and ceremonial regalia stood on the stage beside the master of ceremonies and the director of the art gallery. They were all smiling and chatting.

The master of ceremonies began to speak. Millie felt ill, wondering if anyone would notice if she went home to bed. She was just creeping away through the crowd towards the bathroom to hide when a loud voice hailed her.

'Millie,' Aunt Jessamine cried. 'I'm so sorry I'm late. There was terrible traffic on the freeway.'

'Hi, Aunt Jessamine,' said Millie. She hung her head and scuffed her ballet slipper on the floor.

'What a night,' said Aunt Jessamine. 'I had no idea there would be so many important people here.'

'I know,' Millie whispered, her voice croaky with fear.

'As promised, I brought you the charm bracelet,' Aunt Jessamine confessed.

Millie smiled. Memories crowded in of the wonderful scenes that she had witnessed while wearing the bracelet.

'I thought you might like to wear it to give you courage tonight?'

'Yes, please,' said Millie.

Aunt Jessamine slipped the bracelet off her own arm and clasped it around Millie's narrow wrist.

'To remind you where you came from, and where you are going . . .' Aunt Jessamine murmured.

Millie took a deep breath and shook her wrist. The bracelet gave a reassuring jingle. 'I'm ready . . .'

Aunt Jessamine held out a bouquet wrapped in dusky-green tissue paper. 'I brought you some flannel flowers . . . to match the painting.'

Millie took the flowers and stroked their velvety petals. She smiled, her eyes brilliant with emotion.

'Thank you, Aunt Jessamine,' Millie said, kissing her on the cheek. 'Thank you for everything.'

The director of the art gallery stood up to begin his speech. Aunt Jessamine and Millie went and stood beside Mum, Dad and Bella. Mum squeezed Millie's hand.

'I acknowledge and pay my respects to the Gadigal people, the traditional owners of the land on which we meet, and pay my respects to the elders, both past and present . . .' the director began. He went on to discuss the importance of art in Australian culture and to praise the outstanding talent of the young generation.

Then the mayor stood up and added her own words of encouragement.

'Now,' said the mayor. 'It is time for a drum roll . . .'

In the crowd, Millie could see the other hopeful young artists clutch each other and thrum with anticipation.

Mum leant over and whispered, 'Good luck, sweetie. No matter who wins, you'll always be our favourite artist.'

Millie smiled weakly. The charm bracelet seemed to tingle.

'I am thrilled to announce the winner of the inaugural Margaret Forsyth Young Artist Award is . . .' The mayor paused dramatically. 'Millie Mitchell!'

Millie stood there stunned, feeling arms pushing her forward. In a dream, she climbed onto the stage, a broad smile across her face. She felt the bracelet tingle on her arm, and its warmth spread right through her body — a sensation of hope, joy and relief. Cameras flashed. People cheered and clapped.

Down below in the crowd, Millie could see Mum crying and Bella cheering. She could see Mrs Boardman with tears in her eyes, hugging the teacher beside her. She could see Aunt Jessamine beaming and congratulating Dad. The mayor and the director of the art gallery shook her hand.

The blonde television presenter pushed forward with the microphone, the cameraman looming behind her.

'Millie, tell us about your painting?' asked the presenter.

Millie looked at *The Dream Girl* and paused. She turned to the presenter and smiled.

'This painting was inspired by my great-great-great-great grandmother, Charlotte Elizabeth Atkinson,' Millie began in a clear voice. 'Like so many girls and women in the early nineteenth century, she and her family faced almost impossible difficulties. Yet she faced these obstacles with courage, strength and dignity, and fought for what she believed in.

'Charlotte reminds me that I, too, have a secret strength within me,' Millie continued, beaming down at Aunt Jessamine. 'Charlotte reminds me of where I came from, and where I am going . . .'

Fast Facts about Australia in the 1840s

- Australia experienced a financial depression from 1841 to 1845 caused by a severe drought, the recession in England and a slump in the price of wool, livestock and wheat. Many previously prosperous settlers were ruined. By 1844, approximately 200,000 sheep, which had previously provided a high income from the export of fine wool, had to be slaughtered and boiled down to make tallow for soap and candles.
- Women in the 1840s had no legal rights to property, education or profession. Until 1882, the common law of coverture meant that a married man could do anything he wished with his wife's property, even the money she earned herself. He could sell it, destroy it or give it away without her consent.

- Divorce was not legalised until 1857, and it was considered scandalous for a woman to leave her husband — even if he mistreated her and her children. In the 1840s, a woman's profession was marriage, so by leaving her husband a woman was perceived to have failed in the eyes of society.
- In the early 1840s, less than half of the children in the colony received any form of education. Education for wealthy girls was often restricted to domestic skills and decorative arts — music, drawing, singing and needlework.
- The transportation of convicts to the colony of New South Wales was suspended in 1840. Between 1840 and 1843 the number of assigned convicts shrank from 22,000 to about 4,000. The issue of transportation was the cause of much political debate during the next decade, with landowners wanting cheap convict labour and workers fearing the effect on wages and crime rates. The last convicts arrived in 1849.
- In the 1840s many of the local flora and fauna were still known by the names of English plants and animals, for example native dog for dingo, native bear for koala, native cat for quoll and native squirrels for possums. I have used the names we know now to avoid confusion, though I have used their 1840s names in dialogue.
- In the 1830s, the population of New South Wales was about 60,000 people, with only 12,000 people of European descent who were born in Australia. The population swelled rapidly during the early 1840s with mass immigration, particularly from Ireland due to the

potato famine. The city of Sydney was proclaimed in 1842 when approximately 35,000 people lived there.

- In November 1841 alone, approximately 2,000 immigrants arrived in Sydney. There was not enough accommodation or employment for such a large influx of people. Hundreds of immigrants were sleeping under the rock overhangs near Lady Macquarie's Chair. Caroline Chisholm became famous for her work with female immigrants, organising protection, accommodation and employment.

- Most of the labour was provided by convicts transported from England, Scotland and Ireland, as well as ticket-of-leave workers (ex-convicts).

- Bushrangers, often escaped convicts, made travel within the colony dangerous. Newspaper reports show that the Southern Road in the vicinity of Oldbury was frequently the scene of robberies, armed hold-ups and murders.

- John Lynch was arrested on 21 February 1842 for the brutal murders of at least eight people in the Berrima district. He was executed on 22 April 1842. *The Sydney Herald* published an article claiming that those people would not have died if George Barton had not been too drunk to give evidence against Lynch at his first trial for the murder of Thomas Smith at Oldbury in March 1836.

- For thousands of years, the Gandangara people lived in the Southern Highlands around Camden and Goulburn. They lived a nomadic life hunting animals such as goannas, possums and koalas, and gathering tubers and seeds. The local Aboriginal people were severely impacted by European settlement through disease, violence and dispossession of their lands. An influenza epidemic in 1846, the year the Atkinson family returned to Oldbury, killed most of the remaining Indigenous population in the area. By 1856, the local Aboriginal population was considered to be almost extinct.

Acknowledgements

When I was a child, my grandparents, Nonnie and Papa, several times took me down to the Southern Highlands to Sutton Forest to visit Oldbury with my younger sister Kate. We would peer through the hedges at the grand old house which had been built by my great-great-great-great grandparents James and Charlotte Atkinson in about 1828. By then it was looking neglected and forlorn. We would visit the churchyard where the family was buried. On the long drive down and back, they would tell us romantic stories about James and Charlotte, and their four children.

Over the years, these stories would be added to and enriched by my mother, Gilly, and by snippets from distant aunts and uncles at family gatherings. These anecdotes included James Atkinson wrapping Charlotte in his cloak on board the ship shortly after they met — and I was thrilled when this detail was confirmed in Charlotte Waring's journal.

When my grandmother Nonnie died, she left me a pile of her treasures. Among them were a painting of Oldbury and a pile of old books. One had been written by James and one by Charlotte.

Two years ago an extraordinary heirloom came to light, which had been inherited by a distant relative, Jan Gow. It was Charlotte Waring Atkinson's sketchbook, filled with exquisite sketches. Three generations of my family went to view the sketchbook before it was auctioned. In complete awe we examined the book, as the curator explained the significance of the drawings. It was more than a sketch-book. It was Charlotte's teaching book — that she used to instruct her four children about the natural world around them, about the local Aborigines and about her own family stories.

There are two illustrations which I particularly remember. One was of a graceful Aboriginal mother, clad in a possum skin cloak, carrying her child on her back. In her hand she held the glowing ember from a campfire, which would be used to start the flame of the new home fire. There was such beauty and respect evident in this drawing.

The other was a drawing of Charlotte's own mother, Elizabeth, as an unusually small child travelling with her father. This was the illustration for a family story about her mother, who died when Charlotte Waring was just two years old.

Many of the stories which Charlotte told her children are preserved in *A Mother's Offering to Her Children*, Australia's first published book for children, and in the writings of her own daughters Louisa and Charlotte.

My mother has a beautiful rose gold charm bracelet which has been handed down through her family. One of the charms is a red-brown pebble, which, according to stories from our childhood, Charlotte Waring picked up from the river bank just before she left England forever.

The Atkinson family members did not write about this pebble. However, Louisa several times wrote about the charm stones that the local Aboriginal women always carried — 'the smooth white stone she carries in her wallet . . . a reference to spirits . . . which shall be carefully kept a mystery from the curious white invader' ('Recollections of the Aborigines', *Sydney Mail*, 19 September 1863).

This story is a work of fiction, based on the life of this extraordinary family. The key events in this book are based on true happenings. For example, Oldbury really was the scene of murders and multiple bushranger attacks. It was the terrifying attack on Charlotte Atkinson and George Barton near Belanglo which triggered their hasty marriage. A convict did shoot at George Barton through the drawing room window, narrowly missing him, and the bullet hole in the window was recorded as still being there as late as the 1930s. Charlotte did flee Oldbury on horseback through impenetrable wilderness down the Meryla Pass with her four young children, an Aboriginal boy called Charley, their pet koala called Maugie, and Charlotte's writing desk. And Charlotte really did have to fight through the law courts for the right to keep her children — a battle that went on for years and drained the extensive fortune that James Atkinson had bequeathed. Charlotte Waring

Atkinson was an inspiring woman of immense courage and determination.

Her daughter Charlotte was also a strong, talented woman. Her outstanding academic results were recorded in the *Sydney Morning Herald* in 1842. She was engaged to William Cummings when she was only fifteen, but they did not marry. She eloped with Thomas McNeilly, a charming Irish coachman, and was married on her nineteenth birthday. Some of her paintings and sketches still survive, as well as an account she wrote about her family published in the *Australian Town and Country Journal* when she was in her late seventies.

I chose to tell this tale as stories within stories to acknowledge the importance of oral history within families, passing down wisdom and knowledge from generation to generation.

I would like to thank many members of my extended family for sharing their own anecdotes and research but particularly: my mother Gilly Evans, Jan Gow, Neil McCormack, Paula MacMillan-Perich, Kaye McBride, Margaret Broadbent, Jen Paterson and Elaine Johns.

As well as the oral history of my own family, I was able to draw on many details recorded in the prolific writings of the family — books, journals, newspaper articles and letters written by James Atkinson, Charlotte Waring Atkinson, Charlotte Atkinson McNeilly and Louisa Atkinson. Some of these publications included *A Mother's Offering to Her Children* by A Lady Long Resident in New South Wales (Charlotte Atkinson), *Journal written on board the Cumberland* by Charlotte Waring (her maiden name), *An Account of the State of Agriculture and Grazing in New South*

Wales by Charlotte's first husband James Atkinson, novels by Louisa Atkinson including *Gertrude the Emigrant*, *Tom Hellicar's Children* and *Debatable Ground*, as well as Louisa's collection of newspaper articles including *The Native Arts, Excursions from Berrima, Recollections of the Aborigines* and *A Voice from the Country*. The Atkinson family left an incredible legacy for future generations about life in the nineteenth century.

I owe a huge debt of gratitude to Patricia Clarke and her wonderful book: *Pioneer Writer – the life of Louisa Atkinson: Novelist, journalist, naturalist*. The extracts of letters in this book are from actual correspondence between the executors of James Atkinson's estate (Alexander Berry and John Coghill) and Charlotte Atkinson, which were quoted in *Pioneer Writer*. Another invaluable modern source was *The Natural Art of Louisa Atkinson* by Elizabeth Lawson. In addition, many books gave me an insight into everyday life in the mid-nineteenth century including: *Mrs Beeton's Book of Household Management*, *The Letters of Rachel Henning* and *What Jane Austen Ate and Charles Dickens Knew* by Daniel Poole.

I spent many hours searching Trove – the National Library of Australia's digitised collection of newspapers. *The Sydney Herald*, *Australian Town and Country*, *Sydney Mail* and *Sydney Gazette* have dozens of newspaper articles about Oldbury, the Atkinsons, the protracted legal battle, John Lynch, the Cummings family, letters written by George Barton and even his death notice. The staff at the Berrima District Historical and Family History Society were very helpful, particularly archivist Linda Emery and volunteers Philip Morton and Nancy

Reynolds, who shared her own childhood memories of Oldbury.

The Atkinson family was fascinated by the Indigenous people of Australia. James Atkinson wrote letters to the Colonial Secretary about the local Aborigines and his fear that 'in a short time (they) will be nearly extinct' (12 May 1828). Charlotte Atkinson wrote about the Aborigines in *A Mother's Offering*, and in her journal on board the *Cumberland*. Her first entry describes her meeting with James Atkinson and mentions his colonial estate 'called by himself Oldbury, by the natives Jillynambulla'.

Louisa wrote a series of articles about her childhood recollections of the local Aboriginal clan and their culture. By today's standards, their attitude to Aborigines might be perceived as patronising and racist. However, by the standards of colonial society, their attitudes were unusually sympathetic, concerned and affectionate. They recognised that the Aborigines had been dispossessed of their land, and that colonisation had brought widespread death, disease and destruction of Aboriginal culture. Louisa referred to her Aboriginal 'friends', acknowledged their relationship to the land and expressed her concern for their future — attitudes which were rare in nineteenth-century Australia.

I have drawn on the writings of the Atkinson family as the source for the descriptions of the Aboriginal characters and scenes in this book. They used nineteenth-century terms such as kings, chiefs and tribes to describe Aboriginal society, so this is reflected in dialogue. I have tried to reflect the spirit of the family's affection for the Indigenous people, while also conveying the horrific treatment of the Aboriginal people of the area by the white settlers at the time.

As well as the writings by the Atkinson family, I drew on *Aboriginal Legends* by C.W. Peck — a number of Aboriginal folktales collected in the Shoalhaven area during the 1860s, including the two waratah stories — and *Illawarra and South Coast Aborigines 1770 to 1900* by Michael K. Organ, University of Wollongong, 1993.

Thank you to the current owner and 'custodian' of Oldbury, who has renovated and restored the estate to its former colonial glory. Charlotte Atkinson would be proud.

Finally, I would like to thank the many people who helped in the writing of this book. My first readers were my family — Emily Murrell, Rob Murrell and particularly my sister Kate Forsyth, who gave me much help, advice and encouragement in writing this story based on our shared family history.

As always a huge thank you to my incredible publishing team: Zoe Walton, Brandon VanOver, Pippa Masson, Dorothy Tonkin, and my talented cover designer, Nanette Backhouse.

Apology

In the 1840s most European Australians used disparaging and patronising terms to describe the Indigenous Australians. These terms and attitudes are now considered racist. I have included some of these attitudes and terms, particularly in dialogue, not with the intent to offend any readers but to provide a reflection of attitudes prevalent during the early nineteenth century.

I acknowledge that my ancestors settled on land of the Gandangara people. I would like to pay my respects to the Gandangara people, both living and dead.

About the Author

At about the age of eight, Belinda Murrell began writing stirring tales of adventure, mystery and magic in hand-illustrated exercise books. As an adult, she combined two of her great loves — writing and travelling the world — and worked as a travel journalist, technical writer and public relations consultant. Now, inspired by her own three children, Belinda is a bestselling, internationally published children's author. Her previous titles include four picture books, her fantasy adventure series, The Sun Sword Trilogy, and her four time-slip adventures, *The Locket of Dreams*, *The Ruby Talisman*, *The Ivory Rose* and *The Forgotten Pearl*.

Belinda's family has recently celebrated the 140th anniversary of the first Australian children's book, *A Mother's Offering to Her Children*, written by Belinda's great-great-great-great grandmother, Charlotte Waring. Writing runs in the family with both Belinda's brother, Nick Humphrey, and sister, Kate Forsyth, being published authors.

Belinda lives in Manly in a gorgeous old house overlooking the sea with her husband, Rob, her three beautiful children and her dog, Asha.

Find out more about Belinda at her website:
www.belindamurrell.com.au

THE LOCKET OF DREAMS

When Sophie falls asleep wearing a locket that belonged to her grandmother's great-grandmother, she magically travels back to 1858 to learn the truth about the mysterious Charlotte Mackenzie.

Charlotte and her sister, Nell, live a wonderful life on a misty Scottish island. Then disaster strikes and it seems the girls will lose everything they love. Why were the sisters sent to live with strangers? Did their uncle steal their inheritance? And what happened to the priceless sapphire — the Star of Serendib?

Sophie shares in the girls' adventures as they outwit greedy relatives, escape murderous bushrangers, and fight storm and fire. But how will her travels in time affect Sophie's own life?

Shortlisted for the 2011 KOALA awards
OUT NOW!

THE RUBY TALISMAN

When Tilly's aunt tells her of their ancestress who survived the French Revolution, she shows Tilly a priceless heirloom. Tilly falls asleep wearing the ruby talisman, wishing she could escape to a more adventurous life . . .

In 1789, Amelie-Mathilde is staying at the opulent palace of Versailles. Her guardians want her to marry the horrible old Chevalier to revive their fortunes. Amelie-Mathilde falls asleep holding her own ruby talisman, wishing someone would come to her rescue . . .

Tilly wakes up beside Amelie-Mathilde. The timing couldn't be worse. The Bastille has fallen and starving peasants are rioting across the country. The palace is in chaos.

Tilly knows that Amelie and her cousin Henri must escape from France if they are to survive the Revolution ahead. But with mutinous villagers, vengeful servants and threats at every turn, there seems nowhere to run. Will they ever reach England and safety?

OUT NOW!

THE IVORY ROSE

Jemma has just landed her first job, babysitting Sammy. It's in Rosethorne, one of the famous Witches' Houses near where she lives. Sammy says the house is haunted by a sad little girl, but Jemma doesn't know what to believe.

One day when the two girls are playing hide-and-seek, Jemma discovers a rose charm made of ivory. As she touches the charm she sees a terrifying flashback. Is it the moment the ghost was murdered? Jemma runs for her life, falling down the stairs and tumbling into unconsciousness.

She wakes up in 1895, unable to get home. Jemma becomes an apprentice maidservant at Rosethorne — but all is not well in the grand house. Young heiress Georgiana is constantly sick. Jemma begins to suspect Georgiana is being poisoned, but who would poison her, and why? Jemma must find the proof in order to rescue her friend — before time runs out.

A CBCA Notable Book
OUT NOW!

oved the book?

THE FORGOTTEN PEA

When Chloe visits her grandmother, she lear
the Second World War came to destroying
Could the experiences of another time help Chl
her own problems?

In 1941, Poppy lives in Darwin, a peaceful parad
from the war. But when Japan attacks Pearl Harbor,
Australia, everything Poppy holds dear is threatened —
family, her neighbours, her friends and her beloved pe
Her brother Edward is taken prisoner-of-war. Her home
town becomes a war zone, as the Japanese raid over and
over again.

Terrified for their lives, Poppy and her mother flee to
Sydney, only to find that the danger follows them there.
Poppy must face her war with courage and determination.
Will her world ever be the same again?

OUT NOW!